Heidegger's Fascist Affinities

HEIDEGGER'S
FASCIST
AFFINITIES

A Politics of Silence

Adam Knowles

Stanford University Press
Stanford, California

STANFORD UNIVERSITY PRESS
Stanford, California

Printed in the United States of America on acid-free, archival-quality paper

Library of Congress Cataloging-in-Publication Data

Names: Knowles, Adam, author.
Title: Heidegger's fascist affinities : a politics of silence /
    Adam Knowles.
Description: Stanford, California : Stanford University Press, 2019. |
    Includes bibliographical references and index.
Identifiers: LCCN 2018026467 (print) | LCCN 2018027735 (ebook) |
    ISBN 9781503608795 | ISBN 9781503608191 | ISBN 9781503608191
    (cloth : alk. paper) | ISBN 9781503608788 (pbk. : alk. paper)
Subjects: LCSH: Heidegger, Martin, 1889-1976—Political and social
    views. | National socialism and philosophy. | Totalitarianism—
    Philosophy. | Fascism—Germany.
Classification: LCC B3279.H49 (ebook) | LCC B3279.H49 K623 2019
    (print) | DDC 193—dc23

Typeset by Kevin Barrett Kane in 10.9/13 Adobe Garamond Pro

Contents

Acknowledgments

Many people, too many to name, have played a role in shaping this book, portions of which were conceived and developed as a work of philosophy at the New School for Social Research. I sincerely thank Claudia Baracchi, Walter Brogan, Simon Critchley, James Dodd, Lynne Huffer, Julia Ireland, Eduardo Mendieta, Andrew J. Mitchell, Dmitri Nikulin, and Richard Polt for their help, support, and invaluable contributions in the earliest stages. I would also like to thank the audiences and hosts of all the venues where I have presented parts of this work: the Heidegger Circle, Boston College, Emory, Stony Brook, KU–Leuven, University of Vienna, Tilburg University, O. P. Jindal Global University, and the Society for Phenomenology and Existential Philosophy (SPEP), among many others.

But . . . the best-laid philosophies go to waste in the hands of historians. Wendy Lower delivered the decisive blow when she advised me to consult the archival record on Heidegger's denazification. I would especially like to thank Alexandra Israel and Benjamin Frommer of the Holocaust Educational Foundation (HEF) of Northwestern University. A Sharon Abramson Research Grant for the Study of the Holocaust from the HEF enabled me to do intense archival work in Germany. Thanks in turn to Alexander Zahoransky, at the Freiburg University Archives; Christina Morina, especially for arranging a research stay at the Duitsland Instituut, in Amsterdam, where Ton Nijhuis, Charlotte Broersma, and Jeffrey Herf provided support and insight. I thank Karel Berkhoff, of the Netherlands Institute of War, Holocaust and Genocide Studies, in Amsterdam, where a grant from the European Holocaust Research Infrastructure facilitated work. Michiel Bot has been a wonderful friend and interlocutor in Amsterdam, and Benjamin Hirschfeld also deserves thanks, though I know not quite what for.

This book was made possible in part by funds granted to the author through a Judith B. and Burton P. Resnick Postdoctoral Fellowship at the Jack, Joseph and Morton Mandel Center for Advanced Holocaust Studies of the United States Holocaust Memorial Museum. The statements made and views expressed, however, are solely the responsibility of the author. I am also grateful to the Emerging Scholars Program at the Mandel Center for its support in the preparation of the manuscript and of the book proposal.

At the Mandel Center, Vicki Barnett, Ron Coleman, Jo-Ellyn Decker, Deborah Dwork, Judith Gerson, Irene Kacandes, Megan Lewis, Jürgen Matthäus, Vincent Slatt, and Elliot Wrenn all contributed their time, dedication, and expertise to this project. Special thanks to Steven Feldman and Adam Seipp for coaching it along, and to Jeff Love and Michael Meng for their detailed feedback on early drafts. Thank you to Emily-Jane Cohen of Stanford University Press for her immediate enthusiasm about the project and to Faith Wilson Stein for her editorial assistance. Special thanks to my copyeditor, Peter Dreyer, for his patience and close attention to the manuscript. Most especially, I am grateful to my two anonymous readers, whose thorough critiques helped reshape this book entirely.

Thank you to Penn State University Press for permission to reprint portions of my article "The Gender of Silence: Irigaray on the Measureless Measure" from the *Journal of Speculative Philosophy*. Thank you to SUNY University Press for permission to reprint portions of my article "A Genealogy of Silence: *Chōra* and the Placelessness of Greek Women" from *philoSOPHIA: A Journal of Continental Feminism*.

At Drexel University I would especially like to thank my colleagues Peter Amato, Jacques Catudal, and Flavia Padovani, from the Philosophy Program, and Rakhmiel Peltz, of the Judaic Studies Program, for creating a collaborative scholarly environment. The Office of International Programs provided much-needed research support. My enthusiastic students are a constant source of inspiration. My apologies and appreciation to the family members and loved ones who put up with my absences while I finished my book on "headgear."

My parents, Stan and Linda Knowles, deserve more thanks than words can express. This book is dedicated to them in appreciation for their generosity, understanding, and unflagging patience. May the parents of the future be so willing to foster budding philosophers with all of the love I received from mine. For Gran, I might never have left school, but perhaps this book will make some sense of what I have been doing there for so long. Tapan and Bandana Bhattacharyya provided endless warm meals for the weary and observed the foibles of academic life with equanimity and generosity, albeit with a much-appreciated dose of skepticism about the meaning of it all. Thank you to Chris, Melissa, Avery, and Hannah Knowles for being ever-stable models of sanity and the art of relaxation. There is one reader whom I will never satisfy, a reader relentless yet kind, a reader whose imprint is on every page of this work, as a historian, a thinker, and a friend—Debjani.

Acknowledgements

Abbreviations

Unless otherwise noted, all German citations of Heidegger are from the *Gesamtausgabe* (*GA*) published by Vittorio Klostermann. Citations include the *GA* volume number, followed by the German/English pagination. I have often modified the published translations or provided my own translations for the sake of terminological consistency.

BT	Martin Heidegger, *Sein und Zeit* ([1927] 1979); *Being and Time* ([1996] 2010a)
CL	Martin Heidegger, "Schöpferische Landschaft: Warum bleiben wir in der Provinz?" (2002e); "Creative Landscape: Why Do I Stay in the Provinces?" (1981c)
GA 13	Martin Heidegger, *Aus der Erfahrung des Denkens* (1983a)
GA 16	Martin Heidegger, *Reden und andere Zeugnisse eines Lebensweges, 1910–1976* (2000b)
GA 19	Martin Heidegger, *Platon: Sophistes* (1992b); *Plato's Sophist* (1997a)
GA 33	Martin Heidegger, *Aristoteles, "Metaphysik" Theta 1–3* (1981a); *Aristotle's "Metaphysics" Theta 1–3* (1995a)
GA 29–30	Martin Heidegger, *Die Grundbegriffe der Metaphysik: Welt, Endlichkeit, Einsamkeit* (1983c); *The Fundamental Concepts of Metaphysics: World, Finitude, Solitude* (1995b)

GA 36–37   Martin Heidegger, *Sein und Wahrheit* (2001); *Being and Truth* (2010b)

GA 38   Martin Heidegger, *Logik als die Frage nach dem Wesen der Sprache* (1998a); *Logic as the Question of the Essence of Language* (2009a)

GA 54   Martin Heidegger, *Parmenides* (1982c); *Parmenides* (1992a)

GA 60   Martin Heidegger, *Phänomenologie des religiösen Lebens* (1995c); *The Phenomenology of Religious Life* (2010c)

GA 65   Martin Heidegger, *Beiträge zur Philosophie (Vom Ereignis)* (1989); *Contributions to Philosophy (of the Event)* (2012b)

GA 79   Martin Heidegger, *Bremer und Freiburger Vorträge* (2005); *Bremen and Freiburg Lectures* (2012a)

GA 83   Martin Heidegger, *Seminare: Platon, Aristoteles, Augustinus* (2012c)

GA 94   Martin Heidegger, *Überlegungen II–VI (Schwarze Hefte 1931–1938)* (2014a); *Ponderings II–VI, Black Notebooks 1931–1938* (2016)

GA 95   Martin Heidegger, *Überlegungen VII–XI (Schwarze Hefte 1938/9)* (2014b); *Ponderings VII–XI, Black Notebooks 1938–1939* (2017a)

GA 96   Martin Heidegger, *Überlegungen XII–XV (Schwarze Hefte 1939–41)* (2014c); *Ponderings XII–XV, Black Notebooks 1939–1941* (2017b)

GA 97   Martin Heidegger, *Anmerkungen I–V (Schwarze Hefte 1942–48)* (2015)

HA   Walter Homolka and Arnulf Heidegger, *Heidegger und der Antisemitismus* (2016)

IM   Martin Heidegger, *Einführung in die Metaphysik* (1976b); *Introduction to Metaphysics* (2000a)

LH Martin Heidegger, "Brief über den Humanismus" (1976a); "Letter on Humanism" (1998)

Met. Aristotle, *Metaphysics,* trans. Hippocrates G. Apostle (1966)

NE Aristotle, *The Nicomachean Ethics,* trans. Hippocrates G. Apostle (1984c)

OWL Martin Heidegger, *Unterwegs zur Sprache* ([1959] 1982d); *On the Way to Language* (1982b)

Parm. Plato, *Parmenides,* trans. Albert Keith Whitaker (1996a)

PW Martin Heidegger, "Der Feldweg" (1983b); "The Pathway" (1981b)

RA Martin Heidegger, "Rektoratsrede: Die Selbstbehauptung der deutschen Universität" (2000); "Rectorial Address: The Self-Assertion of the German University" (1993)

SL Silvia Montiglio, *Silence in the Land of Logos* (2000)

SW Luce Irigaray, *Speculum of the Other Woman* (1985)

Heidegger's Fascist Affinities

Prologue

Hidden in Plain Sight

In order to keep silent, one must first have something to say. "Silence," Martin Heidegger writes, "is a manner of not speaking, but not every instance of not speaking is silence" (*GA* 36–37, 109/86). On this account, silence is made possible because one does have something to say, a situation that is impossible for an entity such as a stone or—Heidegger's own example—a window. The stone does not have the power to keep silent, because it does not have the power to speak. Yet in Freiburg im Breisgau, a city in the German state of Baden-Württemberg ineluctably attached to Heidegger, the stones do in fact speak; they do have something to say. They speak from their dull glistening, from their concealment in their inconspicuous everyday settings in the old city's bustling commercial district surrounding Freiburg University. They speak from the spaces dispersed among the houses, shops, classrooms, academic departments, and administrative buildings of the university. They speak from the very spaces where Heidegger taught, wrote, and served as rector of the university while National Socialism solidified its power in the era of *Gleichschaltung* (ideological coordination, compulsory conformity), a violent process of ideological assimilation imposed upon German society and institutions.[1] "The world of our people and Reich is being rebuilt," Heidegger writes in April 1933, on the cusp of assuming his own position of power in the burgeoning Nazi state. It is the duty of "everyone who still has eyes to see and ears to hear and a head to act . . . to bear this reality into the spiritual world of the Reich and into the secret mission of the German essence."[2] In contrast to the philosopher Heidegger, who flourished under National Socialism and went on to produce a *Complete Works* of more than one hundred volumes, these stones tell stories that are terse, abbreviated, and concealed beyond the few words that are stamped into their surface line by line. Often they tell very little, because only little is known, yet in their brevity, they also speak volumes.

In German, these stones are called *Stolpersteine*—"stumbling stones," figuratively in English, "stumbling blocks."[3] Conceptualized by the artist Günter Demnig and mimicked by many others from Holland to Hungary, these stumbling stones are brass plaques the size of a cobblestone that are set into the street to commemorate the stories of Holocaust victims, integrating the memory of the Holocaust into the everyday lives of the inhabitants of European cities. Placed in front of sites of deportation or a victim's last verifiable residence, they tell what is known about individuals deported: name, birth year, and, if possible, the date, manner, and place of death. In their inconspicuousness, the stumbling blocks serve to remind us that the Holocaust involved, not only mass death, but also mass complicity, with recent research estimating the involvement of some two hundred thousand perpetrators (Bajohr and Pohl 2008, 10). The stumbling these blocks cause is metaphorical, for despite their surface joining flush with the surrounding sidewalk, they bring us to a halt and confront us with the unspeakable by embedding it in the physical terrain of the city.

At one corner in Freiburg, three stones are set inartistically, almost haphazardly, in the asphalt of a busy commercial street. This cluster tells the story of the Kaufmann family: Louis born in 1899, Yvonne born in 1894, and Manfred, presumably their son, born in 1923. Having fled to France in 1935, as the stones inform us, Louis and Yvonne survived the Holocaust, while Manfred was first interned at the Drancy detention camp in suburban Paris and later deported to the Majdanek concentration camp in German-occupied Poland. He was murdered at Majdanek in 1943. Heidegger—whose only public remarks about the Holocaust were brief and cryptic—would have said that he did not *die* there for according to Heidegger, there was perishing and liquidation in the death camps, but no death, since, for him, to die "means to carry out death in its essence" (*GA* 79, 56/53).[4]

Around the corner, a set of six stones, tapered at the edges from the wear of countless feet making their way to and from Freiburg's main train station, are set crookedly in asphalt among the cobblestones. They speak of the twin fates of the Abraham and Grumbacher families. Albert and Lina Abraham fled Freiburg in 1932 and were murdered in Auschwitz in

1942. Let us have the generosity to say they died there. The remaining stones speak voluminously of the Grumbachers. Benjamin, Kiara, Rita, and Sedy Grumbacher fled Freiburg in 1934. Benjamin returned in 1935 but was dead, the stone reports, without mentioning a cause, by 1938. Kiara, Rita, and Sedy, along with Fanny Grumbacher were murdered in Auschwitz in 1942. The stones tell us this. They have little difficulty telling their abbreviated stories, which narrate themselves to the attentive listener who walks the streets of Freiburg, and so many other parts of Europe, with an eye trained on such stumbling blocks.

Elsewhere in the old city of Freiburg, one encounters two haunting talking stones placed side by side, hinting at a story all the more powerful for its prosaic brevity:

HERE LIVED	HERE LIVED
THEKLA LION	SELMA LION
NÉE STEIN	BORN 1896
SUICIDE	SUICIDE
02/24/1936	02/24/1936

Stumbling block in Freiburg, Germany. Photo by the author.

Were Thekla and Selma Lion a mother and daughter incapable of flee-ing, or unwilling to flee? Why? History tells us that in response to threats and extortion, they stepped into the Rhine and drowned themselves on February 24, 1936 (Meckel 2006, 153). The stones use the euphemism *Freitod* to describe their suicide instead of the more common German terms *Selbstmord* and *Suizid*. While *Freitod* seems to imply a peculiar form of freedom, *Selbstmord* is far more metaphysical in its self-referentiality, translating literally as "self-murder." "*Sui caedere*: to kill oneself," as Jean Améry writes in his analysis of suicide. "Remarkable how the Latinized forms always suck the reality out of something" (Améry 1999, 2). But re-gardless of the word chosen, it would seem inappropriate to assign Thekla and Selma responsibility for their own murders. Neither word captures what they endured at the hands of the Nazis and neighbors who exploited their vulnerable situation, provoking them to end their own lives.

In "We Refugees," a short personal account of the experience of exile, Hannah Arendt, who fled Nazi persecution by way of the French camp of Gurs, sums up this experience in a tone of disarming insouciance. Discuss-ing the rash of suicides by Austrian Jews following the German annexation of Austria, she writes: "Unlike other suicides, our friends leave no explana-tion of their deed, no indictment, no charge against a world that forced a desperate man to talk and to behave cheerfully to his very last day. Letters left by them are conventional, meaningless documents. . . . Nobody cares about motives, they seem clear to all of us" (Arendt 1994, 112).[5]

What mask of cheerfulness did Thekla and Selma Lion wear? What was their "quiet and modest way of vanishing" (ibid., 114)? What was it that they did not explain, in a silence chosen for them before a death chosen for them (*fabricated* for them, Heidegger would say)? What words can capture the monstrous truth hinted at by Thekla and Selma Lion's stone?

The stones of Freiburg speak. They speak against Heidegger, who de-spite—or perhaps because of—his immense philosophical talent, also served as a ruthless Nazi administrator who coldly and efficiently implemented the Aryanization laws as rector of Freiburg University, a law euphemistically deemed "The Law for the Restoration of the Professional Civil Service." He enthusiastically declared his allegiance to the Führer in 1933, only months into the reign of National Socialism. "The greatness Hitler is growing into as a statesman reveals itself from day to day," he writes in April 1933.[6] At approximately the same time, he makes the following note in his philosophi-cal diaries known as the *Black Notebooks*: "The great experience and fortune that the Führer has awakened a new actuality, giving our thinking the correct course and impetus. Otherwise, despite all thoroughness, it would have remained lost in itself and would only with difficulty have found its way to effectiveness. The literary existence is at its end" (*GA* 94, 111/81).

Hitler shows Heidegger the way, gives his thinking a direction. Finally, Heidegger's philosophy will have an impact. Yet while Heidegger seeks to take on his own stature of greatness as a statesmanlike philosopher by distancing himself from his literary existence, the Abrahams, Grumbachers, and Kaufmanns of Germany had fled or were preparing to flee. These stones thus speak against the *Rektor-Führer*, as he was officially designated in the bureaucratic terminology of the Nazis. As rector, Heidegger Aryanized Freiburg University in a manner considered exemplary by the Ministry of Culture in Berlin (Grün 2010; Seier 1964). As a bureaucrat, thinker, and public figure, Heidegger contributed both directly and indirectly to the deportations and murders recounted in the terse messages of the stumbling blocks. It is thus perhaps all too convenient for him to wish that stones could not speak. As an early devotee lending intellectual credibility to the Nazi "revolution" (*GA* 16, 151/286),[7] as—in his own brother's words—a "celebrity" and a "hot stock on the world market of public opinion," Martin Heidegger, the thinker and the man, is woven into the fabric of the crimes of Nazi Germany.[8] The local Nazi party propaganda organ *Der Alemane* announced Heidegger's entry into the Nazi party in May 1933 with great fanfare: "It strikes our consciousness with infinite satisfaction that this great man stands in our ranks, the ranks of Adolf Hitler."[9]

1   Heidegger's Politics of Silence

Heidegger's Fascist Affinities analyzes Heidegger's place in the ideology and intellectual history of National Socialism by focusing on his philosophy of language, and in particular on the topic of silence in his philosophy of language. There are a number of historical and philosophical reasons for selecting silence as the focus of analysis, some of which are immediately obvious, and some of which will only become clear in the course of the analysis. First, the book seeks to make a case for Heidegger to be read as a thinker of silence by showing how the question of silence is, in his terminology, "equiprimordial" to the question of being in his work. Heidegger calls this thinking "sigetics," a term he derives from his readings of ancient Greek philosophy. By making the case for the primacy of sigetics in Heidegger's work, I will show how his thinking undergoes a number of fundamental shifts in the early 1930s that place silence, and more broadly speaking the question of language, at the center of his politics. This politics is based on Heidegger's vision of the spiritual and linguistic revival of the German people through an attunement to the Greeks, achieved by overcoming the dissevering affects of modernity—which includes, in Heidegger's words, "world Jewry" (*GA* 96, 243/191). By arguing that Heidegger's *Black Notebooks* must be treated as integral to his sigetic philosophical project, I then show why they ought to be regarded as a central component of his philosophy, and not merely as autobiographical texts unworthy of philosophical consideration. By drawing together Heidegger's teaching, writing, and political activities during the era of National Socialism, I will demonstrate how he employs a laden philosophical language to express a clear affinity to the conservative, antisemitic *völkisch* movements of the 1920s and 1930s.[1] By reading

Heidegger's politics and philosophy in the light of the *Black Notebooks*, and reading the *Black Notebooks* in light of their *völkisch* affinities, the point is not to prosecute the "Heidegger case" once again, but instead to show how his philosophy and National Socialism share a common set of fundamental commitments. Through a reading centered around the theme of silence, I will ultimately argue that Heidegger's politics and philosophy are not separate entities, but instead constitute an integral, yet complex whole, even despite his own skilled and politically expedient postwar attempts at dividing his thinking from his political activities.

Yet while the book does primarily focus on Heidegger, it is worth mentioning from the outset that it would be a miniscule, almost useless "discovery" finally decisively to declare Heidegger a Nazi if that study is not accompanied by some further illumination about the nature of National Socialism, university and cultural politics, the humanities under authoritarian regimes, or the nature of the discipline of philosophy.[2] This book seeks to examine Heidegger's philosophy in order to draw larger conclusions about the response of the humanities to totalitarian regimes, and in particular about philosophy's historical contribution to ethno-nationalist authoritarian regimes. As one of the most prominent academics to embrace the rise of National Socialism in early 1933, Heidegger has long occupied a central place in discussions about coming to terms with the past in Germany, especially with regard to academic complicity. For better or for worse, the name of Heidegger has often served as a placeholder for discussions about the complicity of the German professoriate.[3] Numerous academics from the humanities, especially in the fields of philosophy, history, anthropology, and German studies, enthusiastically embraced the rise of the National Socialist regime.[4] However, many of these figures disappeared into postwar obscurity, and none were able to match the kind of postwar reputation Heidegger enjoyed. Analyzing the question of silence in relation to Heidegger's trajectory, from the Weimar years through the National Socialist era, and ultimately denazification, thus tells a larger story about Germany, German universities, and the transformation of the humanities under Nazism. Moreover, the "Heidegger case" calls attention to the persistence of right-wing thinking among German academics from the Weimar era to the postwar Federal Republic of Germany. It is important to underscore from the outset that Heidegger approached National Socialism as a philosopher and, moreover, as a full professor of philosophy.[5] To underscore this means to say that he approached the rise of National Socialism by mobilizing the full weight of the credibility that the German public sphere at the time associated with the professoriate and with the venerable German philosophical tradition. Heidegger's political intervention into what he called the "situation" was from the outset both academic and philosophical (*GA* 94, 1/5). His entry into politics was not merely a move to advance his career, nor a form of opportunism—though it may have been those things as well. Richard Rorty long ago advised Heidegger's readers that "we should hold our noses, separate the life from the work"; this book argues, however, that by holding our noses we have, so to speak, shut off our sensitivity to some of the more unsavory elements in Heidegger's thinking (Rorty 1990, 21). The *Black Notebooks* reveal how Rorty's approach relies upon an ultimately illusory division between life and work that serves Heidegger's own skillful occlusion of his past.

With regard to such unsavory elements, one cannot speak about Heidegger and silence for very long without mentioning his own purported postwar silence about the Holocaust (see, e.g., Lang 1996).[6] If this silence has garnered so much fascination, that is because Heidegger, once again, has served as a conduit for a broader discussion of postwar silence in Germany. The process of "coming to terms with the past" in Germany has long been characterized as breaking silence about complicity among perpetrators (see, e.g., Frei 1996). As the philosopher Hermann Lübbe described the situation in 1983, in the postwar Federal Republic of Germany there was a general and palpable "silencing" of such discussions, while it was "politically less important where one comes from than where one is willing to go" (Lübbe 1983, 341). With regard to Heidegger's silence, *Heidegger's Fascist Affinities* takes a twofold approach. First, the *Black Notebooks* have ultimately rendered the thesis of Heidegger's silence untenable, given his defiant political tone in the postwar notebooks. Secondly, the book will show how Heidegger positions himself publicly and politically through a complex play with silence as early as the 1920s. The nature of this concealment and the silences it engenders will become clearer when read in terms of Heidegger's philosophical analyses of silence.[7] In other words, Heidegger was not merely silent as an unrepentant antisemite or as a stalwart adherent to at least some portion of National Socialism's political agenda, he was also silent as a philosophical act. Ultimately, what the *Black Notebooks* reveal is how Heidegger embedded his vision of what, even in 1952, he referred to as the "the inner truth and greatness" of National Socialism within complex layers of silence and silencing (*IM*, 152/213).[8] *Heidegger's Fascist Affinities* is dedicated to elucidating the philosophical nature of Heidegger's silence as a political act. This follows a principle stated eloquently by Charles Bambach: "I will hold that Heidegger's texts present themselves as a call for action and that Heidegger's own actions are rooted in the philosophical commitments expressed in these texts" (Bambach 2003, 25). *Heidegger's Fascist Affinities* extends this principle by showing how Heidegger's many silences should be counted among the actions that need to be taken into consideration, demonstrated by analyzing the texts in which that silence is preserved.

In order to unearth these layers of silent philosophical action, the analysis that follows will focus on the complex ontological, ethical, and political place of silence in Heidegger's philosophy, and especially in his influential interpretations of ancient Greek philosophy. From the time of his earliest lecture course in 1920–21, Heidegger exhibited a distinct interest in the question of silence (*GA* 60, 314/336). This intensified in *Being and Time* (1927), culminating in the sigetic texts of the 1930s, which deal with silence as a primary ontological concern. Concurrent with the emergence of silence as a theme in Heidegger's work, a thematics of silence also arose in the contemporary *völkisch* movement. For Heidegger, silence is neither some particular thing nor a sort of fixed entity. Rather, it is a performance enacted through and with words, whether written or spoken. By the early 1930s, a time when his thinking begins increasingly to utilize terms and themes about language, noise, and modernity that resonated with the ethno-nationalist *völkisch* political movements of his time, Heidegger begins to refer to this performance of silence as the "handicraft" of thinking. This performance of the handicraft of silence is a distinctly philosophical act and one that for Heidegger serves to link the Germany of his day to what he refers to as the "Greek inception." By learning to "hearken back to the voices of the great inception," Heidegger writes, the Germans will learn to "perceive the primordial laws of our German ethnic essence in the most simple exigency and greatness" (*GA* 36/7, 89/72). As the medium of spiritual and linguistic renewal, silence binds the Germans to the Greeks, and Heidegger regards himself as the essential link to this "occidental essence" (*GA* 97, 54). In his autobiographical works, Heidegger describes certain key moments of his life in terms of their relation to silence, including the ebbs and flows of his relationship to National Socialism. Simultaneously, many of Heidegger's philosophical colleagues, including Ludwig Ferdinand Clauss, Raymund Schmidt, and Herrmann Schwarz, invested the topic of silence with overtly antisemitic connotations.

Clauss, Schmidt, and Schwarz all approached National Socialism as academically trained philosophers, and they provided philosophical descriptions of what they regarded as a peculiarly Germanic form of silence threatened by a noisy, distracting, and dissevering (Jewish) modernity. The *Black Notebooks* make Heidegger's philosophical affinities to this movement clear. This clarity demands a renewed examination of key fundamental terms in Heidegger's work. *Heidegger's Fascist Affinities* is dedicated to examining a constellation of terms that include silence, reticence, quiet, scattering, and gathering.

To Silence and Back

Given his immense philosophical investment in the topic of silence, the way Heidegger characterizes his entry into and exit from National Socialism in terms of a complex layering of forms of silence, which he amplifies and attenuates according to his desired affect, is telling. In 1933, on the verge of assuming the Freiburg rectorate, Heidegger states the connection between National Socialism and silence in the *Black Notebooks*: "*National Socialism is a genuinely burgeoning power only if it still, behind all of its action and talk, has something to keep silent about—and if it operates with a firm deviousness aimed at future impact*" (*GA* 94, 114/84). Silence, he asserts here, is essential, not only to the National Socialist movement, but to his own relationship to that movement. Silence is the central motif running through the *Black Notebooks* from the years 1932 to 1948. Indeed, the *Black Notebooks* are a tapestry woven out of countless threads of silence. The patterns formed by these threads are complex and deeply intertwined with Heidegger's philosophy of language, readings of ancient Greek philosophy, teaching activities, and research agenda in the Nazi years.

Beginning in 1932 in the earliest entries of the *Black Notebooks*, Heidegger decisively links his writings to the notion of silence. In the opening pages of the first notebook, he proclaims that he will "[w]rite out of a great reticence" (*GA* 94, 28/22). Around 1940, when Germany was launching into its war of genocidal annihilation and imperial expansion, he speaks of the time as one of "*essential active silence*" (*GA* 96, 54/42). As the notebooks progress, they reveal themselves to be an elaborate, multilayered repository of Heidegger's many philosophical, political, and personal silences. They coalesce into the most intense textual site in which he talks about his silences, reaffirming that silence is one of the most essential concerns of his work (cf. Smith 2013, 84–98; Baracchi 2013, 92–121). This reaches its peak in the early 1940s, when Heidegger—seemingly having returned to his literary mode—writes elliptically:

> To once again know more than we say or speak. To once again be silent, to silence over the idle chatter, the language of metaphysics. Once again the word. Once again the listening answer—
> Stillness—instead of noise—*through* writing and speaking?
> With one's own obstacle constantly in the way!
> Thus to give the "illusion" and appearance:
> Silence—nothing published—not going any further—unproductive, helpless, at the end. Failure.
> "Further"—further on to where—to begin with here and there where we are—first the there—to remain, in the there—not going any "further" and no progress.
> *Being* there. Where then? The where for the where. (*GA* 97, 56)

This passage is replete with some of the multiple forms of silence that this book analyzes with the tools of critical phenomenology:[9] a silence that silences over noise and chatter, a silence produced by not publishing academic works in order to produce the "illusion" of philosophical confusion bringing his academic productivity to a halt, and a stillness produced in opposition to chatter. Most important for the task of this book, these silences are produced through writing and speaking, not in opposition to them. Since these silences are an operation of language, acquiring the capacity for them requires, as Heidegger writes in the *Black Notebooks*, "the assumption of an insidious ambiguity" (*GA* 95, 27/21).[10] These silences, and the insidious ambiguity out of which they arise, reach a particularly acute tension in the *Black Notebooks*, setting Heidegger's other writings in relief. From their perspective, Heidegger's work as a whole can be read anew, with an ear attuned to what remains unspoken in them. Moreover, the silences of the *Black Notebooks* ebb and flow in a current tied to the rise and fall of both the National Socialist movement and Heidegger's own career within it. *Heidegger's Fascist Affinities* seeks to show how this "insidious ambiguity" relates to the "firm deviousness" of a movement that, in order to maintain its "greatness," must have something to keep silent about, which it holds in reserve. Demonstrating this connection requires, not only attentiveness to how the specifics of the political and historical moment inflect Heidegger's performance of silence, but a detailed analysis of the ontology of speech and silence developed in his lecture courses on Greek philosophy.

Heidegger regarded the rise, evolution, and fall of National Socialism as enabling various channels of speech, while closing off others. His silences reflect his navigation of these transformations. Confronted with the administrative tasks of the university rectorate, he had to "let his own work slip into the background." Yet, as he wrote to his brother Fritz on May 4, 1933, just three days after being granted membership in the Nazi party, he replaced that work with a new public role and a cooperative task: "But at the moment one cannot think of oneself, rather only of the whole and the fate of the German people, which is at stake."[11] In the early months of the Nazi solidification of power, Heidegger discovered for himself a robust public voice in speeches, Nazi party assemblies, radio addresses, and writings in periodicals.[12] This helps to explain why, after President Paul von Hindenburg named Hitler chancellor of Germany on January 30, 1933, Heidegger quickly assumed a leading role in crafting a political platform for an organization of radical professors known as the Cultural-Political Working Community of German University Professors. In March 1933, this group declared itself to be a "community of conviction, work and struggle" and sought to transform universities into a "site of national-political education" guided by "ethnically German university professors" (Bundesarchiv Berlin-Lichterfelde, file BArch R8088/1155). Beyond these local organizations, Heidegger also successfully built alliances with Nazi party representatives at the local, state, and federal levels, thus revealing himself to be anything but "naïve," as much recent literature still contends.[13] This transformation may have struck many observers as peculiar given the fact that, throughout the 1920s, and especially in *Being and Time*, the work that solidified his international reputation and secured his place in the philosophical canon, Heidegger expressed great skepticism about involvement in the public sphere and about the distortion one necessarily undergoes as a result of entering a realm in which "the they unfolds its true dictatorship" (*BT*, 126/119).[14] In 1924, Heidegger declared philosophy to be in a "battle against idle talk," but by the early 1930s, he seems to have been promoting its rapid spread (*GA* 19, 16/11). This indicates that Heidegger was more strongly attracted to National Socialism and its antisemitic agenda than repelled by its method of delivery. In other words, he was not so much disturbed by dictatorship per se as by the rule of the wrong kind of dictator. Much like many intellectuals in Weimar Germany, Heidegger was a staunch critic of the universalist assumptions of modern liberal democracies (Sontheimer 1957). "There is a clear line separating

Right from Left," he wrote to his brother Fritz. "Being in the middle is treason."[15] *Heidegger's Fascist Affinities* seeks to analyze the philosophical stakes involved in this declaration.

Heidegger's notion of "the they," the average, everyday public realm into which we are thrown, and from which we must withdraw in order to return to our authenticity, is one of the most famous terms he coined in *Being and Time*. In his description of "the they," Heidegger echoes a theme common among Weimar intellectuals concerned about the distracting effects of modern technologies, the increased tempo of modern life, and the anonymity of urban existence (Simmel 1969, 47–60; Kracauer 1995, 323–30). The primary snares of "the they" involve a pernicious form of idle talk that interprets everything it encounters in advance and transforms it into an average, easily repeatable and consumable message. "The they" produces endless information, jingles, sound bites, headlines, bursts of information, and shocking revelations about the latest hot topics. Consequently, this anonymous mass consisting of nobody and everybody destroys whatever element of patience, thoughtfulness, or intellectual complexity passes through it. The message of "the they" is ordinary and fleeting, leveling off whatever is unique in a particular utterance to fit it into preexisting molds and expectations. A population trained to anticipate the latest bursts of information, memes, GIFs, and tweets is but the most recent instantiation of an ever-evolving set of tactics employed, according to Heidegger, to draw us away from what he calls our "ownmost" existence and into the scattered existence of the public realm. *Being and Time* coupled this suspicion of the public realm with a critique of the forms of technology that allowed for the easy mass distribution of chatter and idle talk, including the radio, newspaper, popular periodicals, and—in a different manner—forms of rapid transportation such as automobiles, trains, and airplanes. In Heidegger's reading, the process of reducing great distances to technological challenges to be overcome by transportation logistics disturbs our rootedness in a particular place. Given this suspicion of both technology and easily repeatable mass messages, which Heidegger expressed so clearly in 1927 and reinforced in many lecture courses in the 1920s and early 1930s, it may at first seem peculiar that he would align himself with a regime that was at the forefront of rapidly embracing technological innovations to spread an easily repeatable political message (Herf 2006).[16] Indeed, Heidegger not only aligned himself with the regime but, as a public figure of significant international renown, deemed "a towering thinker in our eminent schools," he also made use of the very modes of technology that he had previously denounced so vehemently.[17]

How could a philosopher so thoroughly suspicious of mass media become so enamored of using it in the service of National Socialism? What does it reveal about Heidegger's philosophy of language that he was willing to submit certain messages to the mass media but keep other messages concealed within his notebooks? What does this layering and selective distribution of texts and messages reveal about how Heidegger conceptualized the task of philosophizing and the role of the philosopher in society? Heidegger's embrace of National Socialism and the manner in which he did so are far from being mere biographical curiosities without philosophical relevance. They are deeply rooted in a complex set of philosophical commitments that emerge from his peculiar understanding of the ontological relation between speech, silence, and idle talk. Heidegger turns to silence through an overlapping set of ideological commitments involving antisemitism, anti-modernism, and anti-liberalism, while revering the German language and landscape as sources for the spiritual renewal of the German people.

Heidegger as a Thinker of Silence

My working hypothesis in this book is that in his philosophizing, Heidegger was concerned, not just with the question of being, but with silence. As we have seen, Heidegger calls this thinking "sigetics," deriving the term from Greek *sigē*, usually translated as "silence," but applied to a vast range of phenomena (*GA* 65, 78–79/62).[18] Yet as a thinker deeply indebted to Aristotle, Heidegger's ongoing sigetic project initiated in the early 1930s demonstrates that theoretical knowledge of sigetics is useless if it is not coupled with a silent comportment, much in the same way that theoretical knowledge of virtue is useless for Aristotle if it is not embodied in virtuous action. Through Heidegger's actions and ontological descriptions of silence, he demonstrates that theoretical knowledge of the philosophy of silence is meaningless if it is not also practiced silently. This is the core of Heidegger's performance of silence: silence requires an essential space of utterance, and, for him, Nazi Germany was that space. For Heidegger, National Socialism's arrival heralded the renewed possibility of restoring essential silence to its essential place by enabling him to put the performance of silence into practice in the service of what he called the "handicraft of thinking." Of course, the irony does not go unnoticed that Heidegger draws this philosophical lesson from—of all places—Aristotle's ethics.[19] Yet this should not be too surprising given that, for many supporters of National Socialism, the movement was based on a distinct form of morality privileging the good of the German people above everything.[20]

Tracing this trajectory through Heidegger's works written during National Socialism and during the early phases of the postwar occupation of Germany reveals something I call a "logic of inversion" at the heart of Heidegger's philosophy of language: the less essential something is to his thinking, the more likely he is to expose it to the mass media. Conversely, the more essential something is to Heidegger's thinking, the more carefully he shields it from exposure to the public realm.[21] Such inversion is a central element of the performative aspect of Heidegger's sigetics. Heidegger states the principle of his inverted politics of language outright in an entry from the *Black Notebooks* written in early 1946, on the eve of receiving the final judgment of the Denazification Commission. After calling the public sphere the "most turbulent perversion which the openness of being tolerates," he goes on to state the principle that guides the analysis of this book: "The more public the public sphere, the more closed the openness of being" (*GA* 97, 68). Roughly speaking, one could classify the degree of public exposure in Heidegger's diverse range of texts to include, in descending order: radio speeches and public speeches given during his rectorate, works published during his lifetime, large lecture courses, smaller courses with advanced students, private seminars, manuscripts not intended for publication during his lifetime, personal correspondence, and, finally, the manuscripts that include his writings on the event and the *Black Notebooks*. The point here is not to posit a rigid system of classification, but instead to suggest the possibility of a spectrum that would place his public appearances in various formats—on the radio, in popular periodicals, in public speeches, open telegrams—as rector at one extreme and the *Black Notebooks* at the other extreme. Within this spectrum, the *Black Notebooks* serve as a site for the preservation of a politics and language not exposed to the more "vulgar" formats.

Throughout the *Black Notebooks*, Heidegger describes himself as speaking through various masks including, most ominously, the mask of a thinker who declared in 1934 that "we will remain at the invisible front of the secret spiritual Germany" (*GA* 94, 155/114).[22] If Heidegger wore masks on this invisible front, this does not mean to say that the words spoken under that, or any other particular mask, are somehow to be dismissed.

Instead, it indicates that Heidegger's message is inflected by his preemptive assumptions about how essentially the medium involved will distort it. Hence the mask and the silence it engenders are figures, not merely of occlusion, but also of modulation. In other words, at the latest with the inception of National Socialism, Heidegger was perfectly willing to make strategic alliances with the distorting influence of the public realm, which he regarded as a space for a particular voice or set of voices as he entered the "situation" (*GA* 94, 1/5). In *Being and Time*, he observes harshly: "Publicness obscures everything, and then claims that what has been thus covered over is what is familiar and accessible to everybody" (*BT*, 127/119). Given this assessment, is it possible that Heidegger sought a certain obscuring or occluding effect within National Socialism? Or did he regard National Socialism as the authentic public realm in which his thinking would first find its essential place? Is it possible that he sought both at the same time? And if the Weimar democracy was a space of noise, distraction, and the leveling affects of sameness, then what kind of quiet, resoluteness, and difference would National Socialism restore to the German people?

Before attempting to answer these questions we should recall that Heidegger depicts exposure to the public realm as a matter of necessity, and not merely as an avoidable inconvenience. This is because the public realm of "the they" is constitutive of who we are as human beings "proximally and for the most part," even if it alleviates the burden of dealing with our ownmost existence.[23] In the *Black Notebooks*, Heidegger describes the public realm as destructive of philosophy, even though it effectively disseminates a certain kind of philosophy: "Fame—to be under surveillance by the demands of the public sphere and simplified, i.e., to be simplified by its implacable opining that claims that everything should take part in everything else" (*GA* 97, 109). A person cannot retreat from the scattering effects of the public sphere, for that scattering is only the intensification of the dispersal of language itself. Even in the mode of authenticity, a term that diminishes in importance in Heidegger's thinking after *Being and Time*, one can modulate one's intensity of exposure to the public realm or use it intentionally to one's own ends. In other words, while there is no space that maintains the purity of either silence or speech, since both are primordially contaminated, there are nonetheless political situations that can at least abate this contamination. For Heidegger, the Greek world preserved a particularly intense form of silence, while National Socialism, in its "inner truth and greatness" promised to restore silence—and thereby the power of saying—to the German language and people.

In 1933, this promise, alongside the party's overtly antisemitic platform, motivated a particular intensity of exposure to the public realm.[24] This is because the public realm is deeply tied to the *Volk*, a people who would have to be trained to listen and to question anew. Heidegger makes what is perhaps his clearest statement regarding the link between the people, the public realm, thinking, and silence in the lecture course he held after withdrawing from the Freiburg rectorate: "Hence, the further question is: what is speaking? And which speaking constitutes the reality of language? Is language then real, if only this one or that one speaks, or is it real, when all members of a linguistic community speak at the same time? Does it cease to be when there is silence?" (*GA* 38, 31/29).

What does it mean for the members of a linguistic community to speak at the same time? It does not mean speaking in unison, nor speaking over one another, but instead speaking from the same space of attunement. This fundamental attunement arises for Heidegger from a place, from a landscape, and from a historical meditation on the "Greek-German essence." Heidegger turns to the public realm qua the *Volk* because it is the space of the essential saying of language for those who are rooted in that space. Yet this saying requires an attunement that is disturbed by those who are portrayed as homeless and uprooted. Following long-standing antisemitic stereotypes, reinforced by Nazi propaganda, the Jews were this homeless, "wandering" people disturbing the German essence. In one of the more infamous antisemitic passages from the *Black Notebooks*, Heidegger states this explicitly: "The question of the role of world Jewry is not a racial question, but the metaphysical question about the kind of humanity that, without any restraints, can take over the uprooting of all beings from being as its world-historical 'task'" (*GA* 96, 243/191).[25] For Heidegger, protecting Germany from this uprooting required the preservation and restoration of the German language, infused with the "voices of the great inception" (*GA* 36–37, 89/72).

Heidegger's Fascist Affinities is devoted to identifying and analyzing the philosophical context from which Heidegger's antisemitism emerged, and within which it was performed.[26] If what is most essential in Heidegger is indeed precisely what is most concealed, it is noteworthy that his antisemitism is most prominently expressed in his *Black Notebooks*, and that his antisemitic statements in these are more frequent and vehement after

Kristallnacht in November 1938, the first act of mass antisemitic violence in Nazi Germany.[27]

The modes of expression Heidegger employed to create a space for the unsaid in his speaking and writing structure his life and work. Heidegger was a philosopher who worked through and with a vast array of silences, including philosophical, political, and personal silences. As a result, we can often learn more about him by investigating what he did not say or refused to say than from what he did in fact say. As rector of Freiburg University, he wielded silence as a tool of administrative power, blocking, for instance, an investigation into the violence initiated by a Nazi student group against a Jewish fraternity in May 1933.[28] This play with concealment and unconcealment culminated in a form of writing that he referred to as the "handicraft" of thinking and writing.[29] Heidegger developed this handicraft of silence as a phenomenological recovery of a Greek experience of silence developed primarily through his readings of Aristotle and Plato in the lecture courses he held as a professor in Freiburg, which erected a linguistic and political bulwark against modernity's effect of diluting language and proliferating idle talk. Exercising this handicraft, Heidegger structured the *Black Notebooks* as a cryptic and multilayered repository for his silences. While the Greeks provided Heidegger with an ontology and pedagogical practice of silence, the *Black Notebooks* provided the textual space for these silences to unfold. These silences set the entirety of Heidegger's oeuvre in relief and help us further to map the terrain of the unsaid in his works. Though this encompasses much of Heidegger's thinking, ranging at least from the 1920s to the 1950s, I focus here primarily on the particularly intense period of philosophical productivity and transformation from the publication of *Being and Time* until the end of World War II. These were both the years in which he developed his phenomenological recovery of silence most explicitly and those in which Germany transitioned from the liberal democracy of the Weimar era to a totalitarian state. If this work integrates the study of the person Heidegger so deeply into the philosophical analysis of Heidegger's thinking, that is because his thinking changes so profoundly at a time of great upheaval for Heidegger as a person and for Germany as a whole.

Given the widely held assumption that Heidegger is first and foremost a thinker of being, it may seem peculiar to read Heidegger through the lens of silence. Heidegger himself confirms this assumption in variations on a refrain repeated throughout his work: "the question of the truth of *being*, is and remains *my* question and is my *unique* question, for at issue in it is indeed what is *most unique*." For Heidegger, this is "*the* question of all questions" (*GA* 65, 10–11/11). In calling Heidegger a thinker of silence, I am not so much attempting to question this claim, already substantiated by both Heidegger himself and a great deal of literature on him. Rather, I am drawing a series of conclusions that emerge from the assumption that he is a philosopher primarily concerned with the question of being. Heidegger certainly dedicates a great deal of philosophical effort to the ontological task of posing the question of being, yet from his earliest attempts to do so, he also recognizes that the question of being is always accompanied by concern for the degree and manner of sayability applicable to the inquiry. That is to say, in order for the inquiry to achieve its proper measure, it must be aware of the limits of sayability of the matter under examination. In following this logic, Heidegger overtly relies upon a principle stated in Aristotle's *Nicomachean Ethics*: "it is the mark of an educated man to seek as much precision in the things of a given genus as their nature allows" (*NE* 1094b, 24–26). This hermeneutical insight shapes Heidegger's phenomenological practice from very early on. From his first attempts to recover the question of being in the 1920s, he is always highly attentive to the language appropriate to the task of philosophically recovering the question of being. This entails a concomitant concern with the role of silence in the philosophical process, and with silence as a medium of philosophical expression. Recovering this question is always a matter of acquiring the grammar in which the question can be posed by listening—as Heidegger puts it—to the speaking of being. Yet this was never simply a private endeavor, and we must keep in mind that when Heidegger speaks briefly of the *Volk* in *Being and Time* §74, he links the *Volk* to the necessity of communication: "In communication and in struggle the power of destiny first becomes free. The fateful destiny of Dasein in and with its 'generation' constitutes the complete, authentic occurrence of Dasein" (*BT*, 384–85/366).[30] The *Black Notebooks* help illuminate how this communication worked with and around complex layers of silence. Heidegger's affinities to the *völkisch* movement help show how this destiny was tied to a particular landscape. Although he maintained a degree of distance from the doctrine of the blood in Nazi blood-and-soil ideology, he nonetheless shows himself in thrall to the mythological powers of German soil, often endowed by the *völkisch* movement with a peculiar stillness.

Silence and Politics

Silence is also a particularly revealing lens through which to view Heidegger's philosophical activity in the era of National Socialism, inasmuch as he explicitly narrates this period as being bookended by it. In 1946, Heidegger was an embittered, isolated man receiving psychological care in the Sanatorium Hausbaden in Badenweiler, south of Freiburg. In January 1946, the university's Denazification Commission gave him specific directives to "hold back from the public realm," and he dutifully complied (*GA* 97, 68). Writing in April 1946 from the Sanatorium, he describes his descent into silence: "Everything remains strange around me, and for days on end I only speak the most necessary words at the table. But this estrangement and disengagement is necessary for me to confront what I have worked through in two decades of silence with increasing freedom."[31] Up until Germany's defeat in May 1945, Heidegger had been living relatively comfortably and securely in the Reich, continuing a robust teaching agenda, despite all of his seemingly unfounded claims of persecution by the Nazi security apparatus.[32] Heidegger certainly felt inconvenienced during the wartime state of emergency, such as when Dibionta, the ersatz chocolate product he consumed as a nutritional supplement while meat was strictly rationed, disappeared from the market.[33] He was also upset by what he regarded as the dwindling quality of the students at the university as the wartime draft drastically shifted the gender demographics of German universities, leaving him to question the value of teaching "a tutorial for a few young girls,"[34] if "one can at all call a stable of 120 cackling girls" a tutorial.[35] When drafted into the domestic work service in 1944, he complained that in those surroundings "no conversation is possible."[36] Under National Socialism, Heidegger would occasionally face annoyances at the hands of the Nazi surveillance apparatus, including one instance in 1942 when the publication of his essay "Plato's Concept of Truth" in an Italian collection was blocked until none other than Benito Mussolini intervened through the Italian ambassador to request that Joseph Goebbels approve the publication.[37] He also had repeated difficulties receiving clearance to travel for lecture tours in Italy, Spain, and Portugal in 1942,[38] while his letters to his brother complain of his publisher Niemeyer using the pretext of not receiving approval for requisitions of paper, a scarce product in wartime Germany, for reprinting editions of his Hölderlin lecture.[39]

Despite these inconveniences, for the most part he lived the compara-
tively peaceful life of a philosophy professor in the years after his Freiburg
rectorate. Heidegger himself admits this, even in the final stages of the war
in January 1945: "Many thoughts are becoming clear, and despite all of
the disruption and threat, I trek across the high cliffs, clear and beckoned,
unhindered by the professorial existence."[40] This unhindered balancing
act of the professor's life was possible for Heidegger since he had been
officially designated as "politically reliable," though not overtly National
Socialist, by the regime in 1942.[41] He received this designation because
he not only tolerated but also actively fostered many of the fundamental
goals of National Socialism. Even if Heidegger disagreed about the precise
nature of some of National Socialism's tenets, it was not necessarily because
he had more moderate aims than the ones the regime was actively pursuing. Moreover, with his lecture courses and seminars on Kant, Nietzsche,
Schelling, Leibniz, and Hölderlin, Heidegger established a research and
teaching agenda under National Socialism that satisfied both the demand
for Germanic studies (*Heimatkunde*) and Nazi philhellenism (Bialas and
Rabinbach 2007, xxiv; Marchand 1996).[42] Thus, while Heidegger's defenders often tend to echo the sort of assertion recently made by Arnulf
Heidegger that "the lectures of Martin Heidegger in the late years of National Socialism were regarded as 'critical of the current moment' and
'courageous'" (A. Heidegger 2016, 12),[43] his chosen topics fit quite nicely
into the overall "ideologically prescribed themes" of National Socialist
cultural politics (Bialas and Rabinbach 2007, ix).

Despite his relatively comfortable life as a professor under National
Socialism, Heidegger did suffer some inconveniences during these years.
No doubt he was unsettled by the bombardment of the town of Freiburg
by the Allies and by the disruption of the university's operation in 1945
due to the chaotic situation at the war's end. Yet despite this disturbance,
his primary concern at this time was teaching a group of radically loyal
students in the Cloister Beuron in the Black Forest, while frantically scout-
ing for a suitably isolated spot in which to stash his manuscripts, lest they
be destroyed or fall into the hands of the enemy.[44] By and large, National
Socialism for him was a period of philosophical flourishing, whose end he
bitterly mourned, for he regarded the years of Allied occupation, with the
looming threat of "Americanism," viewed as German self-betrayal (*GA* 97,
51, 143, 150, 161, 181, 230, 390, 446), as "worse than the Nazi time."[45]
Yet perhaps most important for the present study, it was during the years of

National Socialism that Heidegger devoted himself most fully to the study of silence, while simultaneously developing a practice for rendering silence in language in his copious writings on the notion of the event, primarily in the 1930s and early 1940s.

One might at first be tempted to read this cultivation of a silent language as an act of resistance, or as a way of developing new forms of saying to skirt the censorship mechanisms of a totalitarian regime. However, portraying Heidegger in this way would assume that what he refused to say would have been objectionable to the regime. The *Black Notebooks* have proven this to be untenable.[46] They reveal that what Heidegger refused to say, at least at times, was such an extreme version of nationalist, proto-Germanic rhetoric that the Nazis would perhaps neither have comprehended it, approved of it, nor even had any use for it (cf. Nancy 2017, 40). Writing to Bernhard Rust, Reich minister of science, education, and national culture, the rival ambitious, power-hungry philosopher Erich Jaensch mocked Heidegger in 1934 as "one of the greatest scatterbrains and most prominent eccentrics whom we have in the realm of higher education" (Geheimes Staatsarchiv Preußischer Kulturbesitz, HA, Rep. 76 IVa, Nr. 71). The same year Baden's Nazi Ministry of Culture sidelined Heidegger for "appearing too radical" (Dahms 2009, 220). True, the Security Service doubted whether Heidegger's "radical form of questioning is capable of promoting National Socialist science" (Bundesarchiv Berlin-Lichterfelde, BArch R4901/12444), but he was by no means the target of significant political suspicion. After the fall of Nazi Germany, Heidegger was subjected to intense scrutiny under the rules of denazification because of his role in the "Aryanization" of Freiburg University and his membership in the Nazi party from 1933 until 1945, and he resented this perceived interference in his personal and professional life. Things became so uncomfortable for Heidegger that he went so far as to declare that "everything is rotten and worse than during the Nazi period."[47] Eventually, he would undergo two denazification procedures, with the second resulting in a teaching ban, a ban on entering university premises, and forced retirement as a result of being declared a Nazi "fellow traveler."[48] Heidegger responded to this judgment in private with characteristic indignation by declaring himself to be a "fellow traveler of being."[49] Meanwhile his status as a former Nazi party member subjected him to the mandatory requisitioning of a portion of his home for the lodging of a French officer's family. In a peculiarly Heideggerian fashion, he wrote a "most urgent" request in 1947 to the French occupation forces regarding the noise made by the French officer's family stationed in his "acoustically sensitive house" (*GA* 16, 426–27). In July 1945, he had complained offhand to his brother that "[w]e have to take in concentration camp people [*KZ-Leute*] in the apartment."[50] At a larger national level, Heidegger regarded the fall of National Socialism as the end of an era and the beginning of a foreign occupation that—as he repeatedly writes in the volume of the *Black Notebooks* covering 1942–48—he regarded as "more disturbing than any 'crime' that can be publicly 'decried,' a guilt that no one in the future could forgive." For Heidegger, the occupation of Germany was the most significant crime, and Germans bore responsibility for it as an act of self-betrayal. From Heidegger's perspective, this act of self-betrayal began as early as 1934 as Nazism moved away from what he perceived as its essential task of the spiritual renewal of the German people and language. In 1946, in an elaborate orchestration of scare quotes, Heidegger proclaimed that "the German people and land are already a single '*concentration camp*' [emphasis in original]—of a sort that 'the world' has not yet 'seen' and 'the world' does not want to see" (*GA* 97, 99–100; cf. di Cesare 2015, 316–22).

The themes that course through Heidegger's embittered and embattled writings at this time, especially in the *Black Notebooks*, are of betrayal, desolation, and the retreat into silence. He felt betrayed by the Nazi movement, while holding onto a vision of the "inner truth and greatness of National Socialism." Heidegger would frame his eventual banishment from the university by the Denazification Commission as a withdrawal—a withdrawal from publicly philosophizing and a withdrawal into silence: "*Saying and— writing*—Why write? In order to publish? No. To communicate what has been thought? No. To preserve what is to be thought? Yes. But for whom? For thinkers? If they stay away? Then it would be far better if what is to be thought is never publicly torn apart in speech as a set of opinions and is thereby ruined for any tradition" (*GA* 97, 161).

Heidegger now shunned the public realm he had once embraced, instead choosing to preserve his thinking within the space of a form of silence. With his withdrawal into a postwar silence, he had come full circle, retreating back to a mode of silence he had abandoned in 1933. In a clever act of self-reinvention, he moved from being a thinker of violence to one of letting-be and serenity (Morat 2007). This shift helped lay the groundwork for Heidegger's postwar rehabilitation. The *Black Notebooks*, however, reveal a much more straightforward national-conservative thinker, with an unwavering set of fidelities, not to National Socialism per se, but to the political inclinations that brought him to National Socialism in the first place.

Anticipating the decision of the university's independent Denazification Commission in July 1945, either overtly defiant or seemingly unaware, during the "miserable weeks of waiting," that the outcome would not be his to choose,[51] he wrote to his brother: "The question remains whether I should once again 'teach' for a decade under such pressure, that is to say, should I speak indirectly and in a reticent manner—or whether the formation of the saying remains the only essential matter, without regard for impact or contemporary understanding."[52]

Heidegger thus portrays himself as choosing between two forms of silence. On the one hand, he has the indirect speech of his lecture courses, which require him to speak about what is essential reticently, through what he called "the mask of historical interpretation" (GA 94, 243/178). The other form of silence is the conversation with himself in his manuscripts in which he approaches the question of being in a language comprehensible to none, other than a group he refers to using such terms as the "most unique ones," "the most futural ones," "the invisible ones," "the race to follow," the "concealed Germans," and a "race of the concealed guardians of stillness" (ibid., 338/246; GA 94, 370/269; GA 94, 346/252; GA 96, 31/25; GA 95, 27/21). In a short fragment entitled "My Removal," described as a draft of a 1946 letter, whose recipient is not known, Heidegger reinforces the link between his silence, his work, and removal from the university: "I have kept silent in my thinking not only since 1927, since the publication of *Being and Time*, but also *within Being and Time* itself and constantly before that. This silence is the preparation for the saying of what is to be thought, and this preparation is the movement of experience, and this, in turn, is an activity and undertaking. It is indeed 'existing,' but without need of engagement" (GA 16, 421–22).

After the Denazification Commission deprived Heidegger of the first of these two options by banishing him from the university, he describes the second—the conversation with himself—as a form of silence broken. Speaking of the possibility of publishing his essay collection *Off the Beaten Path*, Heidegger envisages its potential reception in these terms: "They will say that Heidegger has broken his silence; he said what is decisive. But this very communication is that act of keeping silent. We betray silence as long as we keep silent."[53] What they say about his work in their chatter may actually preserve it. He quotes Hölderlin's poem "Patmos": "But where the danger is, there grows also what saves" (*GA* 79, 72/68; cf. also *GA* 97, 340; Hölderlin 1967, 483).

As paradoxical as it might seem, I place the notion of a silence betrayed by silence at the center of this work and argue that comprehending the paradoxical nature of this silence helps us to unravel an entire hermeneutics of reticence at the core of Heidegger's life, teaching, politics, and thinking. If silence is betrayed by silence, then Heidegger must keep talking, thinking, and writing to preserve his silence. This silence, in other words, requires a terrain and landscape of speech to preserve it as silence, and this, in turn, requires an elaborate, sustained play with concealment and unconcealment.

Heidegger conceptualized his work after *Being and Time* as an attempt to recover an ancient Greek experience of silence through a phenomenological examination of Greek sigetics, especially in Aristotle (discussed in detail in chapters 4, 5, and 6). However, this process was accompanied by a growing awareness of the very impossibility of that task. *Heidegger's Fascist Affinities* examines this paradoxical and impossible process of recovery. At the same time, the book traces the immense impact that the *Black Notebooks* have had on Heidegger scholarship, arguing for their central place in the Heideggerian oeuvre.

As he often does when discussing matters that are essential to his thinking, Heidegger describes this silence in a series of open questions in the *Black Notebooks*: "To keep silent out of the rigor of an abundance of saying—who understands that? Who is pliant enough not to pounce upon and misconstrue such silence?" (*GA* 97, 123). As Heidegger admits, this play with concealment may justifiably be interpreted as an "insidious ambiguity." Beginning in 1934, after decisive transformations occur in his philosophy of language through a return to Aristotle's *Metaphysics* in the early 1930s, Heidegger describes this performance of silence as the capacity for silence. Heidegger's life, teaching, texts, and politics embody this silence that seeks not to betray itself by never being too silent. Through his inverted relation to the chatter of the public realm, Heidegger preserves an essential form of speech in his thinking, most fully in the *Black Notebooks*.[54] Although this book is not a reading *of* the *Black Notebooks*, in the sense of a comprehensive exegetical analysis of their content, it does intend to be a reading *through* the *Black Notebooks*.

The *Black Notebooks*

Since their publication in 2013, there has been a great deal of debate about why Heidegger preserved the *Black Notebooks* despite their damning testimony to his antisemitism. Peter Trawny, for example, defends the view that Heidegger intended to preserve and publish them as an honest engagement with his own mistakes and in order to document his errors (Trawny 2015a). Without discounting this interpretation, I would like to posit another motivation behind Heidegger's preservation of the *Black Notebooks*, a motivation revealed within the *Notebooks* themselves. Perhaps the most pervasive theme in the *Notebooks*, aside from attention to the development of the National Socialist revolution, is the author's persistent obsession with the belletristic and philosophical reception of *Being and Time*. This obsession is paradoxical, because Heidegger evidently wanted *Being and Time* to be read as an untimely work, as a work that could not yet be understood, yet at the same time, he also wanted to reserve the right to express his displeasure about the many misreadings to which the book was subject. He expresses his greatest frustration early in the first volume of the *Black Notebooks*: "Objection to the book: I have even today still not enough enemies—it has not brought me a great enemy" (*GA* 94, 9/8). Eventually, he goes on to describe his frustrations with a dash of humor: "People are waiting for the second volume of *Being and Time*: I am waiting for this waiting to cease and for people to finally confront the first volume" (*GA* 94, 184/135). Heidegger specifically mentions Karl Jaspers and Jean-Paul Sartre as among his misguided readers,[55] and he rails generally against *Existenzphilosophie*, and specifically targets the "'detective' work" of hunting down influences in the text (*GA* 94, 74/56). Heidegger's anxiety about the public reception of *Being and Time* shows how consistently attentive he was to his place in the philosophical world, and how deeply concerned he was with his philosophical legacy. A quotation from 1942 captures this succinctly, while also presaging a number of themes of overproduction and overspecialization (see chapter 2):

> The number of "books" that purportedly depict my "philosophy" is increasing day by day. Yet nowhere has anyone thought to grasp and define the question of *Being and Time* from the fundamental trait of occidental thinking. Instead, they get by with random, groundless perspectives drawn from contemporary opining, from the bonds of which *Being and Time* sought to free thinking. It is the same approach that was immediately applied in 1927 upon the publica-

tion of *Being and Time*: the hunt for conceptual influences and long-winded explanations of specific terms. Nowhere is there even a hint of genuine questioning! (*GA* 97, 13)

In his typically paradoxical fashion, Heidegger reveals a yearning to be an institution, even while prima facie rejecting the institutionalization of his own thinking. And all of this occurs while he basks self-indulgently in his status as a thinker already considered an institution, or a "hot stock," as his brother Fritz put it in 1933, to whom the philosopher wrote with great bravado that "success among contemporaries is an objection, perhaps even the objection to everything that aims to endure."[56]

Given Heidegger's paradoxical urges, I regard the publication of the *Black Notebooks* as a targeted attack—a potential ticking time bomb—meant by Heidegger to destroy the institution of Heidegger studies once it had established and normalized itself within the scholarly terrain of philosophy.[57] Heidegger himself speculated about what this might look like in the *Black Notebooks*:

Would that a thoughtful grounding again became a sort of compilation of sayings, well protected against idle talk and unharmed by all hurried misrepresentation; would that the works of twenty or more volumes including all the concomitant snooping into the author's life and the gathering of his casual utterances (I mean the usual "biographies" and collections of correspondence) disappear, and the work itself will be strong enough and will be spared the disfavor of being explained through the introduction of the "personal," i.e., kept from being dissolved into generalities. (*GA* 94, 328/238–39)

There is little doubt that Heidegger would include this very book among the kind of works that need to disappear, for it is a work that keeps rummaging about in the author's life. With the preservation and publication of the antisemitism of the *Black Notebooks*, Heidegger sought to destroy what Jacques Derrida refers to as the "machine," or the "machinery interpretation of Heidegger" (Derrida 2005, 139). Yet in his peculiarly delusional fashion, Heidegger sought to enact this destruction in order to pave the way for a more essential Heidegger for his readers, who must wait, as Heidegger says, for "two or three generations" (*GA* 94, 356/260). As he writes with characteristic immodesty to his brother Fritz in August 1945: "The premonition is becoming ever clearer to me that our home, the heart of the southwestern land, will be the birthplace of the occidental spirit. That may sound strange, but it cannot be otherwise."[58] What is unsaid in this declaration is, not that his homeland will be the birthplace of the so-called occidental spirit, but that nothing less than his very own work will be its eventual birthplace. Given this conviction, it is not surprising that Heidegger would preserve even his *Black Notebooks* and would have little interest in the judgment of his contemporaries about what he disparagingly calls the question of German guilt (Jaspers 2001).[59]

Of course, I fully admit that this interpretation risks assigning Heidegger the status of a sovereign over his own texts, as if he were overseeing them from above long after his death. However, I nonetheless assert that this interpretation captures the peculiar mixture of sovereignty and serenity that is Heidegger's legacy, which is, in part, its insidious ambiguity (Davis 2007). It is as if Heidegger wished to show, in a gesture of profound hubris, that once his thinking had been institutionalized into the "business" of modern philosophy, that is, into the entire routine philological business of conferences, journals, and publication series, only a thinker of his stature would have the power to destroy it. Yet deciding whether or not Heidegger is indeed the maniacal mastermind rising up from the grave to jam the machinery of routine Heidegger scholarship is less important than how Heidegger's readers respond to this disruption.

It would not be an exaggeration to say that the *Black Notebooks* have put Heidegger studies into crisis mode. So much writing on the *Black Notebooks* has emerged over the past few years that a survey of it would be a task for a separate work.[60] Among this vast literature, those scholars who doggedly seek to deny that Heidegger was deeply antisemitic, despite the clear evidence to the contrary, require no detailed response.[61] Many scholars have acknowledged the depth of Heidegger's antisemitism, conceded the importance of the *Black Notebooks*, and confronted the task of rethinking Heidegger in the light of what they reveal about his relation to National Socialism. However, much of the literature nevertheless seeks to engage in philosophical and professional damage control by means of what one might call a "quarantining" of the *Black Notebooks*.

One sees quarantining at work, for example, in Holger Zaborowski's call to "more strongly differentiate between different types of texts in the future" (Zaborowski 2016, 437). This tactic primarily involves conceding to the biographical importance of the *Black Notebooks*, while denying their philosophical relevance. By enforcing this neat divide, it is possible to return to business as usual based on a steadfast distinction between the biographical and the political. Such interpretations draw on an oft-repeated apothegm from Heidegger's 1924 lecture on Aristotle: "Regarding the personality of a philosopher, our only interest is: he was born at a certain time, worked, and died" (*GA* 18, 5/4). This is a convenient evasion: there is little reason to classify the *Black Notebooks* as belonging to the category of texts that inform us only about the philosopher's personality.

David Farrell Krell's essays on the *Black Notebooks* are symptomatic of the employment of quarantining to justify an interpretation of Heidegger that centers around *Being and Time* and seeks to downplay the philosophical relevance of not only the *Black Notebooks* but the entirety of Heidegger's later writings (Krell 2015, chaps. 4 and 6; Krell 2016). In this way, Krell duplicates a common strategy of diminishing the importance of Heidegger's later works in favor of an interpretation of Heidegger centered around the analytic of Dasein in *Being and Time*.[62] In his review of the fourth volume of the *Black Notebooks*, Krell makes sure to stress that the volume represents "remarks," "asides," or "footnotes" (Krell 2016, 309) and then goes on to lament "that many supervisors of doctoral candidates in philosophy are sending their students to read the *Black Notebooks*" (ibid., 334). After a lifetime of studying Heidegger, Krell writes, one "will need to spend at least several weeks" on the *Black Notebooks* (ibid., 335). Krell justifies dismissing the *Black Notebooks* based on their quality, which strikes me as rather convenient. This dismissal allows for a double-handed gesture of admitting the importance of Heidegger's antisemitism but diminishing the necessity of confronting it as part of a philosophical reading of Heidegger.

Quarantining can also be found in Daniela Vallega-Neu's approach to the *Black Notebooks* (Vallega-Neu 2016, 127). I choose Vallega-Neu's work because one could, with only a minor tweak, modify her hermeneutic approach to Heidegger's sigetic works in order to expand it to encompass the *Black Notebooks*. Moreover, I focus on Vallega-Neu because she has established herself as one of the leading scholars on Heidegger's thinking of the event through her unmatched quality of translation and scholarship (Vallega-Neu 2001; 2013).[63] Vallega-Neu has long argued that Heidegger's *Ereignis* manuscripts in the 1930s pursue the essential task of Heidegger's thinking, exceeding the linguistic and ontological limitations of *Being and Time*. Her work thus forms a cornerstone of the thesis developed in the present book, for she also identifies Heidegger's sigetics as central to Heidegger's work and regards the silent saying of the event as Heidegger's most originary attempt at sigetics. According to this interpretation, the philosophical apex of Heidegger's sigetic practice is to be found in the manuscripts on the *Ereignis* (*GA* 65–71), and the *Black Notebooks* "should be clearly distinguished from his poietic writings" (Vallega-Neu 2016, 127). She argues persuasively that there is a clear distinction "between the thinking of the event and his reflections on his times" (ibid., 135) and uses this difference subtly to exclude the *Black Notebooks* from the scope of her *philosophical* analysis of Heidegger's sigetics. Her interpretation is justified by asserting that the thinking of the event is the most essential task in Heidegger's work in the 1930s, while she classifies the *Black Notebooks* as preparation for the saying of the event, as sketchbooks, or as "reminders that Heidegger gives himself" (ibid., 132). In other words, she justifies segregating the *Black Notebooks* from Heidegger's philosophical project by first assuming that we know what Heidegger's thinking is about. This is the point where I diverge from her interpretation.

My divergence is based on a fundamental question: should not the arrival of close to two thousand pages of new material give us pause to question our assumptions about what is central to Heidegger's philosophical work? In other words, I argue that the *Black Notebooks* should give us impetus to reorient our understanding of the nature of Heidegger's philosophical project. Even while they may seem to be easily written off by philosophers as "reflections on his times," we should take into account the gravity of those times, along with the upheaval and revolution occurring around Heidegger. Furthermore, it is important to be attentive to the fact that Heidegger himself played such an important role in that revolution, acting as a philosopher, a professor, and a university administrator, when he began to write the *Black Notebooks*. We may be tempted to take recourse to the category of the "biographical," for it has the convenient by-product of producing a narrative that makes us comfortable with Heidegger's behavior, or at least with our own continued involvement with his thinking. After all, Heidegger was a thinker of place, time, and the moment, and we should analyze the particular place, time, and moment in which he developed his philosophy.

The fact that the ongoing publication of Heidegger's *Gesamtausgabe* has led to revisions and shifts in our assumptions about Heidegger is nothing new. For example, an existentialist interpretation focused on the analytic of Dasein long dominated Heidegger scholarship under such towering figures as Jaspers and Sartre. This existential interpretation began to shift as philosophers such as William Richardson and Otto Pöggeler helped to reorient the analysis around the question of being (Richardson 1963;

Pöggeler 1963). With the 1989 publication of the *Contributions to Philosophy (of the Event)*, a later group of scholars such as Vallega-Neu and Richard Polt argued for the centrality of the event to Heidegger's philosophical endeavor (Polt 2006; Vallega-Neu 2003). This recentering was only possible because of increased access to new textual material. More recently, Andrew Mitchell has sought to reorient Heidegger scholarship around the notion of the thing, arguing quite persuasively that Heidegger's 1949 lecture series "Insight into That Which Is" constitutes a "third, decisive milestone along his path of thought" (Mitchell 2015, 3). Once again, Mitchell is able to make this argument because of access to textual material unavailable to previous generations of Heidegger scholars. Of course, I have painted the history of this scholarship in very broad brushstrokes in order to make the following point: given that revising common assumptions about the nature of Heidegger's thinking based on the publication of new material has been a defining attribute of Heidegger scholarship from the very beginning, what authorizes us to treat the *Black Notebooks* any differently? Why should we regard the arrival of the *Black Notebooks* as something other than encouragement—if not the burden—to shift the focus of Heidegger scholarship? What, other than political motivations, could enable us to not treat them as yet another arrival of new textual material that will cause us to question our assumptions about Heidegger's thinking? After all, his thinking is a thinking in motion, a thinking under way. Moreover, Heidegger did everything possible to frustrate our attempts to fix his thinking in place, including preserving and publishing the *Black Notebooks*.

Instead of diminishing the place of the *Black Notebooks* within Heidegger's thinking, I take them as impetus to rethink what is central to Heidegger's work. What they show is that not only the thinking of the event is essential to Heidegger's work in the 1930s, but also sigetics broadly speaking. Heidegger portrays sigetics as a practice of an ethics of silence developed out of his encounter with Greek thought and potentially enacted within a space of speech under National Socialism. I therefore diverge from Vallega-Neu based on the question of scope. While the thinking of the event is always deeply tied to Heidegger's sigetics, Heidegger sigetic practice is not restricted solely to the event, for it is also tied into his understanding of the *Volk*, and specifically the *Volk* of the "universal-destinal essence of the Germans" (*GA* 97, 63). Hence if Heidegger is a thinker of silence, then the *Black Notebooks,* as the most concealed of his writings, preserve the essential saying of what he chose to reserve for the greatest silence, or for the most delicate operations of the handiwork of thinking. "The handiwork of thinking is the writing of the poietic saying of 'being,'" Heidegger writes explicitly in the fourth volume of the *Black Notebooks* (*GA* 97, 118). In arguing that the *Black Notebooks* not only cannot be excluded from Heidegger's sigetic project, but ought to be recognized as the center of his sigetics, I rely upon a hermeneutics that Heidegger himself articulates: "Precisely because the Greek essence of man is fulfilled in 'having the word,' Greek man could also have and retain the word in the preeminent way we call silence. The Greeks are often silent, especially about what is essential to them. And when they do say the essential, they say it in a way that is simultaneously reticent" (*GA* 54, 116/79).

With the ancient Greeks as his model, Heidegger is also most silent about what is most essential to him. This is the essence of his sigetic practice. However, since every act of non-saying for Heidegger takes place in a space of speech and writing, the *Black Notebooks* cannot be read in isolation, for the speech that preserves the silences they contain is also integral to the performance of those very silences.

In other words, Heidegger's two divergent roles within National Socialism—as, on the one hand, its self-styled intellectual leader who speaks of the "Führer *giving* the people its immediate potential for the highest free decision," and, on the other hand, its silent scribe of spiritual purity—enable one another (*GA* 16, 188). The point therefore is not to decide which is the "real" Heidegger, but instead to understand their intertwined nature in all of its insidious ambiguity. This means to say that Heidegger was at one level an opportunistic academic and devout National Socialist attempting—in his own words—"to get closer to Hitler,"[64] while on another level he was also a genuine, though idiosyncratic, ideologue who regarded the Nazi revolution as the proper vehicle for achieving the spiritual-philosophical reawakening of the German essence. For Heidegger this revolution was tied not only to the German soil, but specifically to the soil, place, and landscape of the Swabian homeland. As National Socialism progressed ever further into a technological branch of what he called the machination, as the war became more violent, and the universities more thoroughly devoted to scientific-technical knowledge, Heidegger felt himself to be increasingly isolated and betrayed (*GA* 97, 82). Gradually, he began to regard himself as the final bulwark, the lone voice of thinking silently preserving the "occidental essence" and "occidental destiny" (*GA* 97, 40, 45; *GA* 97, 76, 98).

The *Black Notebooks* as the Essential Space of Silence

I explicitly endeavor in this book to describe Heidegger's recovery of silence in terms that Heidegger most likely would have rejected. However, the project as a whole does take as its starting point a moment from Heidegger's 1933–34 lecture course. The moment occurs as something of an aside in the midst of one of Heidegger's most detailed analyses of the ontology of silence. For the sake of establishing the context, I will quote the long passage in full, though I will leave aside any discussion of Heidegger's comments on *Being and Time* for now, since that topic is pursued in detail in chapter 2. I have emphasized the most relevant remarks in the long quotation that follows:

> Note that with this proposition, I pass decisively beyond what is said in *Being and Time*, § 34, page 164 and following. There, language was indeed brought into an essential relationship with keeping silent; the starting point for a sufficiently originary conception of the essence of language was laid down, in opposition to the "philosophy of language" that has reigned until now. And yet I did not see what really has to follow from this starting point: keeping silent is not just an ultimate possibility of discourse, but discourse and language arise from keeping silent. *In recent years, I have gone back over these relationships and worked them through. This obviously cannot be explained here. Not even the different manners of keeping silent, the multiplicity of its causes and grounds, and certainly not the different levels and depths of reticence.* Now only as much will be communicated as is needed for the advancement of our questioning. (*GA* 36–37, 110/87)

What would Heidegger have written had he in fact carried out an analysis of the "different manners of keeping silent, the multiplicity of its causes and grounds" and "the different levels and depths of reticence"? Why does silence become such a burning topic for Heidegger at this particular juncture? Why does he suddenly sense an urgent need to start developing new ways of keeping silent, especially when the archives show that Heidegger's international stature gave him greater leeway for taking liberties in speech than were allowed to other Germans under National Socialism? I argue that the *Black Notebooks* in fact constitute a version of this project. The *Black Notebooks* are Heidegger's most sigetic work.

Labeling the *Black Notebooks* as Heidegger's most sigetic text places them directly at the center of Heidegger's philosophical project, for it assigns them a particularly crucial role within the development of his

phenomenology of silence. The *Black Notebooks* are the space for the performance of a reticence in which Heidegger says what is most essential to
him. In their pages, Heidegger states the pedagogical principle behind the
cultivation of silence: "The only futural 'education' to 'philosophy' in the
present age is the one aiming at a grounded capacity for silence, a silence
that measures itself according to the highest standards" (*GA* 95, 228/117).
By understanding how Heidegger analyzed the nature of Greek silence,
we can begin to see what Heidegger expected his own silent and futural
thinkers to be silent about.

In order to answer these questions, I trace the contours of what
Heidegger either left unwritten or unpublished by writing with and alongside Heidegger, but always against him as well. In pursuing this project
I am interested, not only in what Heidegger recovers from the manifold
senses of silence in his work, but also in what he occludes. That is to say,
I am interested not only in what was unsaid by Heidegger, but also in
what was unsayable by him as he was on the way to developing his own
philosophical capacity for silence. In short, this book is guided by three
questions that will structure much of what follows: what did Heidegger
not say in his performances of silence, how did he not say it, and why did
he not say it? Answering these three questions will help us triangulate the
content of Heidegger's politics of silence.

2 *Völkisch* Affinities and Renewal
of the German Spirit

Ludwig Ferdinand Clauss opens his 1923 book *Die nordische Seele: Eine Einführung in die Rassenseelenkunde* (The Nordic Soul: An Introduction to Racial Psychology) with a vivid parable about what he calls essential Nordic silence. "Once upon a time," Clauss writes, "at an inn somewhere in the Black Forest, two siblings, the son and daughter of the innkeeper, were quarreling" (Clauss 1940, 7). In this brief tale, Clauss portrays the son as the image of Nordic purity, painting him with great physiognomic detail as tall, sinewy, broad in the shoulders yet narrow in the hips, and with deep-set eyes that "captured the world with a steely clarity." In describing the sister, whose physiognomy inspires no rapturous prose from Clauss, he simply states that with her "everything was short and round and dark." "Her little eyes," Clauss writes, "almost disappeared when she wrenched up her face" in anger. As different as these two are in appearance, they differ even more in style. While the tall and angular brother "did not speak much and calmly went on with his work" in the midst of the quarrel, the sister "let out an ever-increasing volley of words, which ended ultimately in a shuddering spasm." The brother's response is characteristically terse: "She's grousing her head off." Brought to a fit of rage by her brother's calm and collected tone, the sister casts her glance about the room, finding only figures that are foreign to her, the guests as alien as her own Nordic family. "Red race," she blurts out, not to anyone in particular, but to the entirety of this supposedly foreign race around her. "Red," Clauss writes, "was to her an insult aimed at the reddish blonde hair of her brother." This quarrel between the so-called red race and this peculiarly un-Nordic girl who instinctually feels out of place is one, Clauss contends, that would never end as long as these foreign elements are forced to mingle.

Clauss intends this tale of a seemingly harmless spat between siblings to serve as an allegory for the racial struggle he identifies in the German soul. In Clauss's "scientific" analysis of race, the brother and the purportedly foreign sister demonstrate the ultimate incommensurability of different racial elements embedded in the Germanic stock. The sister, with her dark complexion, rounded features, and boundless loquacity, reveals the supposed hidden impurity of the racial stock, which contained the indistinct non-Nordic elements responsible for producing her as a "foreigner" in her own Black Forest family. In contrast, the taciturn brother displays the most admirable Nordic features and, in particular, a distinctive silence, which Clauss describes as a fundamental trait of the Nordic soul. This silence emerges from that soul's characteristic distance, a distance "he cannot violate without violating his type, the law of his race" (ibid., 26).

Describing the Nordic soul in more detail, Clauss associates it with a very particular form of reticence bound together with the Nordic landscape. Unlike the boundless expanse of the Mediterranean, or the boundless world of the nomad, Clauss depicts the Nordic landscape as bounded and circumscribed. The limits of this landscape have in turn created a measured people whose language is in harmonious accord with these boundaries. This conjuncture of measure, stillness, and landscape was not unique to Clauss. Herrmann Schwarz, who in 1923 became the first philosophy professor to join the Nazi party (Dahms 2009, 196), similarly spoke of a "holy stillness" emanating from Germanic nature and described how the ancient Germanic people "sensed in the joyous silence of the forest canopy an ultimate mystery" (Schwarz 1937, 11; cf. *GA* 38, 168–69/139). In his classic analysis of *völkisch* thinking, George L. Mosse elaborates: "Yet, after all the Volk did not have universal dimensions, but was limited to a particular national unit. Not all of nature, therefore, but only its regional manifestations gave the Volk its character, potential, and unity. Nature was defined as landscape: those features of the environment peculiar and familiar to the members of one Volk and alien to all others" (Mosse 1981, 15). For these ethno-nationalist strains of philosophy, the German people are formed by and within this primordial silence of the landscape and are thus imbued with an essentially silent element, which modernity and foreign infiltration threaten to destroy.

Clauss describes this silence in a fair amount of philosophical detail. "The Nordic man," he says, "speaks not only through what he does say, but even more through what he does not say. The pauses in his conversations are meaningful, silence is his most noble form of expression" (Clauss 1940, 34). Nordic silence, he contends, is embodied in a particular reserve, expressed through sparseness of both words and gestures. The Nordic traveling sales- man, for instance, steadfastly avoids ostentation and long-winded sales pitches. He simply strides lankily "into the shop and silently places some- thing in front of him." " 'This is good,' " he tells the shopkeeper. " 'You must order it' " (ibid., 92). The goods, especially if they are a product of German handicraft, should speak for themselves. The less this salesman is required to speak, when his silence is understood, the more fully he expresses his Nordic essence. Indeed, according to Clauss, Nordic souls are more likely to understand one another when they speak as little as possible. Reduced to its bare minimum, Nordic silence cuts out words and gestures altogether, leaving the Nordic soul to speak most essentially "through a silence, not only of speech, but of all forms of expression that do not involve changing color (blushing and turning pale)" (ibid., 59). The whiteness of the Nordic race thus preserves a language threatened by racial mixing, for the slightest degree of tint threatens to occlude the subtle medium of this language of blushing and changing colors. Words may be necessary to communicate with the souls of other races, but between their own kind, Nordic souls communicate their deepest feelings most silently, through subtle changes of color. The Nordic soul is imbued with and preserved in silence.

Völkisch thinkers may seem like an unseemly set of bedfellows for a thinker of Heidegger's stature, but the passages quoted above are drawn from the professional publications of Heidegger's peers. Heidegger may have been so skilled at crafting his self-image that we are often led to be- lieve that his only true interlocutors were the likes of Plato, Aristotle, and Kant, yet it should not be a matter of great controversy to assert that his interlocutors also included his contemporary professional peers—many of whom might now strike us as the most banal of thinkers.[1] Among the ranks of professional philosophers, Heidegger was one among many who shared affinities with *völkisch* authors and who overtly promoted a *völkisch* agenda.[2] In what might be regarded as a direct reference to Clauss, Heidegger includes a similar concept of the soul among the ways of defining the essence of the *Volk* in 1934, noting in a section entitled "*Volk* as Soul" that the people are not simply "placed in an arbitrary, unrelated strip of land" (*GA* 38, 66/58). Clauss followed much of the same academic track as Heidegger himself. Far from being some marginal figure or simply a hack race theorist, Clauss was an academically trained philosopher who served contemporaneously with Heidegger as a postdoctoral assistant to Edmund Husserl in Freiburg.[3] Clauss regarded his racial psychology as an extension and application of Husserl's phenomenology and even attempted to submit *Die nordische Seele* to Husserl as his *Habilitation* (postdoctoral) thesis. Although Husserl refused to accept the work and was troubled by its antisemitism, Clauss nonetheless possessed enough academic legitimacy to be selected to lecture on racial psychology in Dresden in the early 1920s. A fellow southwestern German from the region around Freiburg, Clauss reveals many of the same political commitments as Heidegger with regard to language, race, and landscape. Like many other *völkisch* thinkers, however, he was far more willing than Heidegger to proclaim his antisemitic leanings openly.

Their common belief in essential silence links both Clauss and Heidegger to a larger set of motifs concerning noise, silence, scattering, and distraction that run through much of Weimar thought. While these themes emerge in various ways in thinkers such as Georg Simmel and Sigfried Kracauer as critiques of modern industrial capitalism, technological change, and urbanization, for many *völkisch* thinkers, "capitalism" was a placeholder for "world Jewry." Goebbels's *Das kleine abc des Nationalsozialisten* (The National Socialists' Short ABC) captures the gist of these stereotypes: "Why is the National Socialist Party hostile to Jews? Because the Jew is a corrosive foreign body within the German people, because he poisons the morality of the German people through his mendacious 'Culture Industry,' because he tears down instead of building up, because he is the father of the theory of class struggle, which he uses to rend the German people into two parts in order to rule over them all the more brutally, because he is the creator and supporter of international market capitalism, the primary enemy of German freedom" (Goebbels [1925] 1929, 6).[4]

While different *völkisch* thinkers varied in the extent to which they directly reiterated these assumptions about a Jewish-capitalist world conspiracy, they generally relied on them to underpin their thinking (Volkov 1978, 25–46). Heidegger himself specifically speaks of the "tenacious facility in calculating, hustling, and interfering through which the worldlessness of Jewry is grounded" (*GA* 95, 97/76; Bernasconi 2017, 168–85).

I explore these strands of thinking in four *völkisch* authors here. Three of them—Clauss, Schwarz, and Raymund Schmidt—were academically trained as philosophers, and the writings of the fourth, Walther Darré, a Nazi party official anointed by Hitler as the so-called Reich peasant leader, help substantiate Heidegger's affinity to the Nazi ideology of the German soil. The point is not to offer a comprehensive depiction of these strands of German nationalist and antisemitic thought, but to focus specifically on the question of silence in order to trace the connection between Heidegger's turn to silence in the 1930s and the *völkisch* literary and academic agenda. Heidegger was by no means a doctrinaire *völkisch* thinker, for the simple reason that the loosely articulated movement had no established doctrine (Puschner 2001, 17). Heidegger was quite skilled, however, at endorsing the political commitments of his *völkisch* contemporaries while obscuring his own politics, employing—to use his own terminology—an "insidious ambiguity." This process of occlusion was central to his sigetic practice.

Like many Germans of his time, in the 1930s, Heidegger viewed his present with a heavy pessimism and was drawn to the *völkisch* movement's agenda of restoring Germany's political and spiritual greatness. *Völkisch* thinkers dating back to the middle of the nineteenth century tended to attribute near-mystical powers to the German landscape, and to be suspicious of technology and critical of calculative rationality.[5] *Völkisch* thinking did not valorize nature in general, but specifically the German landscape, in which the German people are rooted. In such thinking, the *Volk* served as the link between the individual and the cosmos, while modern society was regarded as uprooting the people and destroying its links to the earth and the cosmos. The *völkisch* hero was the peasant, rooted in the soil, attuned to the landscape through his labor, or bound to the household and family through her labor. The *völkisch* enemy, in contrast, was the capitalist, the city dweller, and the rootless foreigner. In short, the enemies of the *Volk* were the Jews, but also "Aryans" alienated from their racial essence by the destructive infiltration of German culture by the conspiratorial plotting of "world Jewry." Heidegger's thinking exhibits strong affinities to these movements, and Heidegger admits to having been immersed in *völkisch* literature in the late 1920s and early 1930s.

Heidegger's antisemitic affinities are discernible on two levels. On the one hand, there are his overt, blatant antisemitic pronouncements in official correspondence, private letters, and writings. On the other hand, there are the concealed expressions of affinity apparent in the cultivation of a recognizable *völkisch* language and set of themes,[6] which often persist unabated into his postwar thinking. Investigating these thematic affinities requires focusing on a number of concepts linking Heidegger's philosophy of language to *völkisch* thinking: rootedness, the measure, silence, landscape, and gathering. "Language is the reigning force of the world-forming and preserving core of the historical existence of a people," Heidegger asserted in his 1934 lecture course (*GA* 38, 169/140). This language must be preserved from the overpowering forces and "machinations" of modernity.

Modern society is "the measurelessness of the grounded, of the massive, of the rapid, and of the transitory knowledge and attainment of everything," Heidegger states in the first of the *Black Notebooks* (*GA* 94, 216/158). This draws largely on common motifs of the time, but Heidegger employs them to reflect his own unique set of ontological commitments. To the extent that National Socialism would, in Heidegger's words, still have something to keep silent about, it would restore measure to the *Volk*, and thus to the language of the *Volk*. However, Heidegger's political commitments differ in one significant way from those of the other *völkisch* thinkers analyzed here, and that difference links Heidegger more strongly to strands of Nazi philhellenism than to the strands of *völkisch* thinking that sought to revive Germanic mythology. All of the authors analyzed in this chapter are concerned with the corrosive and dissevering affects of capitalism and urbanization. All of them also ascribe a certain harmony and cohesiveness to what they variously call the Aryan, Nordic, or German people. However, while Darré, Schmidt, and Clauss call for a return to a pre-Christian ur-Germanic essence as the answer to the disruptive effects of capitalism and "world Jewry," for Heidegger the solution lies in a return to a "Greek-Germanic" essence. While for many *völkisch* thinkers, the German landscape provided the measure for the German people, Heidegger sought to reopen the experience of this landscape to what he regarded as a Greek experience. Silence would play a critical role in restoring creative power to this experience. What all of these thinkers have in common, however, although they vary in the degree to which they state this explicitly, is a perception of Jews as a disturbing element that destroys the essential harmonious silence that binds the German people to itself, to its landscape, and to its language. The *Black Notebooks* make this explicit, but in his contemporaneous published writings, lecture courses, and public speeches, Heidegger tends to gesture toward antisemitism less explicitly, though perhaps no less volubly, employing a language laden with affinities to it. Heidegger's turn to silence in the 1930s emerges within this complex set of entanglements bridging *völkisch* thinking with phenomenology and Heidegger's own readings of the ancient Greeks. Within this constellation of political concerns, Heidegger portrays a return to the Greeks as the means to restore to the German people a silence of which the calculative rationality of modernity has deprived it. This process of restoration seeks, in Heidegger's words, to halt the "machination" of "world Jewry" aiming at "the uprooting of all beings from being" (*GA* 96, 243/191).

Nomadic Scattering and Germanic Gathering

Theodor Fritsch's *Antisemiten-Catechismus* (Anti-Semitic Catechism) did much to nurture the antisemitism of *völkisch* philosophy. Retitled the *Handbuch der Judenfrage* (Handbook on the Jewish Question) in 1893, it became one of the most popular books in Germany in the first half of the twentieth century, with forty-nine editions between 1887 and 1944, selling hundreds of thousands of copies (Albanis 2009, 172; Bergmann 1999, 461). Fritsch, an early proponent of eliminationist antisemitism, has been called "one of the vilest German antisemites" (Puschner 2001, 59). His *Handbuch der Judenfrage* rages against the supposed Jewish infiltration of German life, including sections on Jews in the economy, arts, public trendsetting, politics, churches, and German letters, as well as statistics on "Jewish criminality" and a brief history of the milestones of the antisemitic movement. Beginning with its 1935 edition, the *Handbuch* contained a contribution by Raymund Schmidt entitled "Das Judentum in der deutschen Philosophie" (Jewry in German Philosophy), which is especially useful for tracing many of Heidegger's affinities to *völkisch* thinking and academic antisemitism in Weimar Germany.[7]

Schmidt posits a basic distinction between the Aryan and the Jew. The Aryan is rooted in the whole and seeks to "integrate himself with all of the powers of his mind into the great nexus of being." A belief in the "simplicity and harmony" of the whole, which exists beyond rationality, is located "in the blood" of the Aryan, while "contradictions within the phenomena" serve as a "call to the will to strive for action" (Schmidt 1939, 391). The great systematic works of Aryan philosophy (Kant, Leibniz, Fichte, Schelling, Hegel, Schopenhauer, and Nietzsche), Schmidt argues, are like the monumental "gothic cathedrals that strive for completion and totality," serving as the "crowning achievement" of the morality and thinking of their time. What allows these lofty vaults to reach such heights is their anchoring in a firm and stable foundation, the "expansive tranquility of the Aryan peasantry resting on stable ground." This firm grounding in the countryside and this tranquility helps to root another "fundamental trait" of these great systems, their "inborn" ability to "halt in the face of the great mysteries of the world, in the face of the primordial facts" (ibid., 392). The Aryan is rooted in a connection to the whole that is lived directly, experienced without mediation, and transmitted by blood. Like a Platonic philosopher falling silent in the face of the Good, the Aryan thinker knows when to halt the interrogation and to allow language to taper off into silence. According to Schmidt's reasoning, the Jew not only does not have access to this nexus of being, but even threatens to destroy the Aryan connection by insinuating himself into the cohesiveness of German philosophy.

A fundamental opposition between the Jew and the Aryan grounds the logic of antisemitic philosophy, the "Occidental-Semitic divide" (Bergmann 1999, 450). The Aryan represents cohesiveness; the Jew, *Zersetzung*—decomposition, dissevering, corrosion, even putrefaction (Schmitz-Berning 1998, 698; Böschenstein-Schäfer 196). Rootless, "lacking an independent ethnic culture," the Jew is a "parasite" on genuine ethnic cultures, clinging to them for material sustenance. Schmidt goes so far as to assert that the world of the Jew is so fragmented that the he seemingly cannot even focus his eye. His very visual perception of the world is "kaleidoscope-like," dizzying him with a world that "swirls around him," pushing him into the "infinity of existence" (Schmidt 1939, 393). Schmidt depicts this drive toward infinity as typical of the Jews, a supposedly nomadic people, and argues that it stands in contrast with the bounded nature of the settled German peasant. According to this logic, the Jew is thus caught between two possibilities: either he can toss about in this swirling kaleidoscope or he can latch onto something in a parasitic clutch. The Jew, Schmidt contends, opts for the latter, thus developing a dexterity and cunning as regards minutiae, bereft of an experience of the whole. The Jew dissevers; the Aryan gathers together and unites. The former evokes idle chatter, the latter silence.

Caught between the infinitely large and the infinitely small, the Jew orients himself by dividing up whatever he latches onto, dismantling it, and, in the case of philosophy, refining endless "sophistries" in a logic of production that necessarily results in overspecialization, Schmidt claims. Lacking an experience of the whole in his blood, he zeroes in on whatever is rational in a philosophical system and drives it to an absurd extreme. Such an untethered intellect "is capable of proving everything and refuting everything," for it is not restrained by the bounds of conscience. This free-floating intellect is a "corrosive poison" to German philosophy (ibid., 394). According to

Schmidt, this poison has infiltrated the German spirit through philosophy, especially through neo-Kantianism, which he portrays as the logical refinement of Kant's thinking separated from Kant's own anchoring in the sense of (Aryan) duty. Schmidt focuses his attack on Hermann Cohen and the Marburg School, in particular, significantly echoing an earlier antisemitic attack, in the *völkisch* journal *Der Panther*, by the philosopher Bruno Bauch, a professor of philosophy in Jena and a former editor of *Kant-Studien*, the most prestigious German philosophy journal of the time, on Cohen and the Marburg School as "foreigners" (Bauch 1917a).[8] In Schmidt's portrayal, the internationally oriented Jew, after having infiltrated Kant scholarship and turned the most important academic organizations and journals into businesses and cash-cows for private junkets, has penetrated Aryan philosophy—and thereby the Aryan spirit—so deeply that "years of struggle and thorough cleansing will be required" to rid philosophy of this parasite (Schmidt 1939, 401).[9] According to Schmidt, this parasite drives even the good German philosopher to produce blindly, to specialize, to disregard the whole, and—perhaps most important—to forget his inborn instinct and "neglect the essential, the unsayable" (ibid., 294). In its verbosity, German philosophy has become Jewish philosophy. German philosophy will need to say less to return to itself, which it will begin to do by adopting an ethics of silence and reticence.

These themes are not unique to Schmidt. In his book *Zur philosophischen Grundlegung des Nationalsozialismus* (The Philosophical Foundations of National Socialism), Schwarz expresses a similar sentiment, proclaiming to his readers "that we will take mastery over the fog of emotions with which we veil what is, that we will be freed from the fogging over of the soul through the empty production of words by others, which leads to its own yammering heroics" (Schwarz 1936, 21–22). Hans Grunsky, who was installed directly in a professorship by the Nazi party without having the proper credentials (*Habilitation*), against the objections of the faculty (Schorcht 1994, 312–17), repeats similar set of themes in his 1937 book *Der Einbruch des Judentums in die Philosophie* (Jewry's Intrusion into Philosophy). Driving the theme of idle chatter developed by Schmidt to an even further extreme, Grunsky describes the infiltration of the Jew into German philosophy in terms of dissonance (Grunsky 1937), which began to expand after Moses Mendelssohn, a "business manager in the silk trade," popularized an enlightenment vision of sameness and equality. As a result of this popularization, "Jews . . . infiltrated philosophy in numbers that are hard to believe," though Grunsky agrees to "spare" his readers "a list of more than two hundred names that [he] could name." Occupying all of the "key positions" in the field, the Jews have begun their true destruction of German philosophy: "The cacophony has now become so deafening that the majority of those with German blood have begun to play along." The Jews, Grunsky contends, have tricked the Germans into accepting a talmudized version of German philosophy, and thus they have counterfeited and sold their own perverted thinking in the name of German philosophy. In order to combat this supposed infiltration, Grunsky ends his book with a call to action: "For we would once again like to hear the primordially well-formed themes, the *de-talmudized themes of our philosophy*" (ibid., 15).

This brief sketch should suffice to establish the basic lineaments of philosophical antisemitism in Nazi (and pre-Nazi) Germany. In these racist depictions, based on the hypothesis of a fundamental opposition between the Aryan and the Jewish—cohesive and corrosive, rooted and rootless, scattered and gathered—the Jewish philosopher is portrayed as intelligent and with a knack for identifying logical inconsistencies. Jews are productive, moreover—indeed, overly productive of publications, leading to hyper-specialized academic institutions that no longer have the sense of the whole that grounds the Aryan essence. In order to reorient itself and recover its essential, characteristic silence, Aryan philosophy will have to learn to refrain from publication, specialization, and professionalization. This essential silence is produced by the landscape, which is accessible only to the Aryan eye.

Yet aside from a set of terminological affinities, there is also a far more concrete connection between Heidegger and Schmidt's attack on the contemporary neo-Kantians, whose origin can be traced back to Bauch's attack on Hermann Cohen, which was reiterated in 1929 by Othmar Spann, a professor of philosophy at the University of Vienna, at an official event sponsored by a cultural outreach program of the Nazi party at the University of Munich. According to a report in the *Frankfurter Zeitung*, Spann bemoaned the "sad situation that the German people needed to be reminded of its own Kantian philosophy by foreigners" such as Hermann Cohen and Ernst Cassirer (Krois 2002).[10] Shortly thereafter, in his notorious April 1929 Davos dispute with Cassirer, Heidegger pointedly pressed Cassirer to take sides on Cohen's Kant interpretation. John Michael Krois describes how this confrontational action stifled the debate from the beginning by forcing Cassirer to defend Cohen against this implicitly antisemitic attack. A few months later, Heidegger would express these affinities once again in a letter of recommendation. Prior to the publication of the *Black Notebooks*, the documentary evidence for the depth of Heidegger's antisemitism was still rather thin. The most important proof was a letter from Heidegger to Victor Schwoerer, the president of the Notgemeinschaft der Deutschen Wissenschaft (Emergency Association of German Science), the most important funding agency of the day. In the letter dated October 1929, Heidegger uses common antisemitic language to support his student Eduard Baumgarten's application for a scholarship: "I would like to say more clearly here what I could only hint at indirectly in my report. At stake is nothing less than the pressing consideration that we stand before a choice: either to provide our *German* spiritual life once more with genuine forces and educators rooted in the native and indigenous or to deliver it over ultimately (in the broader and narrower sense) to increasing Judification."[11]

This remark is all the more troubling when one considers the context and Heidegger's employment in both private and public of antisemitic language to promote the "purification" of German universities. Heidegger casts himself as a solitary, almost conspiratorial guardian of the German spirit in this letter. By 1933, he would play the same role in a powerful, highly public position.

Walther Darré: The German Peasant as Life Force

In contrast to Schmidt and Clauss, Walther Darré was not a trained philosopher, but an agricultural scientist. With the publication his works *Das Bauerntum als Lebensquell der nordischen Rasse* (1929; The Peasantry as Life Source of the Nordic Race) and *Neuadel aus Blut und Boden* (1930; New Nobility from Blood and Soil), Darré came to the attention of Hitler, who put Darré in charge of agricultural affairs, with the title Reich peasant leader. As an author and speaker, Darré was primarily responsible for reviving the mythology of blood and soil in Nazi ideology. Positing a "primordial enmity between Jews and peasants," Darré claims that "even just a few drops of Jewish blood acquired through lines of marriage" are sufficient "to mark an incomprehension of the essence of the genuine German peasantry" (Darré 1941, 72). Hence, according to Darré, the Germanic peasantry is under siege, directly targeted by its "fundamental enemy." Just as Jews fight against National Socialism as their enemy, they also fight against everything associated with the peasantry, "making it contemptible, and where possible, destroying it" (Darré 1940, 71). This primordial enmity is based on the same fundamental opposition between the scattering of the nomad and the gathering of the settled peasant that operates in Schmidt's text.

Much like Schmidt, Darré portrays Jews in cinematic terms. Echoing many of Schmidt's basic assumptions, he characterizes Jews as a "mobile race," which "needs to negotiate everywhere quickly" and thus possesses a "pronounced eye for the valuation of what is at hand" (ibid., 44). While the nomad can buy, sell, or uproot any individual item from its place without concern for the whole, the German peasant, in contrast, "possesses a feeling for the organic interplay of the forces at work as a whole" (ibid., 279). Opposed to the essential limitlessness of the nomad, the peasant—with his eye trained toward the future—is an essentially measured figure. He calculates based on "the quantities at hand," knows how to predict the future consequences of his decisions properly, "and knows how to get the job done the right way" (ibid., 283). In organic harmony with the people, the peasant is not seduced into the "limitless possibilities for expansion of the single individual," but instead "does not at all know the unbounded I-freedom of the single individual" (ibid., 95).

In contrast to this boundedness and rootedness, Darré claims that the nomad sees the world "as we see the sequential images of a film pass by in a cinema" (ibid., 290). Hence, Darré states that the nomad's vision is simply a superficial vision and amounts to little more than "thinking at the surface." As a result of this superficial perspective, the nomad is skilled at all forms of scientific thought that, like mathematics, "presupposes no spatial thinking or can be carried out solely on paper," as if to say that thinking carried out on a flat piece of paper is by nature flat. This superficial thinking lends itself to a certain logic of quantity and accumulation that requires no depth or grounding. Such a "superficial consciousness tends toward sophistry, that is to say, it exhausts itself in subtleties and clever games." The nomad, according to Darré, glides over things, assigning a superficial value to them, calculating their worth in terms of a universal medium of exchange. The peasant, on the other hand, is "rooted in place and position" and the things around him are "masses which he continually gets to know from many different sides," thus allowing an experience of depth (ibid., 292). Given this tendency to " 'get to the bottom of things,' " Darré draws this conclusion about peasantry: "Genuine peasantry is therefore also always philosophically disposed, and every peasant is by nature a philosopher" (ibid., 293). The German peasant is the primordial philosopher of the German people, and the Jew in turn is the primordial enemy of the peasant's embodied interaction with the landscape. The peasant is not a thinker, but an actor. In the peasant's action, a thinking is revealed. While this thinking can be transformed into an object of analysis, doing so risks severing it from its essential place by objectifying it. As Schwarz describes this fundamental phenomenological insight, "in every German soul there is an imageless Germanness at work," which stands in opposition to an external, "objectified image" (Schwarz 1936, 17). This imageless Germanness is not spoken about, but instead lived. This life is a philosophical life. After 1933, philosophers with a *völkisch* orientation, whether preexisting or newly discovered, sought to position themselves as the translators of this philosophical peasantry by navigating the subtle gap between word and deed. Heidegger seeks to contribute to this through a philosophy of the word in harmony with the deed, a word spoken that does not violate what the peasant would leave in silence.

Darré contends that the pernicious influence of Jewry has put the German people in conflict with itself and has caused far too many Germans to misrecognize their own essence by objectifying that essence. He claims that this is especially true of city dwellers. In contrast to the uprooted Germans of the cities, the peasantry will renew the life source of a people under threat. "To be a peasant," Darré writes, "means to understand handiwork" (Darré 1940, 278). Understanding handiwork does not mean speaking about it, but simply doing it, executing the task without contemplation and unnecessary verbiage. And since the peasant has a knack for getting the job done according to the proper measure, there will be little need to speak about the work. In a famous passage in *Being and Time*, Heidegger depicts a similarly silent process of labor in which a worker signals for his co-worker to pass him the appropriate hammer (*BT*, 157/152). These themes will reemerge in chapter 7 in an analysis of Heidegger's 1933 text "Schöpferische Landschaft: Warum bleiben wir in der Provinz?" ("Creative Landscape: Why Do I Stay in the Provinces?").

The point of this analysis is not to assess the philosophical value of authors such as Clauss, Schmidt, or Darré, if any, but to establish the coherence of a set of terminological affinities with which Heidegger aligned himself. Putting aside whatever obvious weaknesses one might identify in their thinking, these authors represent a set of discourses that were central to well-established strands of *völkisch* thinking that had, in the words of one intellectual historian, "widespread acceptance . . . among mainstream sections of the population, particularly the professional middle classes" (Tourlamain 2014, 9). Many postwar histories—and no less so postwar reckonings with Heidegger's intellectual and political development—may conveniently seek to dismiss Nazi Germany as an aberration, but a subtle understanding of both Nazi Germany and Heidegger's place within it requires one to be attentive to Heidegger's proximity to these termino-logical constellations. While Heidegger may have expressed skepticism about some of the particular strands of biological racism represented, for example, by Darré, he nonetheless portrayed the German people as placed within a harmonious constellation consisting of its language, landscape, and history. In other words, despite his pronounced skepticism at one level, Heidegger exhibits a set of affinities enabled by a proximity to *völkisch* thinkers like Darré.

By the early 1930s, a number of closely related terms assumed a central role in Heidegger's work: silence, harmony, place, landscape, gathering, and scattering. Each of these terms resonated with particular affinities in the 1920s and 1930s. In Darré and Clauss, the German peasant's harmonious relationship to his place protects the German people from capitalism and world Jewry. In Heidegger, it is the Greeks. Before extended analyses of the Greeks in the ensuing chapters, it is therefore first necessary to analyze the role the Greeks play in his thinking as the guardians of a form of silence and a handicraft of thinking.

The Greek-Germanic Essence

On January 30, 1934, the one-year anniversary of the Nazi seizure of power, Heidegger showed up over an hour late to his own lecture course and under the thinnest veil of academic pretense proceeded to excoriate the *völkisch* luminary Erwin Guido Kolbenheyer. The previous day, Kolbenheyer had given a popular address drawn from his 1935 book by the same title to celebrate the Nazi revolution, *Lebenswert und Lebenswirkung der Dichtkunst in einem Volke* (The Value of Life and the Effect on Life of Poetic Art in a People). Denouncing Kolbenheyer in a ten-point rebuttal, Heidegger declared that "what we have here is just bad popular philosophy." "Kolbenheyer is a *völkisch* man, a nationalist," Heidegger proclaims, "and yet he does not stand in the new political reality, but somewhere above it." Heidegger concludes by identifying what he takes to be Kolbenheyer's greatest shortcoming: "He measures everything with his standards and believes: in 1933, the revolution; in '34 and after, the spirit as a supplement" (*GA* 36–37, 213/162). For Heidegger, the space for spirit still had to be remade; it had to be cleared. The revolution was at most preliminary. While Heidegger's vehement rejection of Kolbenheyer may seem to represent his distance from the *völkisch* movement, it is more appropriate to read it as a quarrel between powerful men vying for primacy in a political movement without a coherent ideological vision. Moreover, given that Kolbenheyer's speech revolved around determining "how a language becomes creative" by describing the poet's responsibility to the *Volk*, Kolbenheyer represented the very strand of *völkisch* thinking that Heidegger sought to institute as part of the remaking of German universities. By achieving "*leadership* in *science*," Heidegger sought to create an academic discourse linking the *Volk* to its language through "the clarity of our own *volklichen* essence. *Questioning*" (ibid., 273/207). Heidegger may seek to obscure his *völkisch* fidelities by choosing the spelling *volklich*, but these fidelities run far too deep to be hidden by simple orthographical manipulation.[12] In his public speeches and lectures as rector, Heidegger presented his own *völkisch* vision and vied for primacy on a busy stage of public intellectuals supporting the Nazi revolution.

In his infamous 1933 rectorial address "The Self-Assertion of the German University," Heidegger made perhaps his clearest public pronouncement on the philosophical links between the renewal of the German spirit and Greek philosophy. Presented with all the pageantry of an official Nazi party event, the address was intended to be the crowning moment announcing Heidegger's arrival on the political scene.[13] The restoration of the German spirit is central to the vision of reforming the German university that Heidegger develops in the address, and this restoration relies on many of the *völkisch* affinities identified in the previous section. In order to restore the German spirit, a new kind of questioning will have to emerge, a form of questioning concerned neither with output, performance, and production nor with the safe confirmation of the parameters determined by a particular field of study. Heidegger sees a fragmented university lacking cohesion, where the "university" label "is now just a name" (*IM*, 37/51). Although Heidegger does not specifically use the word in this address, what he is calling for is the handiwork of thinking and questioning, in contrast to the scattered university of knowledge production. While this description of the university is not per se antisemitic, Heidegger infuses it with layers of antisemitic affinities.

The rectorial address develops a vision for how to restore the German spirit to itself through the revival of a Greek form of philosophical questioning (Love and Meng 2015). "Such questioning," Heidegger proclaims, "shatters the division of the sciences into rigidly separated specialties, carries them back from their endless and aimless dispersal into isolated fields and corners" (RA, 111/474). As the speech progresses, Heidegger adds even more detail to describe the spirit that will revive German education: "For 'spirit' is neither empty cleverness, nor the noncommittal play of wit, nor the endless drift of rational distinctions, and especially not world reason; spirit is primordially attuned, knowing resoluteness toward the essence of being" (ibid., 112/474). Read in the light of Schmidt and Darré, the antisemitic resonances in Heidegger's description of spirit become rather clear. Untethered from the place of the German spirit, it is the Jew who rationally dissects, is not committed to anything binding, is boundlessly adrift and suspiciously cosmopolitan. Without needing to mention the Jew as such, Heidegger goes down the checklist of the antisemitic stereotypes well known to his audience. Heidegger makes these links more explicit in the *Black Notebooks*: "To appropriate 'culture' qua means of power and thereby assert oneself and allege a superiority—this is at its bottom a *Jewish* behavior" (*GA* 95, 326/254).

In contrast to this uprooted culture of domination, Heidegger proposes a return to a Greek form of questioning in order to "again place ourselves under the power of the *beginning* of our spiritual-historical being." This beginning, Heidegger writes, "is the awakening of Greek philosophy" (RA 107/470). The Germans, in other words, will return to their ethnic, linguistic, and spiritual roots through the Greeks. This return is necessary in part because one does not relate to this language and to these ethnic roots simply by being born into an ethnicity or language. National Socialism, after all, was a movement of renewal, of revolution, and of removal. Through the Greeks, the Germans would come back to themselves and their language by once again learning the power of silence. In the lecture course Heidegger held during this time, he elucidated the ontological nature of this more clearly by describing what he called the capacity for silence. Through the Greeks, the German spirit would once again be endowed with a capacity for silence, and this silence would bring the blind productivity of philosophy to a halt in order to restore German thinking to itself. This restoration would require the removal of an enemy and of polluting agents from the space of the German spirit.

Standing at the lectern as a representative of the Nazi academic vanguard, as a full professor bearing the party insignia, and as a university administrator vigorously remaking one of Germany's most important institutions, *Rektor-Führer* Heidegger impressed upon his students the necessity of removing the essential enemy. He exhorted his audience to be attentive to an enemy, without naming that enemy. In the course of a seemingly abstract analysis of the pre-Socratic philosopher Heraclitus, Heidegger describes the resoluteness required for the struggle against this enemy:

> The enemy can have attached itself to the innermost roots of the Dasein of a people and can set itself against this people's own essence and act against it. The struggle is all the fiercer and harder and tougher, for the least of it consists in coming to blows with one another; it is often far more difficult and wearisome to catch sight of the enemy as such, to bring the enemy into the open, to harbor no illusions about the enemy, to keep oneself ready for attack, to cultivate and intensify a constant readiness and to prepare the attack looking far ahead with the goal of total annihilation. (*GA* 36–37, 91/73)

There is very little doubt about what Heidegger intended to gesture to in his reference to an enemy attached "to innermost roots of the Dasein of a people," nor is there much doubt about the identity of this essential enemy. Heidegger's use of the cultural codes of antisemitism is at best thinly veiled here (Faye 2009, 166–72). However, it is informative to witness one of the more transparent instances of Heidegger playing with the operation of linguistic disavowal by refusing to name this enemy. Moreover, it is quite telling that he chooses this as the opportunity to enact his most detailed analysis of silence. By attending to the affinities expressed in his teachings and public speeches, Heidegger's politics, philosophy of language, and interpretation of the Greeks converge into a troubling alliance. We risk overlooking this alliance by simplistically dividing life from work in order to create neat divisions in Heidegger's philosophy. Such divisions can only sanction—whether inadvertently or intentionally—a disturbing politics.

Within the very same lecture course, Heidegger describes the silent manner of keeping silent as the capacity for silence, a twofold concept that denotes a power for instances of silence that is empowered by a prior attunement to silence as the measure for speech. Heidegger urges the students present to approach silence with a great deal of hermeneutic caution, for, as he warns, "whoever discourses about silence is in danger of proving in the most immediate way that he neither knows nor understands keeping silent" (*GA* 36–37, 107/85). Both of these statements signal the curious double movement that marks the place of silence in Heidegger's work. On the one hand, Heidegger's thought continually seeks to cultivate a manner of philosophizing that thinks through silence. On the other hand, however, Heidegger recognizes that in order to think *through* silence, one must first know how to think *about* silence. In other words, the scriptural task of sigetic performance is first grounded in a phenomenological account of the nature of silence. Only by knowing what silence is in a robust philosophical sense and by first subjecting silence to a rigorous thematic examination with all the resources that his phenomenological practice has to offer can Heidegger begin to think through silence. Moreover, only by being attuned to the essential enemy in their midst would his students know how to employ that silence. Heidegger's sigetic politics involves cultivating this ethics of silence—an ethics fundamentally rooted in Heidegger's reading of the Greeks.

The Greeks for Heidegger are those who are capable of keeping silent about silence. It is the Greeks whose comportment toward and within language relates silently to silence. Hence he regards the Greeks as not merely ancillary to a phenomenology and politics of silence, but even as the essential starting point for such an analysis. As such the Greeks are also essential to the political project of the spiritual renewal of the German people that Heidegger undertakes as rector in 1933. The Greeks were able to be silent in a silent fashion and for that very reason they fail to conceptualize silence in an ontological manner. As those who dwell in silence, the Greeks have no need to transform it into an abstract concept, for silence is embedded in their *ethos*. The Greeks' world, in other words, is a space of silence, and that silence must be permitted to echo again in the space of the Germanic-occidental essence. The Greeks thus stand at the center of Heidegger's politics of spiritual renewal of the German people.

In order to understand what Heidegger means by "the Greeks," it is useful to avoid the temptation to associate them with a particular place and time (say, e.g., classical Athens), or even to a particular thinker (say, e.g., Aristotle, Heraclitus, or Anaximander). Within Heidegger's conception of the history of philosophy, such designations would be merely historiographical, and not historical. Heidegger defines the historiographical as "information about and acquaintance with the historical, and indeed in a purely technical sense, that is, it calculates by balancing the past against the present and vice versa" (*GA* 54, 94/64). This historical task is far different from merely engaging in the historiographical task of gathering facts and information about the Greeks. In such an analysis, silence would be included in a list of attributes that characterize the existence of the Greeks. In an analysis of this sort, we might falsely assume that our conceptual terminology captures what silence meant to the Greeks, that our words—and hence to a certain degree our worlds—correspond to one another. Instead of this descriptive process, what Heidegger pursues in his historical analysis of the Greeks is the task of translating what he calls the " 'Dasein' of the Greek world" (*GA* 54, 36/25)[14] by measuring the extent to which Greek silence can be captured in the conceptual language of modern metaphysics, if at all.

Heidegger describes this process of translating the Greek world as occurring through a historical-ontological analysis (*GA* 54, 16–20/11–14).[15] The goal of such translation is not merely a matter of transposing words, phrases, or concepts from one language to another. Rather, it involves a translating that "transports us into the domain of experience or field of experience" in which a phenomena is experienced by transposing the ontological structures of one historical Dasein into the structures of another, while being attentive to the ontological gaps that render such a translation impossible (*GA* 54, 16/11). Given the scale of what has been banished to oblivion in an age that, according to Heidegger, can no longer dwell with itself as a result of a technological exploitation of oneself and the word, this process of translating the Greek world is necessarily a process of failure. This failure does not nullify the process of translation, but instead marks a limitation to the process of recovery enacted by any such translation. Yet to the extent that something of the Greek experience of silence can be recovered, silence forms a peculiarly effective starting point for beginning a translation of the Greek world.

Hence in Heidegger's translation of the Greek world, silence is not merely one of many phenomena one could choose for understanding the Greeks. Rather, he regards silence as somehow essential to what it means for a Greek to be a Greek—much the way Clauss identifies silence as essential to the Nordic soul. This is because the Greek *man* speaks of and through manifold senses of silence, but if *he* is essentially silent, then he does not speak about these manifold senses of silence, especially not in the sense of making silence a thematic matter of analysis. For Heidegger, the Greeks are silent about many things, but he focuses on one particular aspect of their silence in his 1942–43 "Parmenides" lecture course: "Granted, the Greek thinkers did not speak of these essential relations as we now are forced to express them. Precisely because the Greek essence of man is fulfilled in 'having the word,' Greek man could also have and retain the word in the preeminent way we call silence. The Greeks are often silent, especially about what is essential to them. And when they do say the essential, they say it in a way that is simultaneously reticent" (*GA* 54, 116/79).

What Heidegger identifies here is nothing less than a Greek silence about silence, at least for men endowed with the power to choose silence. Heidegger's explanation for that absence is simple. The fact that the Greeks did not sense any urgency to engage in an ontological inquiry into silence is precisely proof that they were capable of dwelling in silence. Moreover, it is proof for Heidegger that the Greeks were able to keep silent in the fullest sense of what he characterizes as the capacity for silence. In short, the Greeks were not "forced" to express and explain silence the way those incapable of dwelling in silence are forced to do. The Greeks are not forced to speak about silence precisely because they have the power to keep silent about silence. One could even go so far as to say that the power of the Greek *logos* even rests in this proximity to what Heidegger calls "saying language," a language that gains its power of expression through silence (*GA* 65, 78/62). This logic of nearness is a central element of *Being and Time*, where Heidegger argues that what we dwell closest to is often the most difficult to inquire into because it exists for us in an inconspicuous manner. According to this logic, those things that define our very capacity to be in the world are the ones that are most difficult to render strange through inquiry (*BT*, §22).[16]

What this means for the Greek relation to language is that when they speak most essentially, the Greeks are simultaneously reticent. They produce silence in and through the words they choose by means of a language employed according to the proper measure or mean (*NE* 1104a10–1105a18). Greek silence is voiced and spoken, and it is, according to Heidegger, voiced and spoken so essentially that there is no need to pose the question of what silence is. Heidegger's recovery of a Greek experience of silence occurs by saying what the Greeks themselves do not say about silence for the very reason that they dwell essentially in silence. Standing necessarily outside the space of that silence, modern humans can only measure their distance from that space in the language and conceptual structure available to us. The corrosive elements of modernity identified in the previous section only draw modern humans further away from the space of silence as the harmonious dwelling together of a people. Phrased differently, this means that the capacity to be able to speak about silence also emerges in a significant sense as an incapacity not to be silent about silence. This historical analysis is essential for understanding Heidegger's phenomenology of language because Heidegger's inverted politics of language seeks to restore this capacity to dwell in silence within the essential space of such "abodes of silence" (*GA* 96, 171/135). This is the core of Heidegger's sigetic project, which he invests with profoundly antisemitic resonances. Indeed, Heidegger's sigetics reveals itself to be one of the branches of his philosophy most deeply saturated with antisemitic and *völkisch* affinities.

Conclusion

For the most part, Heidegger assigns the Greeks a special proximity to silence, but occasionally he indulges in a more straightforward *völkisch* characterization of the German peasant as the essential bearer of silence. Yet whether he portrays the peasant or the Greek as the bearer of essential silence, at the heart of Heidegger's sigetics is a fundamental form of failure that marks human nature. We moderns, hopelessly fallen and entangled within the conceptual language of metaphysics, speak about silence because we fail to be able to keep silent about it. In this formulation, one might imagine that idle chatter has spilled its bounds and infected all language with its waywardness, resulting in the "ruination of language" (*GA* 96, 221/174, 233/183).[17] Within the space of such a language, only inauthentic silence is possible, according to Heidegger: "Inauthentic silence—arising from perplexity and ignorance—degrades immediately into rampant chatter. Genuine silence—arising from conscious mastery of the decisions—prepares the essential word. The genuinely silent one builds upon the simple stillness" (*GA* 96, 136/106). As one who thinks of himself as a genuinely silent thinker, or at least as the most genuinely silent thinker still remaining, Heidegger regards his sigetic work as preparing the simple stillness—even if the ears capable of listening to that stillness will only arrive centuries from now. This is what Derrida referred to as the "lost native country of thought," which Heidegger yearns for with "nostalgia" and "hope" (Derrida 1982, 27). This hope drives Heidegger's politics, especially his urge to restore the "universal-destinal essence of the Germans" and to rebuild the "worldwide historical destiny of Germany" (*GA* 97, 63, 84).

For Heidegger, who reminds the audience of his rectorial address that the Greeks needed three hundred years even just to raise the question of what knowledge is, he urges the audience to be patient, for "the elucidation and unfolding of the essence of the German university" would not occur in the current or following semester (*GA* 16, 115/478). Nor, perhaps, would it occur in the course of any individual student's studies at a German university. Yet regardless of the exact amount of time involved, it is essential to recognize that Heidegger regards this task of reading and teaching the history of philosophy as a deeply political task. It is not political in the sense that any education might be considered political, but it is even part of the essential political task that lies at the core of the "inner truth and greatness of National Socialism." This "greatness" is deeply bound up with a number of senses of silence, including the silences of the Greek world, the silences destroyed by the dissevering affects of the agents of modernity, and the silencing of a blindly productive, overspecialized, and peculiarly verbose form of academic inquiry. In other words, Heidegger's entire research project and teaching agenda under National Socialism are comfortably situated within the space of a set of entrenched concerns profoundly linked to the *völkisch* movement. More concretely, both his teaching and research are well aligned with National Socialist cultural policy. "Finally," Heidegger writes to himself as rector, "forged into the creative co-responsibility for the truth of *völkisch* existence. Fundamental attunement" (*GA* 94, 112/82). A little over a year later, in the midst of a lecture course held after his departure from the rectorate, Heidegger returned to this theme: "The voice of the blood emerges from the fundamental attunement of the human being" (*GA* 38, 153/127). This attunement is rooted in a renewal of the force of silence, listening, and gathering. This renewal occurs through a process of pedagogy that involves both a remaking of the university and an attunement to a Greek experience of being.

3   The Unsaid in *Being and Time*

Throughout the 1930s, amid the ebb and flow of his public political life, Heidegger was waging another, private battle with the world around him. Although he remained notoriously tight-lipped in public about the extent to which he engaged with the work of his contemporaries, even when they attacked him either personally or philosophically, in private he devoted a great amount of attention to the reception of his 1927 magnum opus *Being and Time*. The *Black Notebooks* document Heidegger's engagement with his contemporaries in great detail, revealing an attentiveness that even bordered on obsessive when his contemporaries published on his work. At first glance these references to the reception of *Being and Time* may seem like nothing more than scattered remarks with little systemic cohesion, but a closer analysis reveals a contradictory tendency that binds them together, especially in the early 1930s. On the one hand, Heidegger wants his magnum opus to be regarded as an untimely, epochal work, which cannot yet be understood. On the other hand, he is dismayed that it is being read in a manner that levels off the work's fundamental insights. However contradictory these tendencies might seem, they are a fitting response to a book that is itself bound together by a set of constitutive tensions. This chapter is dedicated to unraveling the constitutive tensions that cohere in the analyses of speech, language, discourse, and silence in *Being and Time*. By attending to these tensions, Heidegger creates the phenomenological space for the form of silence that later becomes central to his sigetics, bringing his thinking toward a set of political commitments that are still only latent in *Being and Time*.

Since its publication in 1927, *Being and Time* has been subject to a vast array of readings as a work of phenomenology, existentialism, fundamental ontology, and ethics—to name but a few. The fact that *Being and Time* can be read in so many ways is itself a consequence of how one seeks to unravel—or perhaps even to tighten—the central tensions in the work. More than any other text in the Heidegger oeuvre, on its surface *Being and Time* invites one to pursue a very classical and straightforward reading, based on the seemingly rigid conceptual structure of the work's constitutive terminological pairs (e.g., ontic/ontological, ready-to-hand/present-to-hand, and authentic/inauthentic). Readers approaching Heidegger from a more analytic bent have often tended to focus on this conceptual structure and have sought to work within it, ameliorating any perceived tensions in the work by "correcting" Heidegger's apparent inconsistencies whenever necessary. The tendency of these readings, perhaps best exemplified by Hubert Dreyfus's influential work, is to ascribe a static, logically coherent structure to the movement of Heidegger's thinking. This reading relies on assigning fixed meanings to Heidegger's conceptual terms and on treating the text as a work that intends to be systematic. Once one has entered into this interpretive mode, the primary question becomes determining where the "rational" edge of Heidegger's work is, where he so to speak goes off the deep end and lapses into a poetic mode that is no longer regarded as philosophical. This reading has often also been coupled with the logic of political quarantining in order to salvage certain aspects of Heidegger's thinking from political critique.

On the other end of the spectrum, readers such as Derrida have applied the tools of deconstruction to open up the Heideggerian text to its constitutive tensions in order to intensify those tensions. Such readings reveal *Being and Time* to be a text working against itself, one which dismantles itself from within. The fundamental question pursued in this type of reading is to ask how the text works against itself and undermines its own seemingly rigid conceptual structures. Hence, even while Heidegger's apparently fixed terminology in the work invites the reader in search of a systematic work to reify certain terms, the deconstructive reader will be attuned to how the text's constitutive tensions also point to the possibility of undermining the work's entire structural edifice. Reading with this deconstructive sensitivity does not mean to imply that Heidegger was aware of or gave voice to the book's constitutive tensions—as is precisely the case with the variegated terminology around speech and silence.

This chapter is devoted to examining the tensions that surround speech, silence, discourse, and language in *Being and Time* in order to show how the work lays the groundwork for Heidegger's sigetics. This reading does not mean to imply that Heidegger got something "wrong" or "right" either in *Being and Time* or at any point in his later philosophy of language. Instead, what it seeks to show is that, by confronting Heidegger's early philosophy of language with what it cannot yet say about itself, the contours of his late philosophy of language and politics of silence can be brought into relief. In Heidegger's own words, he "did not see" something about the relationship between speech and silence in *Being and Time* (*GA* 36–37, 110/87). In other words, there was something that *Being and Time* could not yet say about itself. Moreover, this very process of confronting a text with what it cannot say about its own structural blind spots is itself an example of how Heidegger seeks to study the history of philosophy and recover the forgotten question of being from the tradition. The task of this reading is not so much to deconstruct *Being and Time* as to show it to be a work always in the process of deconstructing itself.

The structural tensions of *Being and Time* are a consequence of the ontological commitments embedded in Heidegger's early understanding of silence as a means of alleviating the scattering effect of language, especially language in the public sphere. Throughout the work, Heidegger tends to associate language, which he defines as the "vocalization of discourse," with scattering and dispersal, with being drawn away from oneself (*BT*, 161/156). As a result, the conception of silence formulated in *Being and Time* is primarily oppositional and negative. For the most part, Heidegger portrays silence as withdrawal from a field of chatter toward a purity that he never explicitly endorses, but does nonetheless tend toward. This is because Heidegger's conception of silence in *Being and Time* is very much bound up with his early Christian theological influences. Linked to a sense of inwardness and withdrawal in which one turns toward God and away from the distracting world of sin, this silence is deeply indebted to thinkers such as Saint Augustine, Meister Eckhart, and Søren Kierkegaard.[1] These theological influences are implicitly combined with some of the larger discourses about scattering, modernity, and gathering prevalent in Weimar thought—both in its *völkisch* and more liberal varieties. Nonetheless, another form of silence can be identified in *Being and Time* in the silent voice of the call of conscience from Division II. In this silent voice, Heidegger indicates or points toward a different form of silence, which cannot be expressed within the ontological limits of his explicit concept of silence. Only by proceeding in a distinctly Aristotelian mode of analysis by unfolding the multivocality of silence further toward the many senses of *logos* does Heidegger find the ontological resources necessary for bringing this silence to language.

Heidegger's treatment of silence in *Being and Time* is marked by a curious double movement. While the work's philosophy of language moves in one direction as Heidegger seeks to explicitly define silence in Division I, the movement of the work veers in a subtly different direction in Division II as it begins to indicate and operate within the space of a silence that exceeds the explicit definition offered in Division I. What this double movement reveals is that the way Heidegger thinks *about* silence in *Being and Time* is in deep tension with the way he begins to think *through* silence in the course of the work. This tension leads Heidegger to undergo a significant shift in the course of *Being and Time* from a conception of silence focused around the resoluteness and authenticity of the individual toward a space of silence inhabited by a people. In other words, *Being and Time* helps to lay the groundwork for Heidegger's politics of silence.

Despite the central role that language assumes in Heidegger's thinking by the mid-1930s, language is at most a marginal matter of thematic concern in *Being and Time*.[2] The marginal status of language in *Being and Time* poses an even greater difficulty for an analysis of silence in the work, since silence exists at the margins of the investigation of language, subordinated to the inquiry into discourse primarily in §34 and in the discoursing speech of the call of conscience in §§54–60. The fact that language and silence play such a peripheral role in the thematic analysis of the work is not so much a shortcoming of the work as a result of the inquiry's goal of retrieving the question of being by laying out the fundamental structures of human existence (Dasein). Consequently, the analysis of discourse, language, and silence in §34 emerges as one of the most difficult, entangled, and even elliptical sections of *Being and Time*. These difficulties and entanglements arise as Heidegger attempts to distinguish between discourse and language through a set of terminological distinctions that at first appear quite rigid. The deconstructive reading seeks not only to clarify these terminological distinctions but also to locate the movements that are constantly forcing the distinctions apart.

§7: The Manifold Meanings of *Logos*

Heidegger approaches the phenomenological analysis of language in *Being and Time* with a deeply Aristotelian sensibility.[3] He first begins to address the question of language in §7, "The Phenomenological Method of Investigation," in the process of breaking down components of the term "phenomenology": *phainomenon* and *logos*. Phenomenology, according to Heidegger, is a "*methodological concept*," and it indicates a method that "does not characterize the what of the objects of philosophical research, but the *how* of such research" (*BT*, 27/26). The how of this method is captured by Heidegger through the Husserlian mantra "To the things themselves." With regard to the study of language, this return involves a distinct difficulty, for any attempt to go back to language must be achieved through language, that is to say, through an operation of *logos*.[4] *Logos* is thus doubly implicated in the phenomenological task that Heidegger seeks to carry out, for it serves as both the mode of analysis and the thing under analysis.

Logos takes on a central role in this investigation because it is in and through the manifold meanings of *logos* that we have access to things themselves. Consequently, the "how" of phenomenology, that is, its method, ultimately involves an attunement to *logos*, the primary meaning of which Heidegger translates using the somewhat peculiar locution "letting be seen." By choosing the language of seeing as a way of rendering this common Greek term, Heidegger directly counters a long tradition that has translated *logos* primarily as "reason" or "language," both of which may be regarded as "proper" translations of *logos*, even if they capture only a very specific sense of the polyvocal term. He explicitly stresses that this conception of seeing should not be understood as a form of visual perception, but instead in the sense that seeing "lets beings accessible to it be encountered in themselves without being concealed," and, moreover, that "one can formalize sight and seeing to the point of establishing a universal term which characterizes every access as access whatsoever to beings and to being" (*BT*, 147/142). Whether Heidegger refers to this access to being in its undisclosedness as seeing (as is overwhelmingly the case in *Being and Time*) or as listening (as is more commonly the case in his later works), this seeing and listening share a common phenomenological origin. Returning to the things themselves requires an access that follows the path of *logos* as it reveals itself from out of itself, whether one refers to this as listening or seeing. By privileging a visual language in this manner, Heidegger intends to preempt any hasty association of *logos* with enunciated speech or with *logos* as a statement or assertion. In other words, Heidegger wants to avoid any hasty translation of *logos* into either of the predominate conceptions of language drawn from Aristotle's logical works: meaningful sound and assertion.[5] Heidegger's intention is to render these common philosophical understandings of language unfamiliar, thus distancing the reader from these customary understandings by privileging the language of seeing over the language of listening.[6]

Heidegger then turns to the direct examination of *logos* in the subsection "The Concept of *logos*" (cf. Brogan 2005, 28–30), which begins by announcing the importance of the many meanings of *logos*: "The concept of *logos* has many meanings in *Plato* and *Aristotle*, and indeed in such a way that these meanings diverge from one another without being positively guided by a basic meaning. That is in fact only an illusion which lasts as long as an interpretation is not able to grasp adequately the basic meaning in its primary content. If we say that the basic meaning of *logos* is discourse, then this literal translation becomes valid only through a determination of what discourse itself says" (*BT*, 32/30).

Leaving open for the moment what it is that "discourse itself says," Heidegger then proceeds to take the reader through the manifold meanings of *logos* as they relate to and are founded in this basic meaning, employing the Aristotelian method of addressing the *doxa*, the commonly held beliefs or things that are said about *logos*. *Logos* is said in many ways, which means that it both speaks and is spoken of in many ways, and these ways include such translations common to the tradition of metaphysics as "reason, judgment, concept, definition, ground, relation." Heidegger is quick to delineate such translations as modifications of the basic meaning of *logos* as discourse and to identify how those modified meanings work to conceal the "authentic meaning of discourse" (*BT*, 32/30). By identifying this basic meaning, Heidegger lays the cornerstone for the remainder of the work: at its most primordial level, *logos* must be understood as discourse.

We should take pause here to explicitly lay out the primary question that is situated in the background of this inquiry. The phenomenological analysis seeks to address the following question: what must *logos* be, such that it can be modified into and accommodate these manifold meanings? Bracketing these modified meanings prevalent in the history of philosophy in order to approach *logos* at its most primordial level, Heidegger then sets about identifying a number of different meanings of *logos*, all of which are modifications of the basic meaning that are, even despite their modifications, grounded in that basic meaning. These include: (1) making manifest, divided into the modes of assertion and wishing, (2) speaking or vocalization (*legein*), (3) letting something be seen *as* something, (4) being true and false, (4) reason, and (5) spoken words (*legomena*), divided into (a) that which is said, and (b) that about which something is said.

A full reckoning with all of these meanings cannot be attempted here. given that the condensed examination contains the seeds for Division I's later detailed examinations of such variegated terms as assertion (2), the as-structure (3), language (2), understanding (3, 4), and idle talk (5). However, for the analysis of silence that follows what is most essential are both the operation and the result of the phenomenological analysis that traces the paths of the polyvocality of language. There is a guiding meaning of *logos* that is fundamental to all of these different meanings: discourse as letting-be-seen, in the sense of disclosing. Accordingly, while discourse is Heidegger's primary translation of *logos*, everything else pointed to in the examination of the manifold senses of the term can likewise be regarded as a translation of *logos*, provided that those translations are themselves each regarded as modifications of the authentic and primary meaning of discourse. As is the case with every word, discourse is always already perforated, scattered beyond itself in its manifold meanings. Yet when it is distilled down to the basic meaning that runs through its many modifications, Heidegger asserts that discourse always essentially means letting be seen.

That Heidegger chooses such strange terminology, indeed that he would choose to delineate discourse and language in the first place, in the process giving language the rather restricted definition of "vocalization," is a result of *Being and Time*'s constant drive to render the familiar strange (*BT*, 161/156). Breaking with the traditional conception of language that has privileged the spoken word as the primary meaning of language is a task of utmost importance for Heidegger's fundamental ontology. As he states in §34: "The Greeks do not have a word for language, they understood this phenomenon 'primarily' as discourse. However, since *logos* came into philosophical view primarily as statement, the development of the fundamental structures of the forms and components of discourse was carried out following the guidelines of *this logos*. Grammar searched for its foundations in the 'logic' of this *logos*. But this logic is based on the ontology of what is present" (*BT*, 165/159–60).

Heidegger initiates this project of placing the analysis of language on a more primordial level by situating his own analysis within the manifold meanings of language. The polyvocality of discourse has significant hermeneutical consequences for the interpretation of §34 to be carried out in the following section, for what it reveals is that we should not read discourse as a watertight term ready to be subject to hair-fine distinctions, but instead as a term that is at all times said in many ways and that resonates at all times with this polyvocal saying. In other words, even when he is engaged in his most precise and rigorous phenomenological analysis, Heidegger still leaves his basic terms open to revision. This is because his inquiries do not offer definitions per se, but instead take the reader through the process of defining. This process is itself the end goal of the analysis, not the achievement of final definitions.

§34: Discourse, Language, Silence

DISCOURSE AND LANGUAGE

In §34 of *Being and Time*, Heidegger identifies silence as a mode of discourse. Scholars have variously referred to the condensed analysis of discourse and language in §34 as "frustratingly truncated," "inconspicuous," and "still somewhat tentative" (Dahlstrom 2013, 13; Sallis 1970, 383; Kisiel 1995, 178). Some readers have also found the analysis wanting, faulting Heidegger for abruptly abandoning the questioning of §34, for leading to "no actual result," and even for being contradictory (Aler 1972, 52; Trawny 2003, 120; Pöggeler 1994, 210–10). Indeed, the condensed and frustrating passage has puzzled readers to such a degree that Heidegger himself portrayed the perplexity faced by his readers in his 1953–54 "Dialogue between a Japanese and a Questioner," one of several points at which he turns back to §34 in later works (*OWL*, 136–38/41–43).[7] In the dialogue, the Japanese interlocutor characterizes the analysis of §34 as being "quite sparse" and the questioner urges his interlocutor to go back and take a closer look at §34 (*OWL*, 137/41). If Heidegger claims that he kept silent in *Being and Time*, then §34 is perhaps one of the sites of that silence.

Heidegger defines discourse as "the meaningful structuring of the attuned intelligibility of being-in-the-world" (*BT*, 162/157). He identifies discourse as an "existenzial," his term for a fundamental ontological structure of Dasein's being-in-the-world. As an existenzial, discourse is equiprimordial with understanding and attunement. It is important to be clear on the exact nature of the equiprimordiality shared by discourse, understanding, and attunement, since Heidegger expresses it in various ways, which can at times be confusing. While it seems overstated to say that there is no actual result emerging from Heidegger's analysis, it is indeed the case that Heidegger does not settle the question of this equiprimordiality within *Being and Time*. In §34, he seems to indicate that discourse, understanding, and attunement constitute three similarly equiprimordial existenzials when he writes that: "*[d]iscourse is existentially primordial with attunement and understanding*" (*BT*, 161/155). In this particular formulation Heidegger seems to indicate three existenzials which exist alongside one another without any single one of them being in some way distinct from the other two. However, attention to an earlier formulation from the introductory passages in §28 might give the reader another impression of the relationship between these existenzials: "We see the two equiprimordially constitutive ways of being there in attunement and understanding. In each case their analysis obtains for us the necessary phenomenal confirmation through the interpretation of a concrete mode which is important for the subsequent problematic. Attunement and understanding are determined equiprimordially through *discourse*" (ibid., 133/130).

The key to the distinction here is the phrase "determined equiprimordially" in the final sentence, which indicates that discourse, understanding, and attunement do not simply exist alongside one another, but instead that understanding and attunement are both determined through discourse in the very possibility of their even being there at all. These three elements are thus equiprimordial, but not equiprimordial in the same manner, for discourse in some way determines understanding and attunement. In other words, discourse is somehow primary in this relation. According to this interpretation of the three existenzials, if "*Dasein is its disclosedness*," and this disclosedness reveals to us a world to which we are always already attuned, and which we have always already understood in some way, and if this understanding and attunement are determined in their very ground by discourse, then Dasein is fundamentally discursive (*BT*, 133/129). Heidegger expresses this grammatically by using the German active participle form for "speaking" (*redend*). Dasein is not only fundamentally discursive as an active capacity, but also—using the passive participle form—fundamentally spoken to, immersed in discourse in a way that defies any simple reduction to active and passive modes.

We are fundamentally discursive such that the world reveals itself through *logos*, but this does not mean that we simply possess language as a trait or capacity according to the traditional understanding of Aristotle's description of the human as a rational animal. As Aristotle writes in the *Metaphysics*, " 'to have' has many meanings," and in *Being and Time*, Heidegger reveals his sensitivity to these many meanings in his analysis of Aristotle's definition (*Metaphysics* 1023a9) of the human as a life-form possessing language (*zōon logon echon*): "The later interpretation of this definition of human being in the sense of *animal rationale*, 'rational living being,' is indeed not 'false,' but it covers over the phenomenal basis from which this definition of Dasein is taken. The human being shows itself as a being who speaks. This does not mean that the possibility of vocal utterance is proper to it, rather that this being is in the mode of discovering world and Dasein itself" (*BT*, 165/159).

We do not have language in the sense that we can have a grasp on a thing, nor even in the way that something like fever may be said to have us. In what way, then, do we have language? What Heidegger is trying to recover in his understanding of discourse is an essential relation of having that does not signal possession or mastery over something we take hold of. The transformation away from "logical" thinking that Heidegger calls for in §34 is precisely rooted in relinquishing this perceived—and ultimately illusory—sense of mastery. To have language in this sense does not designate a human capacity or ability, and language understood in this manner is likewise not something to be mastered (Sallis 1984, 80). Since we cannot have language in this way, any attempt to master language will always be founded upon a more primordial relation to language. Indeed, achieving a satisfactory explanation of this primordial sense of language even tests the very power of language, which could itself serve to signal that language is not something to be mastered.

Heidegger's recovery of the relation to *logos* that he designates as discourse indicates something unfamiliar to the kind of philosophy of language which is concerned with the assertive force of statements. This is because the *logos* Heidegger is concerned with is not primarily a human capacity. To the extent, therefore, that language is related to articulation in the sense of enunciation or verbal expression, it only allows for this modification because it is grounded in a prior jointure and scansion—a "meaningful structuring" (*BT*, 162/157). This existenzial structuring makes the world meaningful in the first place and does not indicate *logos* in the limited sense of assertion, which is but one of the many meanings that Aristotle discovered in *logos*. Indeed, the sense of *logos* that Heidegger hopes to recover is not primarily to be found in Aristotle's logical treatises, where assertive language reigns as the privileged mode of *logos*, but instead is more closely related to the sense of *logos* employed by Aristotle when he states in the *Generation of Animals* that "everything that is formed either by art or by nature exists in virtue of some *logos*" (Aristotle 1943, 767a18–19). That is to say, the sense of *logos* that drives Heidegger's analysis here is not to be found in the treatises where Aristotle attempts explicitly to define language, for the very process of definition itself operates within the logical confines of assertive language. The very same structure can be found in Heidegger's sigetics, for his most essential relation to silence in *Being and Time* is not to be found in his most explicit attempts to define silence, but instead in passages where silence is not explicitly dealt with as a topic of thematic analysis.

By developing this understanding of discourse as an existenzial determining our very world in its worldliness, Heidegger distinguishes his philosophy of language from traditional philosophies of language, which he regards as having made the error of limiting the analysis of language to logical treatises while ignoring the ontological dimensions of language, which defy the predetermined parameters of logic. This error is rooted in a fundamental misunderstanding about the nature of Aristotle's logical treatises, which only sought to pursue a specialized analysis of certain meanings of *logos* by intentionally restricting the many meanings of *logos* from the outset. Indeed, as Aristotle himself recognizes, it is because we are discursive that the world is meaningfully structured and hence understood. Words, in turn, accrue to this meaningful structure, which has a scansion or rhythm prior to the accrual of words. In this process of accrual, language as vocalization, as the accrual of words to the prior scansion of a meaningful structuring, begins to emerge as a modification of this primordial structure of meaning. Language is thus conceptualized as the worldly existence of discourse, a relation Heidegger describes as follows: "If discourse, the articulation of the intelligibility of the there, is the primordial existential of disclosedness, and if disclosedness is primarily constituted by being-in-the-world, discourse must also essentially have a specifically *worldly* mode of being. The attuned intelligibility of being-in-the-world *expresses itself as discourse.* The totality of significations of intelligibility *is put into words.* Words accrue to significations. But word-things are not provided with significations" (*BT*, 161/155–56).

Language designates the specifically worldly mode of being of discourse as utterance, expression, and verbal articulation. This leads Heidegger to offer the following definition of language: "The vocalization of discourse is language" (*BT*, 161/156). There is a significant ambiguity at stake here: on the one hand there is vocalization as something like an accomplished speech act, while on the other hand there is the process of accrual or the gathering of words around significations. Discourse, word, and world are thus significantly intertwined in ways that cause the distinction between language and discourse to collapse, even within *Being and Time* itself.

Perhaps the greatest difficulty one faces in distinguishing between discourse and language in *Being and Time* is understanding that what is at stake is not primarily a matter of difference, unless that difference is understood as the ontological difference between being and beings. Discourse, moreover, is only prelinguistic in a very specific sense, even if it is, at its most originary level, pre-predicative. Language and discourse are distinguished by their degrees of primordiality or originality, and Heidegger identifies discourse as that which makes language possible. The distinction between discourse and language is perhaps best understood through the metaphorical language Heidegger employs in the final paragraph of §34: discourse is the " 'place' " of language "in the constitution of being of Dasein" (*BT*, 166/161). The being of beings takes places within discourse, housed within discourse as structured by it. One can become attuned to that place, but one does not objectify it in a logical operation.

Conceptualizing discourse as the ontological place of language, with language in turn as the proximal worldly mode of discourse, helps to explain the puzzling turn that Heidegger takes at the beginning of §35, when he seems to make all the careful work of drawing distinctions in the previous paragraph unravel. Turning to the analysis of idle talk, the mode in which Dasein, immersed as it is in the average everydayness of the they, primarily and for the most part expresses itself, Heidegger says: "For the most part, discourse expresses itself and has always already expressed itself. It is language" (*BT*, 167/162). The sentence must be read with stress on the "is." Discourse *is* language, though language always speaks out of its ontological space, out of a space of *logos*. Language as vocalization is always twofold: it is the ontic revealing of what is prior ontologically to the act of revealing.

Discourse, like *logos*, is said in many ways, and discourse in a certain significant sense is Heidegger's translation of *logos*. However, Heidegger's overarching concern is not to develop a gapless, fully structured, and systematically hermetic terminology for the manifold meanings of *logos*, but rather to work within a strategically elaborated language on a provisional basis in order to follow the articulation of being identified as *logos*. The primary consequence of treating Heidegger's terminology as a temporary strategy—that is, as a set of tools dropped once they have done their work— is that apparent, perhaps actual, terminological inconsistencies in *Being and Time* can be attributed to its overarching phenomenological method. This method is always attentive to the polyvocality of language. In the reception of *Being and Time*, much has been made of how Heidegger quietly distanced himself from the language of discourse in his later understanding of language, and this terminological shift has been regarded as the source of apparent inconsistencies in Heidegger's thinking. Such "inconsistencies" ought to be understood in terms of the movement behind a work that does not operate at the level of the individual word.

In the years after *Being and Time*, Heidegger was forced to rethink the ontological nature of discourse entirely, and to bring it into a new alignment with silence. With regard to discourse, Heidegger not only changes the terminology, allowing discourse to dissolve altogether as a vested term, while language is vested anew, he also significantly alters the *thinking* behind these terms. The tensions around silence in *Being and Time* necessitate this change, and the call of conscience in a certain sense even heralds it. This raises a fundamental question about the place of silence in Heidegger's work: is it because of his changing approach to silence that the distinction between discourse and language ultimately disappears from his thinking?

Silence

In his first mention of silence in §34 Heidegger once again employs a phrase that playfully manipulates the distinction between discourse and language laid down in the very same paragraph: "*Listening* and *silence* are possibilities belonging to discoursing speech [*redenden Sprechen*]" (*BT*, 161/156). Given the distinctions between discourse and language that Heidegger labored over so tediously, what could discoursing speech possibly be? In this sense, it is not vocalization and, as a mode of discourse, does not involve the word, but instead is revealed through a rich disclosedness of oneself in one's being-with and communication with others. This kind of silence as discoursing speech is not understood as a withdrawal in the sense of isolating oneself; rather, it is about giving oneself over further to one's ecstatic being-with. Through the word one scatters oneself in chatter and idle talk, intensifying one's alignment with the topics "they" talk about—the weather, sports, news, political gossip, and countless other topics too fleeting to enumerate. Discoursing speech, in contrast, is about intensifying oneself within one's authentic disclosure and shared understanding of a shared being. This points to an important limitation of Heidegger's conception of language in *Being and Time*: he does not yet articulate the nature of language in terms of gathering, as is distinctly the case by the 1930s, but instead tends to associate the word, and hence language, with scattering.[8] Although "gathering" was to become a central term in Heidegger's thinking by the mid-1930s, in *Being and Time,* he uses it only three times, in an entirely neutral fashion (*BT,* 170/164, 210/202, 266/255).[9] Indeed, if any term represents a notion of gathering in *Being and Time*, it is silence and not any of the manifold meanings of language. This shift in the language of gathering was perhaps the most important transformation in Heidegger's work in the years immediately following *Being and Time.*

As a mode of discoursing speech, silence is limited in *Being and Time,* because it is primarily a negative concept set up in opposition to the chatter of what Heidegger famously called idle talk. Heidegger establishes the oppositional character of silence early in the analysis: "He who is silent in shared discourse can 'make himself comprehensible,' i.e. forge understanding more authentically than one who never runs out of things to say. Speaking a lot about something does not at all guarantee that understanding is furthered as a result. On the contrary, talking at great length about something covers over things and brings what is understood into an illusory clarity, that is, the incomprehensibility of the trivial" (*BT,* 164/159).

Silence clearly stands out against the noise of everyday forms of chatter. Against this clamor, silence fosters understanding, though not in the sense of a cognitive capacity, but instead in the sense of the existenzial that defines what it means for us to be in a world that we have always already in some way understood. As a means of unfolding Dasein's shared disclosedness, silence is fundamentally related to dwelling as being-with in our shared being. In idle talk, in contrast, we are taken out of our authentic being-with and drawn into the public chatter of "the they" in the mode of flight or escape. In *Being and Time*, silence counters this flight or escape, working within and against a vast terrain of chatter, in which the philosopher refuses to participate.

Yet even while this understanding of silence is opposed to a certain manner of speech, it is nonetheless rooted in a capacity for discursive speech. As Heidegger goes on to say in his condensed analysis of silence: "But to keep silent does not mean to be mute. On the contrary, one who is mute still has the tendency to 'speak.' A mute person has not only not proved that he can keep silent, he even lacks the possibility of proving this. And the person who is by nature accustomed to speak little is no better able to show that he can keep silent at a given moment. One who never says anything is also unable to keep silent at a given moment. Authentic silence is possible only in genuine discourse" (*BT*, 164–65/159).

Heidegger approaches his later understanding of silence as an operation of the word here, but his account of speech and silence still remains, to a fine but significant degree, too oppositional and negative to articulate the ontological structure that silence will later assume in his work. In this account, the possibility of silence is guaranteed by language, by having something fundamental to say, but Heidegger does not go so far as to state that silence emerges through language. In this manner, he links the possibility of silence to the capacity for speech, but still separates silence quite distinctly from the word, even if discourse *is* proximally and for the most part in the word. In this conception of it, silence punctuates and structures language, but is still ontologically distinct from language.

In order to be silent, one must have something to say. In *Being and Time*, Heidegger still struggles with what exactly it is that is said through this silence and how it is said, as shown by a later marginal note of his on the statement that "in order to be silent, Dasein must have something to say,* that is, it must be in command of an authentic and rich disclosedness of itself. Then reticence makes manifest and puts down 'idle talk.' As a mode of discourse, reticence articulates the intelligibility of Dasein so primordially that it gives rise to a genuine potentiality for hearing and to a being-with-one-another that is transparent" (*BT*, 164–65/159). Heidegger noted of this passage: "*and what is to be said? (being)" (ibid., 443/159).

When Heidegger poses the question of what is to be said in silence, he answers with nothingness. Yet the ontological valence of this nothingness still remains primarily oppositional. It is primarily concerned with countering "idle talk"—although, he warns, this should not be read in a "disparaging sense" (*BT*, 167/161). What *Being and Time* cannot yet come to terms with is what is to be said. The positive nature of silence as an active instance of non-articulation cannot fully emerge in Heidegger's thinking until the distinction between language and discourse collapses completely. That is to say, Heidegger cannot capture the possibility of speaking through silence until language becomes folded into silence to such a degree that it even requires silence.

It only serves to complicate this story that the distinction between language and discourse was already collapsing, even in §34. Yet despite these complications, it is still possible to conclude that, to the extent that silence is a mode of discourse, even if it is discursive speaking, Heidegger separates it from the word. Silence is not external or contrary to the many ways in which *logos* is defined in *Being and Time*, but it does lie outside of vocalization, and hence outside of the word.

§§ 54–60: The Rupturing of Silence

As the "testimony to one's own capacity to be" (*BT*, 279/268), the analysis of the call of conscience constitutes the climax of *Being and Time*, finally answering the question of the "determination of what discourse itself says," raised in §7 (ibid., 32/30). The call of conscience is a silent call, out of Dasein's immersion in "the they," that summons it back to its own authentic, guilty being-a-self. The call does not speak, at least not in the mode of language, but as a mode of discourse, it does "give something to understand, it *discloses*" (ibid., 269/259). This call corresponds to a possible hearing, and discloses the existence of what Heidegger calls guilt, but it nonetheless says nothing (ibid., 287/275). In this analysis, "guilt," "call," "listening," and "silence" are all ontological terms, and Heidegger does not intend any of them to be heard in an ontic fashion, for the call of conscience has precisely nothing ontic to say. The call is not only incomprehensible to Dasein to the extent that it is immersed in its everyday fallenness and the activity and noise of "the they," it cannot even be heard by Dasein. The call is heard in its silence as a mode of silence.[10]

The silence of the call of conscience is essentially oppositional to the chatter of "the they." The call is a call to reticence, and while this reticence can only be reticence because Dasein has something to say, it is not a reticence that emerges through language. As Heidegger describes the call: "The call does not report any facts; it calls without uttering. The call speaks in the uncanny mode of *silence*. And it does this only because in calling the one summoned, it does not call him into the public idle chatter of the they, but *calls* him *back* from that *to the reticence of his existent potentiality-to-be*" (*BT*, 277/266).

Reticence is both a mode of listening and a mode of discourse, but even as a mode of discourse, it has nothing to say. In fact, what it has to say is the nothing, and what results from the call, even if heard in the proper mode of reticence, is likewise nothing: "That *nothing* ensues means something *positive* with regard to Dasein" (*BT*, 279/280).

At this point the limitations of Heidegger's thinking of silence emerge more fully, for it is precisely this notion of positivity that Heidegger struggles to express in language in *Being and Time*, even though the call of conscience does contain an "abyssal dimension," according to Daniela Vallega-Neu (2013, 124). Heidegger struggles to express this positivity in language because the mode of *logos* appropriate to it is discourse and not language. Consequently, any attempt to express it, or any attempt to apply the word to the saying of the nothing automatically vulgarizes the nothing by reducing it to mere absence—and this vulgarization is the very guilt that the call of conscience discloses. The nothing is understood as disclosed through reticence, but reticence has precisely nothing to say. Reticence is the existenziell mode of the existenzial discourse, which, regarded from the perspective of being as ready-to-hand, is nothing. Heidegger himself recognizes the difficulty involved in saying the nothing in a crucial passage: "Nonetheless the *ontological meaning of the notness* of this nullity remains obscure. But that is true also of the *ontological essence of the not in general*. . . . Has anyone ever made the *ontological origin* of notness a problem at all, or, *before that*, even looked for the *conditions* on the basis of which the problem of the not and its notness, and the possibility of the notness, and the possibility of this notness, could be raised?" (*BT*, 285–86/274). This lays the groundwork for his later turn to nothingness as a thematic clarification of the question of being announced in his 1929 lecture "What Is Metaphysics?" (Heidegger 1976e). However, the project of "What Is Metaphysics?" could only become possible once a significant ontological transformation had occurred in Heidegger's thinking of silence, for in *Being and Time* Heidegger still equates saying the nothing with saying nothing.

What, then, does the reticence of the resolute Dasein called back to itself say? It says the nothing by saying nothing. And what does it not say? Heidegger offers a straightforward answer to this question: "It withdraws the word from the commonsense idle chatter of the they" (*BT*, 296/284). In speaking of withdrawal, Heidegger announces the arrival of a term that will become central to his understanding of language and silence after *Being and Time*. By the time of his 1931 lectures on Aristotle's *Metaphysics*, "withdrawal" has come to mean the presence of an absence, indeed even the presencing of an absencing. Specifically with regard to silence, this means that silence is the presence of the absence of language—a presence that comes to be through the word.[11] It is precisely this twofold nature of silence that escapes Heidegger in *Being and Time* as he struggles to develop a language adequate to the task of bringing silence to language as silence.

Documenting Heidegger's struggles with bringing the positivity of silence to language does not intend to imply that silence is merely reduced to being the absence of speech in *Being and Time*. This is because, as an existenzial, silence lies beyond any distinction between presence and absence. Nonetheless, what *Being and Time* does not yet venture to articulate is the specific ontology of a silence that is not merely posited in opposition to language. By showing that silence is grounded in the capacity to have something meaningful to say, Heidegger does indeed confront his readers with the essential intertwining of speech and silence, yet in this intertwining the strands remain separate: there is speech and there is silence, and while the two touch in such a manner that they mutually determine each other, they nonetheless remain distinct from each other.

The importance of this limitation can be demonstrated through Heidegger's own analysis of the significance of Dasein's retrieval of its ownmost self through listening to the call to conscience. Although nothing occurs through the call to conscience, since what "occurs" occurs in the mode of reticence, Heidegger does nonetheless indicate a consequence of sorts, an ontic result of resoluteness. Heidegger offers this hint while describing the listening peculiar to the call to conscience: "The understanding of the call which listens in an existenziell fashion is more authentic the more Dasein hears *its* being called non-relationally and the less that what it says, what is fitting and valid, distorts the meaning of the call" (*BT*, 280/269). Here Heidegger links the existenzial of the discourse of the call of conscience with an existenziell speech that is all the more authentic the less it distorts the call. The ontological silence of the call is thus brought into connection with an ontic vocalization. What emerges here is a process of translation, a carrying over of the authentic silent message into a language that is, like all language, necessarily always already fallen, that is, primordially guilty. Although this guilt is fallen, it is nonetheless not conceived against any possible concept of purity. Indeed, part of Dasein's guilt is that it will never be able to guarantee the validity of this process of translation, even in reticence. The transparency of discourse is always already obscured and distorted. The purity of silence is always already tainted. As this purity is shattered, the distinction between language and silence begins to collapse, yet this collapse is precisely built into the structures of *Being and Time*. In the wake of this collapse, silence will assume a new meaning, a meaning that will ultimately reorient the task of Heidegger's thinking in the years after *Being and Time* toward the saying of silence, toward silence as the operation of the word, and no less of an operation of vocalization and inscribing. This performance of a worded silence is what he calls the handiwork of thinking. This handiwork is carried out within a profoundly significant political context in which silence and chatter are deeply laden words tied to the spiritual renewal of the German people.

Conclusion: Toward Withdrawal

A fundamental aspect of Heidegger's ontology transforms as he distances himself from the definition of language as "the vocalization of discourse" offered in *Being and Time* (*BT*, 161/156). Defining language in this way results in Heidegger all too often interpreting silence merely "negatively" as the nonvocalization of discourse. Hence the primary limitation of Heidegger's early conception of silence is that it is set up in opposition to the word, and the word, in turn, is all too often associated with chatter. Moreover, to the extent that silence speaks through what Heidegger calls "discoursing speech," neither of the two modes of discoursing speech that he identifies, namely, listening and silence, involve the word (ibid.). Listening and silence are related to *logos* as discourse, but not to *logos* as the word. Yet even while *Being and Time* cannot make space for a worded silence in a thematic analysis, the movements internal to the text indicate or point toward such a silence in the context of the call of conscience, where silence emerges most profoundly in the work as a space of possibility merely indicated, but not expressly articulated.

Heidegger's definition of silence in *Being and Time* remains, in certain critical aspects, beholden to an overly negative concept of silence. This continued fidelity to a negative concept of silence is a result of his terminological distinctions that demarcate silence as distanced from the word and separated from an operation of language: it is nonvocalization set against a vocalization. However, despite the traces of this metaphysics of presence that remain in Heidegger's *definition* of silence in *Being and Time*, the thinking of silence, especially in the voice of the call to conscience, points beyond any mere negative notion of silence. What occurs is that, as the terminological limitation of silence to a mode of discourse ruptures, Heidegger begins to indicate a silence that he cannot account for in his explicit analysis—not least of all because that very silence defies any traditional notion of account, and indeed any traditional notion of conceptuality. After all, what Heidegger was after in *Being and Time* seems to have been, in his own words, an "impossible fiction" (*BT*, 279/268). In the face of this "fiction," the task of thinking does not, as Heidegger himself says, merely involve "the seemingly easily remedied lack of an adequate terminology," but instead involves placing silence and language upon an entirely new ontological footing (*BT*, 16/16). *Being and Time* presents the initial stages of this task.

By tracing these movements in and through *Being and Time*, one can begin to see the origins of Heidegger's sigetics, which already operated in a nascent manner in the work. Silence is rooted in the resoluteness and authenticity of the individual in Division I of *Being and Time*, yet Heidegger's thinking begins to move away from the resoluteness of the individual toward the resoluteness of a people. The call of conscience opens up silence to a space of saying. By opening up silence to a space of saying, silence begins to become a common task of attunement. This suggest two possible ways of assessing the political status of *Being and Time*, although adjudicating between them would require us to indulge in dubious speculation about the author's intention. Either Heidegger's thinking evolved past a concern for the resoluteness of the individual, or *Being and Time* expresses only a certain stage of movement in Heidegger's thinking. Regardless of which possibility is chosen, in the years after *Being and Time*, Heidegger develops a sigetic ontology and sigetic politics, which both relies upon and moves beyond *Being and Time*. Yet perhaps most significantly, Heidegger's nascent sigetics still lacks the political dimension it will later gain. What is lacking is the space of silence as the silence of a people tasked with shepherding what Heidegger refers to as the Greek-Germanic essence.

4   Withdrawal in Aristotle's *Metaphysics*

The years following the publication of *Being and Time* were a heady time for Heidegger. Publication of his long-awaited book brought him philosophical fame, securing the coveted chair in Freiburg for him, and thus bringing him back to his beloved southwestern homeland, after a productive stint as a charismatic young instructor in Marburg (Van Buren 1994). Philosophically, Heidegger undertook a number of ambitious studies after *Being and Time*, including his contested attempt to rethink the notion of temporality in his 1929 book *Kant and the Problem of Metaphysics*, from which he later distanced himself. Perhaps most tantalizingly, in the winter semester of 1929–30, he offered a wide-ranging lecture course under the somewhat innocuous title *The Fundamental Concepts of Metaphysics: World, Finitude, Solitude*, commenting on everything from the flight patterns of bumblebees, to the nature of profound boredom, and the worldlessness of inanimate objects such as stones. Contemporaries may have regarded Heidegger as floundering philosophically without a central project to match the momentousness of *Being and Time* during these years, but it is perhaps more accurate to say that he was experimenting with new terrain and forms of thinking.

Heidegger cultivates this experimental style most clearly in *The Fundamental Concepts of Metaphysics*, which fascinated Jacques Derrida seventy years later, when he held his final seminar (Derrida 2011). Derrida regarded the text as a rich landscape traversed by a multitude of paths of philosophical investigation that do not emerge elsewhere in Heidegger's thinking. Breaking with his often impersonal and rigid style of lecturing, and with many of the mores of the German professoriate, Heidegger paints for his students such scenes as an image of himself returning from a pleasant, all-too pleasant dinner party where "things are witty and amusing." But as he begins to think back over the night upon returning home, casting a "quick glance at the work we interrupted," reflecting on the evening that has just passed, he realizes that—amid the wine, food, and entertaining conversation of the evening—"I was bored after all this evening" (*GA* 29–30, 165/109). One learns some fascinating details, moreover, about how Heidegger passes the time when waiting on a delayed train "in the tasteless station of some minor railway," where "we sit down on a stone, draw all kinds of figures in the sand, and in so doing catch ourselves looking at our watch yet again" (ibid., 140/93). But perhaps most tantalizingly, one learns how a bee navigates its surrounding world in a reading of the contemporary biologist Jakob von Uexküll (ibid., 350–58/240–46). In a break with his normally stern pedagogical persona, *The Fundamental Concepts of Metaphysics* is at times witty and ironic, displaying an uncharacteristically self-referential tone to reflect on the place of the modern philosopher in the production of a form of knowledge served up as a product to be consumed by the modern student, as if they were at "some great marketplace" (ibid., 32).Open-ended, experimental, and fragmentary, at times the work is humble, at times it is bold in its sweeping claims. Perhaps not surprisingly, Heidegger assigned special priority to it when preparing his *Gesamtausgabe* for publication.[1] Yet perhaps the most peculiar aspect of the text is that, in all of its richness, there is little indication as the lecture unfolds that the Heidegger one reads in this lecture course would soon be a significant public representative of National Socialist cultural politics.

In the semester immediately following the bold speculative thinking of 1929–30 lecture course, Heidegger returned to familiar terrain with a lecture course that sharply contrasts with the wide-ranging examinations of the prior year. Heidegger's 1931 lecture course on Aristotle's *Metaphysics* (*GA* 33) was a return to the style of teaching he practiced in the 1920s: a slow, hermeneutical analysis of a classic work of philosophy mediated to the students line by line through his own inimitable style of translation. *Aristotle's "Metaphysics" Theta 1–3* (Heidegger 1995a) is precise, and its pace is slow. While it is easy to overlook it in favor of the speculative fireworks of the prior year's lecture course, close attention to the trajectory of the later course helps to reveal the source of some fundamental shifts that occur in Heidegger's thinking after *Being and Time*.

Fundamental Concepts is fascinating because it is replete with imaginative possibilities that do not appear again in Heidegger's work. *Aristotle's "Metaphysics" Theta 1–3* is important because of the crucial transformation in Heidegger's ontology—and perhaps especially in his philosophy of language—when he lays out the ontological structures demonstrating the positivity of nonbeing, thus lending ontological weight to many of the claims in his 1929 lecture "What Is Metaphysics?" Helping restore a place for nothingness in philosophical thinking, Heidegger proffers an ontology calling to mind Wittgenstein's assertion in his *Tractatus Logico-Philosophicus* that "whereof one cannot speak, thereof one must be silent" (Wittgenstein [1921] 1989, 178). Much like the Platonists, Neoplatonists, and the medieval mystics before him, but also the Jewish scholars of the apophatic tradition in his own time, Heidegger would once again speak of—and through—silence.[2] Aristotle would provide the ontological foundation for that practice of philosophical writing through silence.

As is always the case with Heidegger's assimilation of Greek thinking, one must read *Aristotle's "Metaphysics" Theta 1–3* (Heidegger 1995a) with careful attention to his adoption of power structures of silencing already present in Aristotle. Heidegger regards Aristotle as performing a philosophical operation that lets *logos* speak, but this letting speak is predicated on a fundamental act of silencing that relegates its other to the status of being *alogos*. Hence, even while Heidegger may conceive of his phenomenological practice as the attainment of a capacity for listening, this listening nonetheless relies on a structural closure. Heidegger's reading of Aristotle's *Metaphysics* may not be overtly political, but given his sigetic logic of inversion, that may be the very reason to regard his appropriation of Aristotle as fundamental to his politics of language.

The Impossible Fiction

Chapter 3 concluded with what Heidegger called an "impossible fiction" (*BT*, 279/268). This chapter will consider what Aristotle says "is surprising and is thought to be impossible" (*Physics* 191b16–17). This surprising impossibility addressed by Aristotle is an understanding of privation (*sterēsis*) that folds nonbeing into being. It is so surprising because it articulates a conception of being directed against what Heidegger calls Parmenides's "first decisive truth of philosophy" (*GA* 33, 27/22), namely, the banishing of nonbeing from philosophy. For Aristotle, this constitutes nothing less than the intrusion of nonbeing into metaphysics; for Heidegger, it signals the intrusion of silence into language as the new guiding meaning of philosophical *logos*. These two apparent impossibilities become increasingly intertwined as Heidegger's thinking moves ever further away from the type of phenomenological analysis of silence carried out in *Being and Time* to a thinking that regards itself as an operation of silence. Beneath the surface of the phenomenological analysis of force (*dunamis*) in *Aristotle's "Metaphysics" Theta 1–3*, a crucial transition occurs between distinct phases in Heidegger's philosophy of language (McNeill 2013, 46–62). In the course of analyzing the nature of force and power, Heidegger develops the ontological framework, grammar, and vocabulary necessary to help bring silence to language. As a consequence, with the gradual integration of his manner of thinking about silence into his manner of thinking through silence, his philosophy of language is transformed. This convergence occurs as the performance of a reticent philosophical practice. This manner of expression must attend to the unsayable and unsaid as much as to the sayable and said, and it is precisely such an attentiveness that characterizes Heidegger's so-called "handicraft of writing" as the production of silence. Through his appropriation of the Aristotelian understanding of *sterēsis*, Heidegger develops both the vocabulary and the ontological framework necessary to bring to language what *Being and Time* only indicated: a worded silence. By approaching it as a force or capacity, Heidegger begins to recognize that language is essentially intertwined with silence as its contrary potentiality.

Logos and Gathering

At first glance it may seem strange to argue for locating the shifts in Heidegger's understanding of silence in a work that says virtually nothing about silence. This may seem especially odd since *Aristotle's "Metaphysics" Theta 1–3* is a compact and focused textual analysis, seemingly centered specifically on Aristotle's conception of force. Despite this absence of a thematic analysis of silence, Heidegger's entire philosophy of language begins to profoundly shift as a result of work carried out in the lecture course. In reading *Aristotle's "Metaphysics" Theta 1–3* it is thus noteworthy how quickly Heidegger, in the opening section, steers the inquiry into force directly toward the question of language, even though language is seemingly not at stake in Aristotle's original analysis. What Heidegger then enacts in the course of his ensuing phenomenological investigation involves a complex interaction between his philosophical language and Aristotle's philosophical language carried out while Heidegger is in the process of explicitly rethinking the very question of what it means to have a capacity for language. The lecture course must accordingly be understood as an analysis of an Aristotelian text developed in the course of a simultaneous recovery of an Aristotelian method. In "the peculiarity of Aristotle's approach and way," Heidegger discovers a practice that is fundamental to his phenomenology: the circumscribing of the essence (*GA* 33, 70/59). As *Being and Time* demonstrated, the manner of analysis is, for Heidegger as much as for Aristotle, first of all rooted in attunement to the polyvocality of the matter under inquiry. As "the guiding principle of his entire philosophy," the operation of polyvocality is the fundamental gesture of Aristotle's process of circumscribing of the essence of the matter under inquiry (ibid., 26/21). Heidegger describes this process of circumscription in a later lecture course: "In Aristotle the questioning circles precisely around the fundamental concepts and fundamental principles; more precisely, these are not yet settled, but everything remains close to the substantive essential connections they indicate. And accordingly, we also seek in vain for a system, or even the mere basic outline of one. Such a representation of Aristotelian philosophy is completely un-Greek and arose only later, in the time of the Middle Ages, through Arabic-Jewish and Christian philosophy" (*GA* 36/37, 60/48).[3]

Attunement to polyvocality involves a manner of questioning that allows Aristotle to move within what is unsettled, to gather together a saying around a set of questions that are themselves unsettled. The task of Heidegger's thinking in the lecture course is to recover the possibility of listening to the many ways of speaking of *logos* in Aristotle, where listening does not mean passive receptivity, but writing this polyvocality along the grain of its own self-revealing. What reveals itself to the listeners in this way emerges, not as a finished piece of philosophy, but as a constantly open task of listening and attunement.

This task of attunement involves both a practice of writing and a practice of reading. This kind of philosophical practice therefore always moves in two directions simultaneously, for as Heidegger says of the polyvocality of the being of beings, "beings are addressed in many ways, then being is articulated in many ways" (*GA* 33, 34/28). The phenomenological analysis of polyvocality involves bringing into alignment the manner in which being is addressed with the manner in which it articulates itself. Philosophizing in this sense involves harmonizing these double movements of *logos* as a task carried out without closure. This demands a harmonization of the components of what Brogan calls the "double *logos*" of Aristotle's thinking (Brogan 2005, xiv). In the language of *Being and Time*, that means bringing an ontic sayability into harmony with an ontological saying through a manner of approach that moves back to the origins of the history of philosophy, for "language is the source and wonder of our Dasein, and we may assume that philosophy did not misspeak at the time of its inception or when human beings came into their proper existence" (*GA* 33, 20/16). Heidegger regards this as a process of translation that must always attend to the gap of untranslatability between historical structures of thought. Such a process of translation is always guided by the commitment that we are translating from the genuine speech of the Greeks to the fallen language of modern metaphysics.

It is due to the double implication of an Aristotelian *logos* that Heidegger speaks, in a passage that characterizes philosophy as mankind's greatest presumption, of surpassing Aristotle, "not in a forward direction in the sense of a progression, but rather backwards in the direction of a more original unveiling of what is comprehended by him. With this we are saying further that what is at issue here is not an improvement of the definition, not a free-floating brooding over individual lifeless concepts. Rather, this going beyond which leads backwards is at once in itself the struggle by which we bring ourselves again before the actuality that prevails tacitly in the concepts that have lost for the tradition" (ibid., 82/69).

For Heidegger, this effort to surpass Aristotle from behind involves redefining what it means to offer a philosophical definition, and hence redefining what it means to philosophize as an "Aristotelian." Heidegger finds that there is alive within Aristotle a practice of tracing and circumscribing that allows for being to speak in its manifoldness, for "this philosophizing is still there, not there in the impoverished presence of a supposed Aristotelianism but there as an indissolvable bond and an unending obligation" (ibid., 70/59). When Heidegger speaks of this philosophizing still being there, he means that it speaks to and through the world—and hence the *logos*—it wishes to speak of. One yields to the obligations demanded by this philosophy through a phenomenological sensibility for following "the natural constraints of the matter at hand" (ibid., 91/76). As a labor of writing, this phenomenological sensibility to the matter at hand is made manifest, like any handiwork, though a proper regard for the boundary, through a vision rooted as much in knowledge of what belongs to the work as knowledge of what lies outside its boundaries. This poietic craft is at the core of the handicraft of writing in Heidegger's sigetic philosophy. The vision involved in *poiēsis*, Aristotle calls *epagogē*, a term Heidegger describes as " 'leading toward' what comes into view insofar as we have previously looked *away*, over and *beyond* individual beings? At what? At being" (Heidegger 1976d, 244/187). Such philosophizing is a manner of following the limits revealed within *logos* itself through the many ways of saying. Yet how can Heidegger let these many ways of saying speak when his very understanding of both language and speaking is itself undergoing a transformation?

GATHERING

"[This lecture] course confronts the task of interpreting philosophically a philosophical treatise of Greek philosophy," *Aristotle's "Metaphysics" Theta 1–3* begins (*GA* 33, 3/1). It starts by first bracketing off the common labels and categories applied to Aristotle's inquiry, which include calling it "metaphysical." Calling Aristotle's treatise metaphysical "not only says nothing," but Heidegger even goes on to characterize it as "downright misleading," for "Aristotle never had in his possession what later came to be understood by the word or concept metaphysics" (ibid., 1/3). By resisting the categories commonly applied to Aristotle, Heidegger seeks to recover something forgotten in the tradition of Western philosophy and to prevent us from allowing ourselves to be "swayed" or "talked into anything" by that tradition (ibid., 4/2). This means resisting the temptation to treat Aristotle's *Metaphysics* as belonging to a branch of philosophy known as metaphysics, and refraining from doctrinal assumptions about metaphysical inquiry, particularly interpretations of Aristotle based on anachronistic, non-Greek categories. Heidegger commences by asking: "How else are we to locate the realm of questioning in which the treatise belongs? Or should we leave the matter open and undetermined? In which case, our attempt to enter into Aristotle's inquiry, and thus to inquire along with it, would be without direction or guidance for some time. . . . In what realm of questioning does the treatise belong? The text itself provides the answer in its first few lines" (ibid.).

For Heidegger, philosophizing means inquiring along with the text by moving along with it through a reading enacted as a task of writing and teaching. Inquiring along with the text, Heidegger immediately quotes the opening lines of Aristotle's book 9 in Greek and then offers his translation of those lines in order to discover the terrain of the inquiry: *logos*. This does not mean to say that *Metaphysics* 9 is about *logos*; rather, following what Heidegger refers to as "the natural constraints of the matter at hand," the text reveals itself to be situated within the terrain of the question of *logos* (*GA* 33, 91/76). To reformulate this in a different phenomenological terminology, the inquiry into force and actuality in book 9 of the *Metaphysics* occurs upon the horizon of *logos*—and Heidegger approaches this realm of questioning, just as he does in *Being and Time*, through its polyvocality. What occurs in the course of Heidegger's inquiry is that the very meaning of the polyvocality (*legetai pollachōs*) will change in the course of the inquiry, along with the meaning of the root verb "to speak" (*legein*).

Heidegger translates the beginning of Aristotle's *Metaphysics* 9 as follows, in a formulation that includes his own interjections:

> We have thus dealt with beings in the primary sense, and that means, with that to which all the other categories of beings are referred back, *ousia* [*substance*]. The other beings—please note: *to on*: being (participial!)—the other beings (those not understood as *ousia*) are said with regard to what is said when saying *ousia*, the how much as well as the how constituted and the others that are said in this manner. For everything that is (the other categories besides *ousia*) must in and of itself have the saying of *ousia*, as stated in the previous discussion (about *ousia*). (*GA* 33, 4/2)

Heidegger focuses his interpretive efforts on the second sentence, which is replete with the language about language and speaking: *legein*, *logos*, *legetai*, and *legomena*. These terms encompass the act of speaking, language, and that which is said through speech. In the translations, where he chooses to render these terms in German, he already begins to modify some of the basic terminology of *Being and Time*. While Heidegger translated the common Greek verb for "to speak" (*legein*) as "letting be seen" in *Being and Time*, in this passage the verb becomes invested with an entirely new set of meanings, which are at most nascent in *Being and Time*. Heidegger now associates language with a terminology of collecting and gathering: "*legein* means 'to glean,' that is, to harvest, to gather, to add one to the other, to include and connect with one another" (ibid., 5/2–3; cf. *GA* 94, 100/76). Through this revised set of translations, Heidegger shifts the analysis of *logos* into a new terrain of meaning related to the act of gathering. While marking this shift, it is also important to note the way in which he proceeds to elucidate these terms, for it signals a significant reformulation in the relation of primordiality between discourse and language, if not a complete collapse of the distinction between the two terms. This collapse occurs as Heidegger quietly pulls back from answering the question of the primordiality of the two terms.

Drawing out the precise nature of these shifts in Heidegger's philosophy of language requires close attention to both his language and manner of analysis, especially in a particularly dense passage in §1. There Heidegger follows up the series of definitions quoted above with an explanation that once again exhibits an intentional cultivation of a plurality of terms that defies any attempt to tame the manifold meanings around a simplified terminology. Heidegger operates in this manner because, as his understanding of *logos* moves ever further into the terrain of a language of gathering, the inquiry into polyvocality itself becomes the primary operation for gathering together. Hence, at first glance, Heidegger may seem to offer "a mere collecting of word meanings in order to count them up one after the other," but in following the many ways in which *logos* is said, he will eventually gather these back together in order to analyze them in reference to one another (ibid., 69/58). As Heidegger writes: "Such laying together is a laying open and laying forth (a placing alongside and presenting): *a making something accessible in a gathered and unified way.* And since such a gathering laying open and laying forth plays out above all in recounting and speaking (in trans-mitting and com-municating to others), *logos* comes to mean discourse that combines and explains. *Logos* as laying open is then at the same time evidence; finally it comes to mean laying something out in an interpretation, *hermēneia*" (ibid., 5/3).

At its most primordial level, *logos* means gathering, and this gathering primarily takes on the ontic form of recounting and speaking. Only on the basis of this recounting and speaking does *logos* come to be what Heidegger here refers to as discourse. If we are to assume that Heidegger is attempting to maintain a continuity of terminology with *Being and Time*, an assumption that admittedly is not entirely warranted, then from the perspective of *Being and Time*, the relation of primordiality between discourse and language seems to be completely reversed. Heidegger confirms this in the next sentence: "The meaning of *logos* as relation (unified gathering, coherence, rule) is therefore 'prior' to its meaning as discourse" (ibid., 5/3). Yet what is at stake here is something much more difficult than a mere reversal of the relations of *Being and Time*; rather, it is a complete reformulation of the meaning of language. Consequently, relying on the terminology of language and discourse in *Being and Time* will be a hindrance to following the path of the current inquiry.

Declaring *logos* as relation to be more primordial than discourse seems to constitute a profound shift from the portrayal of *logos* in *Being and Time*, but it also cannot go unnoticed that the use of discourse in this passage is far from the definition of discourse found in *Being and Time*, where it was defined as "the meaningful structuring of the attuned intelligibility of being-in-the-world" (*BT*, 162/157). Indeed, on the very same page, Heidegger offers the following definition of discourse: "*logos* as discourse is the combining and making manifest in the saying, the unveiling assertion about something" (*GA* 33, 5/3). It is remarkable how much these two definitions of discourse vary and no less remarkable that the "meaningful structuring" identified in the definition from *Being and Time* seems to find its place—with a modified focus on the language of gathering—in "*logos* as relation (unified gathering, coherence, rule)," which, as stated above, is "'prior' to its meaning as discourse." What this reveals is that, between the inquiry into *logos* in *Being and Time* and the inquiry into *logos* in the analysis of Aristotle, a profound transformation has occurred that has two fundamental consequences for Heidegger's philosophy of language.

The first major consequence is that the basic or guiding meaning of *logos* has changed from discourse as meaningful structuring to language as gathering. This shift to the language of gathering will prove to have both significant political and ontological consequences. The second consequence is that Heidegger begins to move away from the concern for primordiality toward a gathering together of the manifold meanings of *logos* such that the very concern for a basic or guiding meaning itself becomes less central to the task at hand. Instead, Heidegger shifts the emphasis of his phenomenological inquiry toward a process of gathering, while sidestepping the need to identify a guiding meaning.

THE MANIFOLD SENSES OF BEING

For the time being, this analysis is not primarily interested in the content of the famous passage in Aristotle regarding the manifold senses of being and is instead primarily interested in the operation of the philosophical method Heidegger employs to analyze that passage.[4] This is because the focus of the analysis is on attempting to understand the nature of the inquiry into polyvocality and not necessarily the specific results of the particular inquiry into the polyvocality of being.

Heidegger turns to the manifold senses of being in order to address Aristotle's use of the term "category" in the opening lines of *Metaphysics* 9. In analyzing these lines, he takes care to distinguish the inquiry into force and actuality from an inquiry into the categories, and he states clearly, against the Kantian table of categories, that "*for Aristotle, the question of* dunamis *and* energeia, *possibility and actuality, is not a category question*" (*GA* 33, 9/6). Heidegger takes care to stress this point, since this is where he begins to open up the many ways of saying being by noting that "beings are said and addressed sometimes in the mode of categories, and sometimes in that of *dunamis-energeia*; thus in a dual way, *dichōs*, not *monachōs*" (ibid., 11/8). Beings are addressed in a twofold manner, but Heidegger quickly complicates this twofold division with passages from the *Metaphysics* that introduce beings as addressed in the senses of being true and false, as well as in the sense of being accidental. Being is thus seemingly said in a fourfold manner. Yet after laying this out, Heidegger quickly abandons any attempt to explain the fourfold saying of being and instead dwells for a moment on the operation of saying, noting that what is "[m]ore important is the way that Aristotle introduces the four foldings of beings." Heidegger describes this polyvocal unfolding as "a simple serial juxtaposition without any consideration of their structure or connection, much less their justification" (ibid., 13/10). Thus begins the operation of polyvocality in the analysis, as "a simple serial juxtaposition," a task of laying alongside or gathering together of the many ways something is said. Though Heidegger downplays the importance of what he labels here as "simple," he is in fact performing his analysis of Aristotle's investigative method by mimicking Aristotle.

Heidegger describes this task as follows, stressing its centrality to the entire Aristotelian endeavor: "This sentence, *to on legetai pollachōs*, is a constant refrain in Aristotle. But it is not just a formula. Rather, in this short sentence, Aristotle formulates the wholly fundamental and new position that he worked out in philosophy in relation to all of his predecessors, including Plato; not in the sense of a system but in the sense of a task" (ibid., 13/10).

With this apparent formula—being is said in many ways—Aristotle "explicitly and in no uncertain terms battles against Parmenides," who described the unity of being simply (*haplōs*) (ibid., 26/21). In pursuing the polyvocality of being, Aristotle does not at all seek to deny the unity of being. Instead, by addressing the manifoldness of the ways being speaks within this unity, Aristotle, according to Heidegger, "first truly comprehends" Parmenides (ibid., 27/22). This comprehension does not come to be as a fixed definition, nor as a finished conclusion that can readily be applied to generate philosophical insights; instead, it is manifested through a peculiar philosophical *ēthos* as a task or comportment toward what it is that thinking binds us to: an attunement to the *logos* that speaks and is addressed.[5]

Following this *logos,* Aristotle overcomes the great Parmenidean disavowal of nonbeing, for it is in listening to the polyvocality of being that Aristotle, in his own engagement with Plato, begins to fold nonbeing into being (*GA* 33, 27/22). Heidegger describes this as indicating a distinct ontological shift: "The question about *on* as *hen* comes into sharp focus here for the first time. Of course, it required first a decisive step over and against Parmenides. Plato undertook this, although admittedly at a time when the young Aristotle was already philosophizing with him, and this always means against him. Plato attained the insight that non-being, the false, the evil, the transitory—hence unbeing—also is. But the sense of being thereby had to shift because now the notness itself had to be included in the essence of being" (ibid.).

Leaving aside for the moment Heidegger's treatment of Plato, which has been dealt with capably elsewhere, let us focus instead on what occurs in this passage (Dostal 1985; Gonzalez 2009; Figal 2000). Aristotle follows the manifold senses of being in order to pose the question of the unity of being, and it becomes necessary, through listening to the manifold senses of *logos,* also to listen to the ways in which nonbeing is addressed and addresses us. This moment signals nothing less than what Heidegger calls the "intrusion of notness into the unity," adding that "we modern children, with our short-lived but all the more clamorous discoveries" are no longer equal to the task of this thinking (*GA* 33, 27/22). Heidegger sees this intrusion of notness or nonbeing into the unity of the one, though quickly forgotten and rendered once again an "impossible fiction" after Aristotle, as nothing less than the intrusion of nonbeing into philosophy. Aristotle, drawing on fundamental insights from Plato's *Sophist,* has introduced the strange fiction of nonbeing into philosophy, and the task of Heidegger's analysis is to find the ways in which Aristotle brings nonbeing to language. Nonbeing intrudes into philosophy for Aristotle, while silence intrudes into *logos* for Heidegger.

Being and Time indicates a form of silence that speaks in some way as the "notness" of *logos* intrudes in analysis of its polyvocality. This compelled Heidegger to orient his approach around a new guiding meaning of *logos* as a gathering that folds nonbeing into the many senses of being. In *Being and Time*, owing to the ontological limitations of his conception of silence, Heidegger struggled to adequately articulate the silence that he indicated in the context of the call of conscience. However, in the language of *sterēsis*, Heidegger discovered what he lacked in *Being and Time*: a way to bring silence to the word.

The Withdrawal of Language: Force and Withdrawal

In Heidegger's rendering of Aristotle's concept of force, it is said to be *ausgesetzt* (subjected, given over) to and *verhaftet* (arrested, imprisoned) by withdrawal (*sterēsis*): "*dunamis* is in a preeminent sense exposed and bound to *sterēsis*" (*GA* 33, 112/95). Force cannot escape withdrawal. A particular force cannot be thought other than in relation to its essential contrary, a contrary to which it is inextricably bound. Through this interpretation of force and withdrawal, Heidegger finds a language to express and further unfold what is already latent in his understanding of undisclosedness in *Being and Time*, drawing out more fully what he already thought was revealed in the privative nature of the undisclosed "as a kind of *robbery*" (*BT*, 222/213). Moreover, in withdrawal Heidegger will also find the ontological structure necessary to bring the positivity of silence to language.

Before beginning to work through Heidegger's analysis of Aristotelian withdrawal in the *Metaphysics*, it is worth noting that Aristotle provides detailed analyses of *sterēsis* elsewhere, including in the *Categories*, *Metaphysics*, and *Physics*,[6] the latter of which is central to Heidegger's 1939 interpretation of being.[7] Heidegger makes occasional references to these different treatments of withdrawal in the Aristotelian corpus in *Aristotle's "Metaphysics" Theta 1–3*, although he is primarily concerned with what he calls the "preeminent" sense of *sterēsis* found in the relation between force and actuality. In the discussion below, I avoid the traditional translation of *sterēsis* as "privation," and instead translate the term, following Heidegger, using the language of withdrawal and robbing. This is because Heidegger distances himself from the use of the Latinate German word *Privation* after *Being and Time* because of its association with a traditional metaphysical notion of nullity. I likewise follow Heidegger's preferred translation of *dunamis* as force or ability/capacity. The intention of this analysis is not primarily to offer a reading of Aristotle, but a reading of Heidegger reading Aristotle, while attending to the changes in Heidegger's understanding of *logos* revealed in the course of Heidegger's reading of Aristotle.

Heidegger turns to withdrawal most directly in §12 of *Aristotle's "Meta-physics" Theta 1–3*, which bears the significant title "Force and Unforce—the Carrying Along with of Withdrawal. The Full Guiding Meaning." After his discussion of the polyvocality of being, analyzed in the previous section, Heidegger begins a similar inquiry into the polyvocality of force: "force and to be forceful are said in many ways," Aristotle writes (*Met.* 1046a4–5). Here Heidegger's phenomenological approach mirrors Aristotle's method: the many ways of being said are gathered in the philosophical vision (*epagōgē*) around a guiding meaning. In order to reach the guiding meaning of force, Heidegger first offers a detailed discussion of why Aristotle quickly dismisses the "ones which are called forces by equivocation," including in mathematical relations, but also in reference to language.[8] Because Aristotle is interested in force and actuality as ways of expressing the ontological nature of beings, he dismisses these meanings of forceful and forceless (*dunaton* and *adunaton*) since they are unrelated to motion and are not "a principle of some sort." The guiding meaning is thus a force understood in terms of a principle of change or motion: "a principle of change in another thing or in the thing itself qua other" (*Met.* 1046a9–11). With this guiding meaning, the analysis of polyvocality begins to approach the essential nonforce to which force is steretically bound.

Heidegger bases his analysis of this essential relation of withdrawal on a brief passage from book 9 of *Metaphysics*, 2, quoted here in an English rendering of Heidegger's German translation, including Heidegger's significant extrapolations from Aristotle's condensed phrasing:

> And unforce (forcelessness) and consequently also the "forceless" is a with-drawal as what lies over and against *dunamis* in the sense developed; hence every force, if it becomes unforce, that is, as unforce, is in each case in relation to and in accordance with the same (with respect to that by which force is a force, every force is unforce). Withdrawal, however, is stated and understood in multiple ways. Something is in a state of withdrawal (is affected by and is going through withdrawal) if it simply does not have something else; that is, when it does not have something even though it should have this something (what has withdrawn) according to its essence. (And again this not having

is possible in various ways and respects:) either when what is affected by the withdrawal does not have what was withdrawn at all, or when it does not have this at the moment even though it could have this, or when it does not have this to some extent, for example, when it does not have this, or finally when it does not have what was withdrawn in a certain way. (*GA* 33, 108/91–92)

The potent, namely, the entity that has a particular force, is essentially bound to its contrary in accordance with the same thing in the same respect through the relation of withdrawal. Any force is constituted in its forcefulness through an essential relation to a corresponding withdrawal of force. *Sterēsis*, however, is said in many ways, and Heidegger must be careful to delineate precisely which form of *sterēsis* is, in his words, steretic in a "*preeminent sense*" (ibid., 112/95). The preeminent sense is related to force endowed with *logos*, that is, the kinds of force that possess the principles of change for both of the steretically bound contraries.

Heidegger begins by examining the different steretic relations in the cases of "forces without discourse and forces directed by discourse" (ibid., 117/99). Aristotle offers heat as an example of a force without *logos* (*dunamis alogos*), and the art of medicine as an example of a force guided by *logos* (*dunamis meta logou*). What distinguishes heat from the medical art is that heat, being a force not guided by *logos*, only has the principle for heat; the art of medicine, in contrast, is guided by *logos* and has the principles for both contraries, namely, health and sickness. Both forms of force are steretically bound to their contraries, but the principle for heat is only generative of heat, while the principle for the medical art is potentially productive of both health and sickness. "Heat can only cause heating, but the medical art can cause sickness as well as health," Aristotle writes (*Met.* 1046b7–8). Yet even though the force of heat cannot be productive of cold, the relation between heat and cold can still be understood as a particular form of a steretic relation. This is because for Aristotle the being of heat as a force is not merely regarded as something positive, namely, the presence of heat, but is also understood as something negative, namely, the absence of cold. Stated more precisely, heat comes to be as the *absencing* of cold, or the being-present of cold's absence. A similar steretic relation exists between the contraries of a force guided by *logos*, but with a number of decisive differences, which must be carefully delineated.

As a force guided by *logos*, the medical art has its principle of motion in the soul of the doctor and this principle of motion is potentially a force for producing both health and sickness. *Sterēsis* in this example thus describes a relation wherein sickness is understood as the presence of the absence of health. Moreover, a particular form of *sterēsis* can be utilized to describe the force or power of the doctor. This is because, to the extent that the doctor will need to employ the use of drugs (*pharmakon*), the doctor will likewise be obligated to bring about a certain measure of sickness, for "medicines by their nature work through opposites" (*NE* 1104b18). Hence, a doctor who knows how to be a doctor well, namely, one who produces health through a doctor's action, will know the proper measure of sickness necessary to produce health, and doctors who do not produce health through their activity are, properly speaking, not doctors. The task of the doctor is thus carved out along the mean of health and sickness, and only the doctor who is capable of acting in accordance with this mean can be robbed or deprived of the art of medicine in the preeminent sense of *sterēsis*. That is because a doctor who does not produce health does not possess the craft of medicine in the first place. On the contrary side, the successful doctor only produces sickness in the measured allowance of the cure, and to the extent that this sickness, induced by medication, is produced in the service of greater wellness. Only the doctor who acts in this way habitually can be deprived of the art of medicine, and this deprivation could occur, for example, through injury, loss of memory, or old age. Yet aside from the details of this particular example, what is most essential for Heidegger is the ontological relation between steretic contraries: the medical art is *potentially* productive of both health and sickness. With this concept of potentiality, Aristotle seeks to refute the Megarian school of philosophy's claim that only what is actual is possible (Irwin 1990, 227–30); and by reviving the Aristotelian concept of *sterēsis*, Heidegger assails not only the metaphysical tradition but us, the "modern children" whose "clamorous discoveries" he disparages (*GA* 33, 27/22).

Already we can begin to see how this steretic understanding of the forms of force guided by *logos* allows Heidegger to return with a new level of ontological subtlety to the claim that rings like a refrain through his various treatments of language and silence: "Only what can speak can be silent" (*GA* 19, 15/11). This means that silence of a stone is not essentially steretic, nor for that matter the silence of a mute person, even though both can be described in terms of a certain meaning of *sterēsis*, though not in terms of the preeminent meaning. Most important, both a stone and a mute person lack the capacity to be "properly" silent. The same applies to people who simply repeat endless chatter, who have no more control over their speech than over their silence. Thus, as Heidegger goes on to clarify in reference to Aristotle's analysis of the stillness of mathematical objects in a parallel treatment of *sterēsis* in the *Physics*: "the mathematical is unmoving inasmuch as it is outside the possibility of movement entirely, and only then is it outside the possibility of rest" (*GA* 33, 112/95).[9] In this case, it is meaningless to say that the mathematical (a number or a shape regarded abstractly) is at rest even though it is not in motion, for there is no essential relation of *sterēsis* in such an example: rest and motion do not belong to the mathematical in any meaningful sense. One can say that the mathematical can be robbed of motion only in a very inessential sense, for it cannot be essentially robbed of something it cannot have, just as a person who is already blind cannot be robbed of the power of vision.[10]

After quoting Aristotle describing rest as the *sterēsis* of movement, Heidegger goes on to list some especially fundamental steretic relations, which include among them two different registers of silence and stillness. "Likewise, *skotos*, darkness, is *sterēsis* for *phōs*, light, keeping silent is a *sterēsis* of speech, and quiet a *sterēsis* of noise," he writes (*GA* 33, 112/95). Silence is the withdrawal of speech. Stillness is the withdrawal of noise. As the withdrawal of speech, silence is not the absence of speech, but the presence of the absence of speech. The capacity for speech is steretically bound to the contrary capacity for silence. Speech and silence are rooted in an essential sameness, as are noise and quiet. In the steretic relation between speech and silence, silence is not the outside of language, but is essentially bound to language as its very possibility.

In order to preserve silence, one must speak, but speak in a certain way, much like the doctor who produces a certain amount of sickness in order to produce health. In this speech, silence is not the absence of language, but the presence of language's absencing, or, to follow Heidegger language, the presencing of the absencing of language. Speech and silence are not distinct from each other as worded and wordless, but bound together, given over to each other in this inextricable bond. Heidegger calls this the "decisive thesis" of Aristotle's analysis of force: "This states that unforce is nevertheless bound to the realm of force that remains withdrawn from it. That from which something has withdrawn is related in and through this withdrawal precisely to that which has withdrawn. And despite the negative character of this withdrawal, this withdrawing relation always produces its

own positive characterization for that which is in the state of withdrawal commensurate with the way of withdrawal (which itself is still different in relation to the same thing)" (ibid., 111/94).

In Heidegger's steretic logic, the negativity of silence is its positivity. This negativity is not the form of nonvocalization which tends to associate silence in *Being and Time*, but is instead a speaking through steretically bound contraries. In *Being and Time*, Heidegger portrays privation too privatively, without recognizing the essential intertwining of contraries. He had not yet recognized the "inner essential belonging and notness to the essence of force" (ibid., 158/135). Through the language of withdrawal, Heidegger begins to capture the positivity of the privative relation between speech and silence. By recognizing this inner essential belonging of speech and silence, he significantly alters his ontological analysis of silence, thus setting himself the task of writing and producing the worded silence that first emerges in his ontological analysis.

The Production of Silence: *Poiēsis*

In his analysis of production (*poiēsis*) and craft (*technē*) in §14, Heidegger shows how steretic silence is written and spoken. Production involves an essential relation to contraries enacted through a deed, and productive knowledge (*epistēmē poiētikē*) is a force guided by *logos* as its "innermost framework" (*GA* 33, 136/116). All production involves the proper regard for what Aristotle refers to as the limit or the boundary of what is being produced as a process of "forging into bounds" (ibid., 144/123). In the process of forging something into its bounds, the thing produced is subject to a process of separating out what does not belong to it. Things come to be as a result of forging the work within its limits, "a continual excluding, letting go and avoiding, and that means a relation to contraries" (ibid., 144/123). This process of paring down and gathering occurs by following the *logos* of the form or appearance (*eidos*) of the thing to be produced, for the "'representing' of the *eidos* is a selecting and thus a giving notice (*logos*)" (ibid., 144/123). By selecting, gathering, and gleaning, a thing is produced into what it is by handiwork that is determined as much by what it does not do, by what it chooses not to do, as by what it chooses to do.

This regard for the *logos* seen in the form is *logos* as *"talking to oneself,"* which for the most part goes on silently or as a commentary that gets lost in the work and is often seen only from outside as a bunch of

disconnected words" (*GA* 33, 146/124), recalls Plato's definition of thinking as the soul's silent conversation with itself (Plato 1996b, 263–264a;
Plato 2004, 190a). As Heidegger demonstrated in *Being and Time*, this is
by no means just a solitary task, but is also part of a cooperative task of
labor, especially among those accustomed to working together. Workers
attuned to one another's rhythms often communicate with one another
without words, or with a minimum of words. "From the fact that the
words are absent," Heidegger writes, "we may not conclude that the interpretation is absent" (*BT*, 157/152). In talking to one's self or among one
another in the process of work, one goes over the steps, works through
the process, and gleans out what is and what is not to be done. Wordless
gestures and clipped phrases dominate this space. This silent dialogue
requires the guidance of *logos*, "because it is essentially an activity that
has already taken into its view what is to be done and produced" (*GA*
33, 146/125). As a form of production, it relates to contraries because it
follows a *logos*, and "*logos* is the ground and origin of *enantiotēs*" (ibid.,
140/119).

If production involves the uniting and separating of contraries, how
does this kind of production apply to the employment of words in the
handicraft of writing? In what way are contraries combined in the force
guided by *logos* that is the human capacity for *logos* as the power of speech?
What is the limit of language and how does one forge language into its
boundaries?

Production involves choosing and avoiding certain paths: "The care
which belongs to production *unites* precisely both in itself: holding to
the right path and avoiding going off track and awry. Both what meets
up with the right path and what meets up with the wrong path, both are
constantly seen together, and the two are referred back to the one out of
which the whole producing is set into motion and held in motion, the
orekton prakton" (ibid.,152/130).

This care, which unites our being addressed with the process by which
logos addresses us, is in one sense the very operation of polyvocality. The
polyvocal saying is gathered around and gleaned from a guiding meaning
that is seen and heard, however hazily, much like the form that determines
the borders or boundaries by projecting ahead while going through the
things said. Speaking means echoing the originary gathering of *logos* as a
gathering back toward the originary speech. This gathering and gleaning
sets aside and leaves out. It avoids certain words, while selecting others for

expression. For Heidegger, this means sloughing off metaphysical terminology that would constrain the interpretation of Aristotle's *Metaphysics*
from the outset.

The limit achieved through this process of paring down is understood as
the measure or mean of language—the measure of saying and of sayability,
but also the measure or mean of unsayability. The measure of language is
determined by the capacity for silence, which is developed through listening. This listening requires writing and speaking in a space that is not
overwhelmed by noise and chatter. For Heidegger this space does not refer
so much to a physically bounded area or place, but instead to a people
or community as a space of attunement. The recovery of originary or primordial speech must be circumscribed with a manner of speech, and this
act of speech is determined as much by what it does not say as by what it
says, by what it leaves out as by what it gathers in, but also—to hint at a
significant theme of the following chapter—by the moment when it chooses
to say what it says. This saying occurs through a careful unfolding that is
itself the production of silence through the word—what Heidegger will
later call a "saying not-saying" (Heidegger 1982a, 66/73). The gathering
together of this saying is necessary because *logos* itself is already divided by
what Heidegger calls the "internal divisiveness of *logos*" (*GA* 33, 153/131).
Language has always already been scattered, and reassembling it requires
recognition of this: "the inner divisiveness of *logos* is the origin and root
of the proliferation into individual *logoi*" (ibid., 153/133). Philosophy for
Heidegger thus becomes a gathering of the scattered words (*logoi*—intended
here in the sense of individual words and utterances) back into the primordial assembly of language (*logos*) through a process of gleaning and sifting,
of paring down language. Given the internal fragmentation of language,
"the assumption of an insidious ambiguity" (*GA* 95, 27/21) discussed in
chapter 1 is not to be regarded as a feature of Heidegger's language, but as
a trait of *logos* itself.

Aristotle is particularly important in this context because what
Heidegger is aiming at in his recovery of a Greek understanding of silence
is precisely what he discovers in the Aristotelian method: a productive
practice of saying not-saying, that is, a way of expressing silence through
words. That is to say, what Heidegger regards Aristotle as doing, at least in
certain key moments, is employing a form of writing that—in a formula
borrowed from *On the Way to Language*—"brushes against the essence of
language without violating it" (Heidegger 1982d, 112). For Heidegger

brushing against the essence of language means regarding the proper measure of speech and circumscribing the essence in a worded practice of reticence without violating that measure. If we take a closer look at the passage from the *"Letter on Humanism"* in which Heidegger announces the "handicraft of writing" as the task of thinking, we can see more closely what this means: "Everything depends on this alone, that the truth of being come to language and that thinking attain to this language. Perhaps, then, language requires much less precipitate expression than proper silence. But who of us today would want to imagine that his attempts to think are at home on the path of silence? It would thus be more easily withdrawn from mere supposing and opining and directed to the now rare handicraft of writing" (LH, 344/261–62).

Taking Aristotle as an example of a thinker treading along the path of silence, Heidegger's recovery of a Greek conception of silence reveals itself to be a retrieval of the way in which the Greeks thought through silence and not a recovery of the way in which the Greeks thought about silence. This subtle ontological distinction is fundamental to the gendered pedagogies of silence analyzed in the following chapters. When Heidegger speaks of silence, he always intends to speak of or through the Greeks. Becoming at home on the path of silence means once again becoming at home in the world of the Greeks. This drive for the originary, the authentic, the essential, and the primordial against a form of "internal divisiveness" also draws him to National Socialism.[11]

Conclusion

Through his phenomenological analysis of *logos* Heidegger's ontology of language underwent a transformation as a result of appropriating the Aristotelian understanding of the withdrawal of a force into its contrary nonforce. In the process Heidegger defended an essential relationship of intertwining between speech and silence based on Aristotle's logic of contraries. This helped Heidegger shift his own definition of silence toward a worded silence and away from the type of explicit thematic analysis of silence offered in *Being and Time*, where silence tended to be reduced to nonvocalization. This shift enabled Heidegger to redefine *logos* as a process of gathering, while also laying the groundwork for his sigetic practice of the handiwork of language. Although Heidegger performs it in the most private of his manuscripts, this handiwork also has a number of deeply political dimensions, which emerge out of Heidegger's treatment of gathering.

In his postwar defense of his rectorate, Heidegger describes his attraction to National Socialism in this manner: "At the time I saw in the power of the burgeoning movement the potential for an internal gathering and renewal of the people and a way to find its historical-occidental destiny" (*GA* 16, 374). There is a strong continuity of language between this testimony and the first volume of the *Black Notebooks*, where Heidegger writes of the "gatherdness in the whole of attuning being" and the founding the "space-time of Dasein for the gathered people" (*GA* 94, 48/36, 288/211). This process of gathering and the space-time the gathering produces are both sites for Heidegger's sigetic politics. Sigetic politics both requires and restores the handiwork of silence. This gathering produces the space of the "linguistic community" which speaks in unison and thereby makes language real (*GA* 38, 31/29). As harmonious as this language of attuned being might seem, and as much as it might inspire certain readers to wax rhapsodic about Heidegger's poetic greatness, to stop the analysis at this stage and to celebrate the harmony of attunement to being would be to miss the point of the Aristotelian analysis provided above.

This is because, as Heidegger himself demonstrated on the basis of his analysis of Aristotle, any process of gathering is based as much on inclusion as it is on exclusion. The sculptor hews away the marble to bring out a form. In the process of carving, she creates refuse by brushing away chips, chunks, and dust. The luthier planes the spruce top of a violin to mold a piece of mute wood into a resonant soundboard, coating the floor with delicate, twisted shavings with each swipe of the plane. By chiseling, chipping, scraping, sawing, boring, and carving, the trained hand gives form to the thing forged out of a material that possesses a certain potential. Any form of production requires the employment a certain form of force, if not violence. This involves cutting away, sifting off, and segregating out. Ultimately, it also means disposing of refuse. For Heidegger, this is not simply a description of handiwork in the sense of artisanal production; rather, it involves the very concept of production as guided by *logos*. In a 1934 entry in the *Black Notebooks* devoted to the "secret aim of the other beginning," Heidegger makes the political stakes of this process clear: "gathering: as storage of the actual powers, accumulation of their capacities, and development into structures—creation of the essential *great ability*!" (*GA* 94,

246/180). Just as a carpenter makes a joint in a process that presupposes a certain degree of violence, so too the people must be joined together.

Given that Heidegger defines his attraction to National Socialism in terms of gathering, and specifically in terms of gathering the *Volk*, we should keep in mind the role of the limit and exclusion in Heidegger's own conception of this term "gathering." This limit becomes the distinction between the essential and the inessential, not only in speech, but even within a *Volk*— which likewise must produce itself. Closer attention to Heidegger's exact terminology reinforces this link between the ontological and the political. It is significant that Heidegger translates the Greek *legein* as "gleaning" when he speaks of a "selection, a selective gathering of what belongs together" and "the perfected, the fulfilled, the gleaned, the selected" (*GA* 33, 142/121). The German language of selection (*Auslese*) is itself quite polyvocal, and many of its meanings are drawn from the language of agriculture and selective breeding. *Lese* or *Auslese*, for example, is an important agricultural and vinicultural term used to describe the selection of fruits and the division of the harvest into grades of quality. The production of a quality wine requires the proper selection of the best grapes. One could also apply the term *Auslesen* to refer to soldiers or students being selected out and ranked according to quality—or perhaps according to their political reliability. Heidegger states this directly in his rectorial address, when he speaks of the "selection of the best," and discussing his planned ideological training academy as a site for the "pre-selection" and "selection and reeducation" of university faculty in internal memos (*GA* 16, 112, 312).

"Selection" is, of course, also a fundamental term in the racial politics of National Socialism and of the *völkisch* movement, as well as being a fundamental term in the Nazi language of eugenics, including in *Mein Kampf*, where Hitler speaks of the "struggle for the selection of the best" and the importance of the "selection of humans" for the "ethnic state" (Hitler [1925] 2016, 477, 577).[12] I do not mean to make hasty associations, nor to facilely reduce Heidegger's thinking to *Mein Kampf*, as Emmanuel Faye (2009) and Victor Farías (1991) would like to do. Heidegger's relation to the racial-biological eugenic project of National Socialism is complex, and even with the publication of the *Black Notebooks*, it is still relatively poorly understood. Robert Bernasconi observes eloquently that "when one examines Heidegger's discussion of race breeding, race cultivation, and race ranking in his unpublished manuscripts and sees how he relates them to broader intellectual movements and ultimately to the history of being, it becomes apparent that any attempt to read his texts without reference to this context is to run counter to the direction of his thinking, as well as to invite the usual distortions that arise when context is ignored" (Bernasconi 2000, 63).

Heeding Bernasconi, and to stress the impossibility of portraying Heidegger as "apolitical" (Held 2016: 257), I want to call attention to the terminological continuities between Heidegger's philosophical language and what he calls "vulgar" National Socialism. It is worth remembering that in December 1931, just months after the end of his summer semester lecture course on Aristotle's *Metaphysics* 9.1–3, Heidegger wrote to his brother Fritz encouraging him to read *Mein Kampf*. Moreover, Heidegger seems to have been immersed at the time in what Dieter Thomä calls the "vilest polemical texts" (Thomä 2016, 367), as shown by further letters.[13] It is tempting to describe Heidegger's enthusiasm for such literature as incongruous with his ability to analyze a text such as Aristotle's *Metaphysics,* but doing so makes unwarranted assumptions about "genius" and "great" (male) philosophers (see, e.g., Battersby 1989). Heidegger's reading habits are not germane to the question of his greatness, nor is greatness as a philosophical concept of much value. Doubtless the concern for greatness has only impeded a sober analysis of many philosophers' ethics.

Even more important, this type of assumption would risk misconstruing the nature of Heidegger's relationship to the Greeks and the philosophical place of what he calls the "Greek-German destiny" as so-called occidental destiny (*GA* 39, 151). This language is, of course, highly exclusive and is rooted in a division between the essential and the inessential, that is, in a process of gleaning and selecting. "It can *only* be the Germans," Heidegger writes to Kurt Bauch in 1942, "for in us is preserved the primordial destiny of the Greek world, which is now awakening in its first breaths to the premonition of the historical."[14] This premonition, awakening, and destiny all demand an appropriate language, and Heidegger draws this language directly from the Greeks. He does so, as he states in the first lecture course he held as rector, "not so as to become Greeks and Greek-like, but rather to perceive the primordial laws of our German ethnicity in their most simple exigency and greatness and to put ourselves to the test and prove ourselves against this greatness" (*GA* 36–37, 89/72). Recovering this greatness first requires an attuned listening, recovered within a space of essential silence. For Heidegger, this space is threatened by a great number of clamoring elements—not the least of which is "world Jewry."

5   Being the Measure: The Pedagogy
of Male Self-Mastery

In Heidegger's depiction of ancient Greece, the Greek language is a fundamentally measured language. The measure internal to their language in turn imparts a measured relation to being to the Greeks. By living according to the measure of concealment revealed through a proper attunement to language, life is constricted, bounded, and often shrouded. Much is unknown and mysterious in this world, for living within the measure requires one to refrain from desiring to know too much. This is not the life of an autonomous subject imposing a human image upon the world; rather, according to Heidegger, it is a life of "confinement to the restricted radius . . . of the unconcealed" (Heidegger 1987, 122/94), which requires discipline and renunciation. Such a life is in contrast to the modern age of technical science, which seeks to create a total image of the world, thus "setting into motion the limitless violence of the calculation, planning and breeding of all things" (Heidegger 2002a, 94/71).[1] Heidegger regards this violence as destructive of the possibility of observing the measure of unconcealment determined by language. Whereas the Greeks refrained from committing to the presence and absence of things, the modern subject is not allowed such renunciation. The Greeks' renunciation allows silence to rest in its unconcealment, and Greek philosophy sought to train initiates in the discipline of preserving unconcealment. This training and discipline are at the heart of Heidegger's philosophy of silence.

Self-mastery, specifically mastery of the tongue, "the most difficult of all victories" according to the Neoplatonist Iamblichus ([third–fourth centuries CE] 1818, 38), constituted a significant part of the Greek conception of manliness. Moreover, such self-mastery extended to politics, for moderation is a virtue of harmony in the polis just as much as in the soul (Vernant 1982, 82–101), and outspokenness (*parrēsia*) *does not necessarily contribute to this* (Plato, *Republic* 8.557b). Greek youths learning to be philosophers were taught to cultivate the discipline of silence as an aspect of self-rule. The balance maintained men of measure, *hoi mesoi*, who said neither too much nor too little, stood in contrast to the vulgarity of *hoi polloi*, the many, the chattering of slaves, the garish displays of the aristocracy, and—most starkly—the uncanny, mysterious, and conspiratorial speech of the feminine voice. The feminine voice in classical Athens is marked by an unavoidable contradiction that distinguishes it from the silence of male self-mastery: as paradoxically hyperbolic, it always said both too much and too little. It was a voice beyond measure and thus both out of tune and out of place. The sovereign voice of male authority stood in contrast to this uncanny female voice. In order for a Greek man to be a proper man, in harmony with the place allotted to him, he should say neither too much nor too little.[2]

This analysis of silence serves as the corollary to Michel Foucault's late lectures on the freedom of speech at the Collège de France, in which Foucault analyzes the "active and meaningful silence [that] is required of the good listener of philosophy," though he devotes little attention to the specifically gendered nature of this phenomenon (Foucault 2005, 345).[3] In tracing the often contradictory uses of *parrēsia*, Foucault draws a distinction between a negative form of speaking out, which merely involves saying anything in the sense of saying everything without discretion, and the positive form, which involves the courage to say the truth at any cost (Foucault 2008, 9). A form of silence exists in the space between saying everything as the result of what the Greeks regarded as a feminine garishness and the courage to say anything at any cost. Pythagoras, Plato, and Aristotle sought to cultivate that silence in their pedagogical practice.

Even though—or perhaps precisely because—ancient Greece, and specifically classical Athens, may have been the famously verbose "land of *logos*" where, in Socrates's words "there's the greatest right to speak" (Plato, *Gorgias* 461e), there is nonetheless a silence at the core of Greek self-identity. This silence comes to be within a form of speech and not outside of speech. The capacity for silence that marks both the end and beginning of philosophical training as an attainment reserved for certain freemen does not merely indicate the ability to refrain from speaking as a whole, but also involves the mastery of the proper moment for speech and silence: the right words said by the right person at the right time in the right place to the right person in the right tone. This rightness of the moment is based on a deeply gendered structure of power that excludes certain voices from the "right" to speak.

This chapter is divided into three parts. Firstly, an analysis of the five-year silence of Pythagoras's students will show that silence was primarily manifested through the initiate's entire bodily comportment, involving one's eyes, hands, and bodily posture as much as one's voice. These themes are likewise reflected in the reading of the opening scene of Plato's *Parmenides*, which dramatizes the young Socrates's disregard for the measure and the proper moment of speech. Finally, I argue that a similar form of silence is fundamentally at stake in Aristotle's *Nicomachean Ethics*, especially in Aristotle's concern with the proper amount of precision applicable to the analysis of the matter at hand. Ethics can be regarded as the most "silent" form of inquiry in Aristotle because it is the field of inquiry that allows for the least precision, and thus the field of inquiry that allows for the least amount of discussion of matters in general. For Aristotle, successfully carrying out an ethical inquiry accordingly requires a form of speech carved into a terrain of silence and philosophical training aims at the acquisition of that silence through self-mastery.

In carrying out the readings that follow, I am less concerned with what differentiates Pythagoras, Plato, and Aristotle from one another and more with the common *ēthos* of silence that lies at the core of their philosophical practice, for Heidegger seeks to revive this *ēthos* as a political task. In analyzing this common *ēthos*, I argue that silence cannot be approached from the outside with a method that seizes hold of it as an object of analysis, but instead must be approached from the inside through the very form of language that makes silence possible. For Greek philosophers in general, but especially for Plato and Aristotle, the explicit analysis of silence does not exist in distinction from the performance of silence, but is instead constituted through the very performance of silence. This is especially significant because Heidegger specifically seeks to recover the performative aspect of Greek silence and is less concerned with the analytic aspect. While analyzing some of those performances of silence, it is worth recalling that they resonate against a silenced backdrop of purportedly incontinent and inharmonious voices subject to violent silencing.

Pythagorean Pedagogical Silence

Of the three philosophers analyzed in this chapter, Pythagoras is the one who integrates silence most explicitly into his method of philosophical training. In his *Lives of Eminent Philosophers*, Diogenes Laërtius reports of Pythagoras's pupils that "for five whole years they had to keep silence, merely listening to his discourses without seeing him, until they passed an examination, and thenceforward they were admitted to his house and allowed to see him" (Diogenes Laërtius [second–third centuries CE] 1950, 329). Diogenes uses the term *hēsuchia* (stillness, quiet) to describe the reverential silence expected of Pythagoras's students. The silencing Pythagoras imposes on them involves vision as much as speech, for this stillness is related to wandering both of the eye and of the mouth, effectively seeking to silence both the mouth and eye. According to Aulus Gellius, an individual student's appearance determined the precise duration of the period of silence demanded, with the minimum being two years. Students were "physiognomized" in order—as Aulus Gellius puts it—to "inquire into the character and dispositions of men by an inference drawn from their facial appearance and expression, and from the form and bearing of their whole body" (Aulus Gellius [second century CE] 1795, 46–47).[4] The body was thus under intense scrutiny as potentially producing untoward noise and movement that would interrupt the training of philosophical self-mastery. According to Iamblichus, whose account varies slightly from that of Aulus Gellius, students were subject to a five-year silence "in order that [Pythagoras] might experimentally know how they were affected as to continence of speech"(Iamblichus 1818, 38). The goal was to test the individual pupil's aptitude or even fitness for the study of philosophy, which would be impossible without the hard-fought victory over the restive tongue. For the few who withstood this physiognomic scrutiny, this victory was often won in advance.

According to Aulus Gellius, as auditors the students were neither permitted to write nor speak until they had gained continence in words, training thereby both their memory and their capacity for self-mastery (Aulus Gellius 1795, 47).[5] The tongue, according to this conception of the self, is regarded as an unruly element, something that betrays us, dragging us toward an incontinence that must be countered with the continence both required for and acquired through philosophical training. Since this continence is both the prerequisite for and the goal of the training, a distinct circularity is at work here. In order to prove that one possesses a philosophical constitution, one must already possess a philosophical constitution in some way. Hence the exclusion of certain men as physiognomically ill-suited to philosophical study is but the leading edge of a vast bulwark of exclusion. It is necessary to also draw a further historical distinction, for despite this concern with incontinence, this incontinence must be read without the deep moralistic overtones of the Christian tradition, and the corresponding unruliness should not be hastily translated into a morality of sin or fallenness.[6] What is at stake is not sinfulness, but the care for one's own soul.

Given that silence is not primarily associated with the lack of audible noise in early Greek thought, the stillness of the Pythagorean students reveals a number of attributes. Their reverential silence does not imply a complete silence with respect to the voice, but is instead manifested through what Silvia Montiglio calls "a behavior of the entire body" (*SL*, 47). This stillness enables a form of silence aligned with what Foucault refers to as antiquity's "always unfavorable judgment of fidgeting" (Foucault 2005, 344). Moreover, this stillness also reveals certain attributes of *euphēmia*, a propitious silence that is at times quite verbal. *Euphēmia*, as Montiglio writes, is closely related to ritual forms of silence,[7] and "more accurately signifies speech and silence at the same time: well-omened speech and the silencing of ill-omened words" (*SL*, 16). Foucault's analysis of Pythagorean pedagogical silence supports such an interpretation: "Obviously, five years of silence does not mean that they had to remain totally silent for five years, but that someone who was still only a novice did not have the right to speak in all the exercises and practices of instruction and discussion, etcetera, in short, whenever dealing with *logos* as true discourse and whenever participating in these practices and exercises of true discourse. He had to listen, only to listen and entirely without intervening, objecting, giving his opinion and, of course, without teaching" (Foucault 2005, 341).

Such a silence is perhaps more plausible than five years of not speaking in any fashion while the students learned to speak through listening, for as the Aristotelian author of the *Problems* notes, "the sense of hearing and the voice may be held to arise from the same source" (Aristotle 1984d, 898b29–30). Since hearing and the voice are so thoroughly intertwined, one who cannot listen cannot speak, at least not philosophically.

If the primary task of these pupils was to listen, then what was demanded of them as listeners? Which gestures or signs were forbidden to them, and which were expected from them? What were the demonstrable physical, and perhaps manual, manifestations of their silence? In short, what constituted and defined their silence *as* silence if this silence was not simply the absence of noise? It is perhaps not possible to answer these questions based on the source material available, and this analysis will instead have to content itself with clarifying the necessity of raising such questions even without providing answers for them. Yet even with so many questions remaining, a sketch of the being of silence has already begun to emerge, even if only roughly.

In Pythagorean pedagogy, silence exists as a manifestation or performance that is quite corporeal and even at times quite vocal in nature. Furthermore, silence is far from being merely "negative" in an ontological sense. Instead of being a form of nullity, it reveals itself through a subtle range of signs, gestures, responses, postures, and physical traits that constitute the performance of a capacity for silence.[8] As a physiognomic silence not based upon a modern idea of a mind-body divide, this silence is corporeal and physical, thus raising questions that echo through the *völkisch* tradition about what kind of bodies were excluded from this silence. The subsequent analyses of Plato and Aristotle will show how such signs, gestures, responses, and postures were an integral part of a philosophical practice that cultivated a capacity for silence reserved predominately for particular kinds of men.

Plato's *Parmenides*: The Drama of Extremes

One can easily lose oneself in Plato's *Parmenides*. Indeed, Socrates himself even seems to lose himself in its circuitous exercises. One could likewise lose oneself in the literature on *Parmenides*. In turning to *Parmenides*, my intention is not to enter into any of the various long-standing debates regarding the role of the ideas or forms in the dialogue, a dialogue often portrayed as the key text documenting Plato's so-called metaphysics.[9] Nor is it my intention to deal with *Parmenides* as a dialogue consisting of two parts that do not seem to fit together: the dramatic introduction and the long exercises that Zeno puts Socrates through.[10] I would instead like to call attention to the dramatic details of the opening scene of the dialogue in order to argue for it not only as a work of philosophical education, but also as one that stages the question of the proper measure, thus revealing the pitfalls of disregarding the proper time and place for speech and silence (see, e.g., Miller 1991).

This approach is essentially aligned with Heidegger's brief and fragmentary tutorial on *Parmenides* held in the winter semester of 1930–31—the semester directly prior to the Aristotle lecture course examined in the previous chapter.[11] As published, the tutorial is at best a rough outline and it offers little more than a shadow of how the reading exercise itself must have been carried out in the classroom. In the tutorial, Heidegger tries to situate his reading of the dialogue at a distance from common "professorial" portrayals of the dialogue—an approach similar to his bracketing of the metaphysical tradition in his reading of Aristotle's *Metaphysics*. Heidegger thus announces the following in a statement in which he mentions what he will not mention about common portrayals of Plato in a fragmentary style that reflects the sketchy nature of the published text:

> The *unity of the dialogue* there to such a degree that the question of how to conjoin the "two parts" should *not at all* arise. The unified text in its progression separate from everything that interpretations have brought in, *divided up* and thus torn apart, and only then, upon the basis of that destruction, presented it as a serious problem to ask how the purported second part *fits together* with the first. Hence the insight *is also not* to be presented as a discovery that both parts really do fit together, rather avoid altogether any mention of such interpretations. However: *positive clarity and guidance*. Plato's philosophizing *not* according to the conception of *professors*. (*GA* 83, 32)

Heidegger seeks to offer a reading of Plato that is not the Plato of the professors (as if he were not one himself), not a reading of Plato that generates insights by debunking previous portrayals in the secondary literature, but instead turns to the text itself in its unity. Yet what is most interesting is Heidegger's hermeneutic approach here, for he does not in fact avoid any mention of such interpretations, but instead mentions them by dismissing them. It is as if Heidegger wants to demonstrate that being too silent about such interpretations by not mentioning them at all would accord them too much importance. As he says most pithily shortly thereafter, employing the classical rhetorical gesture of apophasis, "do not speak of all of that" (ibid., 34). I seek here to follow Heidegger's hermeneutic reading of *Parmenides*, not with an eye to insights that might serve to reformulate debates surrounding *it*, but instead to get some insight into the role of silence in Plato's dialogues as works of philosophical training. For Heidegger, the dialogue is primarily concerned with "gaining the proper posture" (ibid., 31). If Heidegger's terminology of posture resonates with traces of the physiognomic language found in Pythagoras, then that is entirely intentional. That posture is critical to the fundamental attunement to *völkisch* existence he spoke of in 1933. What is this posture and what does it have to do with silence?

Parmenides is a drama focused on a young Socrates still developing mastery over the proper measure of speech, vacillating between saying too much and saying too little. In the introductory section one sees the young Socrates either attack like the "Laconian hound" or withdraw into complete silence (*Parm.* 128c). Neither of these two options regards the proper measure for speech and silence. If philosophical education involves a cultivation of an attunement to the moment, then it was necessary to train young philosophers in the proper measure of speech with regard to the time, place, topic, and audience, thus teaching them to express themselves in the right words uttered in the right tone. By focusing on the opening scene of the dialogue, I would like to argue for *Parmenides* to be read as teaching the readers (or listeners) to be lovers of words (*philologoi*). As Socrates makes clear in *Phaedo*, this is of utmost importance for the soul of the philosopher, for "haters of argument," according to Socrates, often "become haters of human beings" (Plato, *Phaedo* 89d). In order to demonstrate what it means to be a lover of words or arguments, one must begin to peel off the layers of silence in which this particular Platonic dialogue is wrapped.

As we begin to unwrap *Parmenides* from its many shrouds of silence, it is first of all worthwhile to devote some attention to its audience. Given its repeated treatment of the forms and overlapping cast of characters, *Parmenides* can be read as the dramatic successor to the *Republic*. According to this interpretation, what was presented for a general group of listeners in the *Republic* is formulated for a philosophical group of listeners in *Parmenides* (Miller [1986] 1991, 18–25). This explains why Zeno assesses the quality of his audience before persuading Parmenides to demonstrate his philosophical exercises, noting: "If there were more of us, it wouldn't be right to ask. For it's unseemly, especially for someone of his age, to speak such things before the many, since the many do not know that without this digressing and wandering through all things it is impossible to possess a mind that's hit upon the True" (*Parm.* 136d–e).

The question of rhetoric as a matter of concern for the audience is powerfully at play in the dialogue, for the gathered group is of a respectable philosophical pedigree, and the discussion can proceed at a more elevated level than was necessary in the *Republic*. All of this influences the proper measure of speech for that particular time and place.

Given the respectable philosophical quality of the gathered men, the dialogue must be understood as staging a philosophical conversation among initiates (Miller [1980] 2004, 2). It is set into motion because Cephalus desires to hear the famous exchange between Zeno, Parmenides, Socrates, and Aristotle (not Aristotle of Stagira, the philosopher, but another man of that name, an eventual member of the Thirty Tyrants) that took place long ago, and he presses Antiphon, who memorized the exchanges as a youth under the tutelage of a certain Pythodorus, to recite the exchange that he purportedly knows so well. It cannot escape our notice that Antiphon, a man with a curiously silent name playing on *anti-phōnē*, at first balks at this task, "for he said it was a lot of work" (*Parm.* 127b). He eventually consents to do so, however, recalling the opening scene of the *Republic* in which, at the behest of Polemarchus's young slave, Socrates turns back and begins the dialogue, though not without a certain amount of arm-twisting.[12] *Parmenides*, much like the *Republic*, thus moves under the sign of a silence refused and a reluctance overcome, and this silence will only deepen before the climax of Socrates's complete retreat into silence as a listener.

In Antiphon's description of the scene Cephalus is so eager to hear recounted, a "very young" Socrates had gone to listen to a recitation by Zeno, and once Zeno had finished, the eager and precocious Socrates begins to attack Zeno's account, specifically his claim that "if the things that *are*, are many . . . they must be both like and unlike." Socrates is in fact accusing Zeno of sophistry, believing that Zeno intends to do "battle against everything that is commonly said by maintaining that there *is* no many" (*Parm.* 127c). At this point in the dialogue the young Socrates is behaving, as Zeno puts it, "like a Laconian hound" (*Parm.* 128c). Socrates here is a callow youth preparing his zealous attack, behaving like a kind of dog that Aristotle in his *History of Animals* would later describe as particularly aggressive and cunning (Aristotle 1984a, 574a17–575a5). In response to this pending attack, the experienced Zeno adds another layer of refused silence to the dialogue, confessing that he wrote the text out of a youthful combativeness, hoping to come to Parmenides's defense by forcing Parmenides's opponents into a logical absurdity. He "couldn't decide whether it should be brought to light," however, until the question became moot after a copy was stolen from him. Once again, the dialogue can be seen as moving under the sign of a silence refused (*Parm.* 128e). Moreover, one should not overlook the fact that this silence is deepened by the additional layer of the silence that is the written word, always an immeasurable form of speech, according to Socrates in the *Phaedrus* (275a–276a).[13]

This dialogue, which is itself taking shape in the face of a silence that could not be, recounts the story of another silence that could not be: Zeno's purloined text. And all the while, as these silences begin to overlap with one another, Socrates presses on with an enthusiasm that evokes smiles of admiration from both of his elders, to whom, it is worth noting, he has been rather rude (Miller [1986] 1991, 38). Socrates persists with a loquacious zeal that exceeds the skill of his philosophical training, and Parmenides has no trouble telling him that "philosophy has not yet grabbed you as it will" (*Parm.* 130e). Socrates's zeal is rooted in youthful philosophical indiscretion—the very sort of youthful indiscretion that accounted for Zeno's early contrarian text. Socrates thus duplicates the very form of zealous desire for speechmaking he seeks to attack. The same Socrates who demonstrates the virtuosity of a subtle dancer in his exchange with Glaucon in the *Republic* is here seen as a brash and precocious hound, regarded with an equal degree of respect and ridicule by his venerable elders.

The rich texturing of silence has already gathered many layers up to this point in the dialogue, but it deepens once again as the inquiry turns to the eventual tyrant Aristotle. Socrates is brought to various impasses regarding the divisibility of forms, the manner in which things partake in the forms, what sort of things have forms, and the potential infinite regress that threatens to make his entire conception of the forms collapse, and Parmenides eventually reins him in. His avuncular praise of Socrates, who has by then been twisted into a great many aporias that he is not yet ready to deal with *as* aporias, reveals a great subtlety and is worth quoting in full:

> "It's because, Socrates," he said, "you are trying too soon, before being trained, to define some Beautiful and Just and Good and each one of the forms. I noticed this even the day before yesterday when I overheard your conversation with this fellow Aristotle. Know well: that zeal which drives you towards speech is beautiful and divine. But you must draw yourself back and train more, while you're still young, in a gymnastic that seems useless and which the many call 'idle talk.' If you don't the truth will escape you." (*Parm.* 135c–d)

Socrates, as Parmenides points out, says too much, which does not only mean that he speaks too much, nor that he uses too many words, but that he also oversteps the philosophical limits of his ability to draw distinctions in what he is saying, even perhaps demanding too much precision from the question at hand. Socrates yearns to grasp too soon. He must learn to say less, to be more reticent by, ironically enough, speaking more, by training himself in speech while young, but not just in any sort of speech. Instead, he needs to practice the very speech that is trained through the exercises. It is not without great significance that sophistry, as Giuseppe Cambiano demonstrates, was regarded by young Greek males as a systematic and sanctioned form of "trying too soon," as a way of shortening the long task of learning how to speak, of being like a philosopher without proper practice. In modern parlance, sophistry was a "life hack"—"the art of learning how to speak as something that could be acquired at an early age" (Cambiano 1995, 109). The task of learning how to speak was above all shortened by skipping over the necessarily slow training of the capacity for silence as the grounding for the capacity for speech. Hence sophistry, to borrow Heidegger's term, is a type of "free-floating *logos*," for it trains a capacity for speech not grounded in the capacity for silence with which it is steretically bound (*GA* 19, 341–42/235). The young Socrates thus seems to stand on the cusp of philosophy and sophistry, between the lovers and haters of words.

Returning to *Parmenides*, it bears noting that Parmenides only agrees to go through the demonstration after a fair amount of convincing and this reluctance closely mirrors the reluctance on the part of Antiphon that had threatened to stall the entire dialogue. Parmenides begins the task hesitantly, even with a certain trembling, but ultimately concedes, based on the philosophical quality of his listeners. As Parmenides says:

> Necessary it is to obey. And yet I seem to be suffering something like that Ibyceian horse, which, as a prizewinner but old, is about to take part in a chariot race and, being experienced, trembles at what is about to happen. Ibycus says that he resembles the horse since, although he is so old and unwilling, Necessity forces him to fall in love. And so I seem quite fearful, since I remember what sort of and how great a multitude of speeches I must swim through at any age. Nevertheless, I must show you this favor, especially since, as Zeno says, we are by ourselves. (*Parm.* 136e–137a)

Eros stares down upon Parmenides, and he is moved to speak. This love, perhaps, is for Socrates, but it is the young Aristotle who is chosen to answer Parmenides's questions, for Parmenides is convinced that the youngest "would say exactly what he thinks" (*Parm.* 137c). Once again, the indiscretion of the youth will be manipulated in the dialogue.

From this point on, Socrates falls completely silent. However, this silence is not mentioned as such by Plato. What Plato calls attention to through this unannounced silence is the obverse of Socrates's initial loquacity, for it seems that the young Socrates knows only the two extremes of language: the bark of the Laconian hound or complete silence. What he must learn, and what Parmenides helps him train in the torrent of arguments that follow in the famous exercise of the eight hypotheses, are the ways of speaking silence through speech. Plato thus effectively demonstrates that the young Socrates knows neither how to speak philosophically nor how to be silent philosophically. Moreover, he does not know this because he still considers speaking philosophically and keeping silent philosophically to be two different things. Socrates must learn that philosophical speech and philosophical silence are one and the same. Above all, he must learn that the challenge of speaking philosophically involves mastering a silence that operates within language. This silence involves withdrawing at the proper moment by tapering into silence neither too early nor too late. This silence is expressed as a matter of a proper posture. This posture involves an attunement to language acquired through philosophical training, even if that posture must first be present in some way to lay the groundwork for philosophical training.

At this point we can return to Heidegger's reading, to a passage in which Heidegger reveals both his insight into Plato and his ontological blindfold as a reader of Plato. As Heidegger writes of the exercises in the "second part" of the dialogue: "The 'exercise': What is being exercised? Logical rules? Neither 'logic' nor rules, not a school exercise. Rather the initial foray into the problem of being: to gain the *right posture* for this and to train the internal manner of seeing. Thus to carry out every comportment proper to every step. In contrast to the universal-vulgar frontal attack and aimless volley of speech" (*GA* 83, 31).

Heidegger is pointing to a speech that both misses the point and makes its point too emphatically. The exercises in the remainder of the dialogue are exercises in unlearning this speech, or, as Heidegger later says: "*Exercises in tuning*. Being able to be attuned to one another. *Attunement*" (*GA* 83, 36). This posture of attunement can only be achieved through a long process of self-mastery, which must first pass through a stage of youthful incontinence by gaining a dual set of closely intertwined capacities: the capacity for attunement with one another as the capacity for silence. According to the Stranger in Plato's *Statesman*, impatience with measure, being out of sync with the moment, and drawing distinctions too quickly might even be regarded as a "sickness," unsurprising in a young philosopher lacking the self-mastery that can only be achieved over time (Plato, *Statesman* 283b).

Aristotle's *Nicomachean Ethics* is also concerned with self-mastery, not so much as an explicit topic of analysis, but as the implicit contour that shapes Aristotle's method—a form of inquiry structured by speaking through silence—in its entirety. Heidegger's sigetics involves an ethics of silence drawn directly from Aristotle.

Aristotle and the *ēthos* of Silence

Aristotle's understanding of silence is very much aligned with the larger Greek *ēthos* he was a part of, sharing both the common suspicion of complete silence and a veneration for the self-mastery that involves knowing when to speak and when to keep silent. Moreover, Aristotle offers rich resources for discussing the being of silence beyond the simple dichotomies of being and nonbeing, or presence and absence, even if Aristotle himself never approaches the question of language in that way. The following analysis focuses primarily on the implicit operation of silence as a regard for the measure of unsayability in Aristotle's *Nicomachean Ethics*. The task of this section is to focus on a number of the silent gestures that define the manner in which Aristotle carries out his ethical inquiry by specifically highlighting three attributes: the concern for the proper amount of precision appropriate to the matter at hand, the disposition of silence, and the proper moment for speaking or and keeping silent.

SILENCE AND PRECISION

Early in the first book of the *Nicomachean Ethics*, Aristotle states the fundamental principle that guides him: "[W]e should be content to indicate the truth roughly and in outline, for it is the mark of an educated man to seek as much precision in things of a given genus as their nature allows" (*NE* 1094b22–23). Although a similar pronouncement can also be found in Aristotle's *Metaphysics* 4.1006a6–8,[14] there is a particular reason why Aristotle advances this claim so early in his ethical inquiry: ethics is the form of inquiry that admits of the lowest degree of precision. Aristotle makes this clear in the *Metaphysics*, where he states that "the sciences with fewer principles are more accurate than those which use additional principles" (*Met.* 1.982a26–27).

Ethics is the field of inquiry that has as many principles as it has moments or instances of questioning. Moreover, as Aristotle makes clear from the beginning of the *Nicomachean Ethics*, the ethical inquiry is simultaneously an epistemological inquiry, for it is constantly accompanied by the question of the nature of knowledge appropriate to the matter it is investigating. In other words, it is constantly concerned with how to know the object of the ethical inquiry, even as it carries out an ethical inquiry. To reformulate this in the Heideggerian terms developed in the previous chapters, ethics is the field of inquiry where the fundamental or guiding meaning of a term is least effective as a principle and attunement to the polyvocality of terms instead becomes most important. Aristotle stresses this point in book 1 of *Nicomachean Ethics* when he writes that the "good has as many senses as being" (*NE* 1096a23–24). The good is thus characterized by a polyvocality the scope of which coincides with the variety of entities that can potentially be. Hence, for Aristotle, attaining the capacity to formulate the ethical inquiry in words is possible only for those advanced in philosophical training, for ethical inquiry is based not on an abstract knowledge about epistemology, but instead on a prudence with regard to speech and silence that is coextensive with its performance. In short, ethics is not something one knows, but instead something one does. The exercise of ethics is a fundamentally linguistic task.

If an ethical inquiry allows for knowing and therefore speaking of its object with the least degree of precision, then this likewise means that ethics is the field of inquiry which must be most keenly attuned to its employment of *logos*. This precision (*akribes*) is a privative phenomenon and is rooted in the verb *kruptein*, concealing or hiding (*Met.* 982a26–27). The attainment of ethical knowledge thus involves depriving the phenomenon about which one speaks of a certain degree of concealment, yet always doing so to the appropriate degree, for the phenomenon will always necessarily remain at least partially concealed. In order to allow the proper amount of concealment appropriate to the matter at hand, a constant vigilance regarding the proper measure of precision accompanies any ethical inquiry. Excess and deficiency—erring both toward the extremes of too much and too little—are precisely what marked the young Socrates's speech in Plato's *Parmenides*. Knowing the amount of unconcealment that is appropriate to the individual phenomenon under inquiry is what constitutes prudence. Thus, in Aristotle's terms, what the young Socrates lacked was prudence, specifically prudence with regard to the measure of speech.

This Aristotelian regard for the appropriate amount of precision does not mean that one must keep silent about ethics, as is patently not the case for a philosopher who wrote multiple ethical treatises. However, it does mean that the ethical inquiry must at all times be aware of the limits of knowability, precision, and sayability of the matter being inquired into. By its very nature ethics deals with individual situations that can always be otherwise, and as the inquiry whose principles are ever-changing, it constitutes the least accurate form of inquiry, the one that inquires into phenomena that must be relinquished to the highest degree of concealment.[15] This lack of accuracy is not a failure or flaw in the ethical inquiry, but is instead simply a description of the nature of ethics. Ethics lets go of language at the right moment according to the amount of precision appropriate to the matter at hand. Yet even while ethics is significantly intertwined with an operation of silence, it never simply relinquishes its object to complete silence. After all, for the Greeks, complete silence is the converse side of an overly precise and verbose speech, for both disregard the measure of language in a specific manner.

This constant regard for the proper degree of precision accounts for such peculiar aspects of Aristotle's writing as the cyclical structure of many of his inquiries and the repeated gestures of beginning the investigation over again by abruptly interrupting it, yet always leaving it open to commence at a later point. According to Baracchi this form of inquiry "keeps an eye on itself, as it were, reflects on itself, practices on itself the same degree of attention brought to the phenomena of human comportment. It is at once a path traced for the first time, *hodos*, and a path looked upon with awareness, *as though* already traced and followed again—a *methodos*."[16]

The path of inquiry may taper into silence, it may even end abruptly in a characteristic Aristotelian fashion, or it may finish with a sly wink, such as the one from the first book of the *Nicomachean Ethics*: "for we have almost said that happiness is living well or acting well" (*NE* 1098b22). The "almost" carries the weight of the sentence, leaving open the future saying of that which perhaps cannot yet be listened to. Ethical inquiry of this kind involves almost saying many things, saying many things roughly or in outline, hinting at them, but often not saying them, and always leaving them open to the possibility of being expressed in a future inquiry. This is central to the Aristotelian method, which is better understood as a strategy of inquiry than as a rigid or fixed procedure leading to final answers. Although this strategy clearly involves a great amount of speaking and writing, it can also be characterized as an operation attuned to silence. Silence even plays such a major role in Aristotle's strategy of inquiry that his ethics could be defined as an operation attuned to silence that is characterized as much by what it does not say as by what it does say. In not speaking further, the philosopher undertaking the inquiry does not so much refuse to speak further, but instead acknowledges that the inquiry has reached the limits of the sayability of the matter at hand.

SILENCE AS DISPOSITION

The pedagogical nature of Aristotle's texts accounts for the seemingly contradictory basis of his entire ethical endeavor in a manner that John Sallis characterizes in a different context as the coincidence of the end goal and the starting point, "of *telos* and *archē*" (Sallis 1995, 133).[17] To become philosophical, in other words, one must already in some sense possess a philosophical disposition, and this disposition involves a capacity for keeping silent as the manifestation of a broader comportment of stillness. In order to listen to an ethical discourse, one must already somehow be ethical, and hence be endowed with the capacity to listen. As Aristotle states at the outset of the *Nicomachean Ethics*, a young man who is prone "to follow his passions" and is lacking in experience "is not a proper student of [lectures on] politics," whether he is "young in age or youthful in character" (*NE* 1095a3–7). Ethics, unlike other fields of inquiry such as mathematics, can only be acquired with age and involves a significant component of time—precisely what the Sophists lured students into ignoring by selling their pupils the snake-oil promises of quick wisdom. Positioned at the other pole, ethics is the field in which speaking properly about ethical manners means the least and acting properly means the most, though not merely acting properly at a particular time, but over the course of a lifetime. As Aristotle writes in a passage distinguishing the types of knowledge demonstrated through *logos* and *praxis*: "A sign of what has been said is also the reason why young men become geometricians and mathematicians and wise in such [fields] but do not seem to become prudent. That reason is the fact that prudence is concerned with particulars, which become familiar from experience . . . and young men have no conviction of their principles but only use words, while the nature of the objects of physics and of wisdom is not unclear to physicists and wise men" (*NE* 1142a11–22).

As a matter of experience gained over time, the prudence that manifests knowledge of ethics—and hence philosophy—is crucially linked to both memory and memorizing. It is related to memory in terms of experiences remembered over time, while this prudence cannot possibly be gained by merely memorizing words. This is because being ethical does not merely consist in saying the right things, but instead involves acting rightly. Ethics does, however, significantly involve not saying the *wrong* things. "Wrong" in this sense does not necessarily refer to something untrue in opposition to something true, but instead refers to the corollary of the rightness of the moment. What is "wrong," therefore is out of place, out of tune, and out of sync. Through experience over time, the virtuous man does not merely *use* language like "young men who have no conviction of their principles but only use words," but instead speaks a language drawn from experience with the things themselves.

For Aristotle, the speech of the prudent man is regulated by a great number of injunctions both imposed by the man upon himself and as a result of his place in society (and, of course, by the very fact that he is a man). The rightness of this man's speech is explicitly tautological and circular in nature. This is because the totality of the attributes of a situation constitute the rightness of the right moment, for rightness according to Aristotle "has many senses" (*NE* 1142b18). It is crucial for the analysis provided in this section to understand that rightness is always measured with regard to the individual attributes of the individual moment. While this individual moment can be grasped, and one can act within it in a proper manner, it nonetheless cannot be defined.[18] Aristotle's description of virtue demonstrates the importance of this rightness: "to have these feelings at the right time and for the right things and towards the right men and for the right purpose and in the right manner, this is the mean and the best, and it is precisely this which belongs to virtue" (*NE* 1106b21–24). This concept of rightness is manifested through prudence (*phronēsis*), which Aristotle defines as a knowing or seeing of what changes and is contingent, as opposed to wisdom, which is concerned with what is unchanging. Consequently, prudence exists in and through being carried out, and not as some sort of static acquisition. As Heidegger describes it, "prudence exists in praxis to a greater degree than in *logos*" (*GA* 19, 139/96).[19]

Even while this capacity to become ethical can only be acquired over time, it is also a matter of a preexisting disposition: the coincidence of the starting and end points that characterizes the self-mastery of philosophy. While one's potential fitness or unfitness for philosophy may not be a matter of physiognomy for Aristotle as it was for Pythagoras (with the significant exception of the question of gender),[20] it is nonetheless a matter of one's disposition, as is indicated by his careful delineation of different types of character in the *Nicomachean Ethics*. This disposition can either be natural or cultivated by habit, for Aristotle states that the first principles of ethics cannot be taught and improper habituation could be destructive of their potential emergence (*NE* 1151a18–20).

Since it requires mastery of a semiotics of address and response that one must already in some way possess in order to learn, silence is not suitable to all character types. As a manner of comportment, it may not be attainable by those who are subject to overly active motions, "whether because of some trouble or because of their time of life" (Aristotle 2006, 450a33–4). The measure or the mean appropriate for different character types is different in each individual case, and if virtue is attained through the philosophical life, then there is likewise a rightness with regard to the amount of virtue for each character type—with some characters being hopelessly ill-disposed to the possibility of achieving happiness. Aristotle makes this clear near the end of the *Nicomachean Ethics*, noting that even those most favorably disposed to virtue may have to content themselves with an imperfect attainment of virtue: "So when all the means through which we can become good are available, perhaps we should be content if we were to get some share of virtue" (*NE* 1179b18–20).

Withdrawal and Speaking Out

As a whole, Aristotle deserves to be characterized as a thinker of silences, in the fullest ambiguity of the phrase, more than as a thinker of silence. Given the manifold meanings of silence that operate in his various investigations, his method can accordingly be regarded as a form of inquiry that mobilizes silence and is rooted in a subtle understanding of manifold forms of silence, even if it does not attempt to thematize silence as such. Silence is perhaps not a vested term for Aristotle, but it emerges as an operative term mobilized repeatedly within various constellations of vested concerns.[21] These concerns underpin the very operation of Aristotle's form of inquiry, which is constantly striving for saying what cannot be said, even while pulling back when necessary, and either tapering into or abruptly announcing silence in accordance with the demands of the moment. *Nicomachean Ethics* is a sustained attempt to say the unsayable, and it operates at all times through an observance of the mean of sayability.

Though Aristotle does not explicitly analyze silence in the *Nicomachean Ethics*, he does repeatedly discuss various circumstances in which the ethical man is obligated either to withdraw from speech or explicitly to speak out. Aristotle illustrates this quite clearly in his description of the virtue of the high-minded in a passage representative of a much larger ethical concern that characterizes much of Greek thought: "He will also be outspoken concerning his hatred and friendships, for secrecy is a mark of fear . . . and he will speak and act openly, because he has contempt for fear and secrecy and falsity. And hence he will be truthful, except when he is ironical, and if ironical, it will be only towards the many" (*NE* 1124b27–29).

In this passage, Aristotle illustrates a silence with regard to the concerns of the many, a silence rooted in a mastery of the self that draws one away from idle chatter. Yet the ethical man does not draw so far away from idle chatter that he tapers into secrecy. This type of silencing as mastery over the self is also reflected in the tactful man, for "it is a mark of a tactful man to say and listen to such things which befit a good and free man; for there are some things which become such a man to say and listen to as a part of amusement, and the amusement of a free man differs from that of a slavish person, and so does that of an educated man from that of one who is uneducated" (*NE* 1128a18–33).[22]

The tactful man and the high-minded man are withdrawn in some manner. They are withdrawn from certain forms of amusement, but also from the types of things discussed by the masses. In order to avoid being carried along in this idle chatter of the many, virtuous men in the Aristotelian sense withdraw or withhold themselves from the many through self-mastery in order not to speak like the many, even while they are likewise obligated to reveal themselves when necessary in order to not err too far toward deficiency with regard to truthfulness, and thereby become ironical (*NE* 1108a20–22).

Aristotle goes on to say that while acts of the legislature may be necessary to silence those disposed to "mockery" and "revilement," the tactful and high-minded man silences himself through self-mastery. Such men are not withdrawn into solitude, but instead into what Aristotle in the *Politics* calls the strange life (*bios xenikos*) of the philosopher who seeks virtue through a certain reserve and reticence (Aristotle 1986a, 1324a5–25).[23] Yet, ironically enough, as the drama of Plato's *Parmenides* demonstrated, the speech of the philosopher is in danger of being regarded from the outside as mere idle chatter even despite this reticence. By means of this reserve and reticence practiced through a form of speech that may seem like idle chatter to the many, the virtuous man does not merely pass words along like an actor on stage. Once again, Aristotle seems to be concerned with those who use language without experience of the things they are talking about. The incontinent man, in contrast, must "be regarded as using language in the way actors do on stage" (*NE* 1147a24). Such speech severs the words from the things at hand, uprooting language as it is passed along from speaker to speaker. This leads to a significant process of forgetting of the matter at hand. Aristotle illustrates the use of language as a means of forgetting in his description of the fleeting companionship sought by bad men: "And evil men seek companions to spend their days with and try to escape from themselves, they recall many distressing things and expect others of this sort." This puts these men, who "have no feelings of love for themselves" into a situation—at once forgetting themselves while recalling themselves—where it is as if the parts of their soul "were trying to break the man apart" (*NE* 1166b14–23). Even though the Greek verb for speaking (*legein*) may mean gathering, speech of this sort scatters and severs both language itself and the speaker from the things that are being spoken about. Ethics demands silence to the extent that it also calls for a distance from the manner of speech that separates *logos* from the matter being discussed. In Heidegger's terms, ethics teaches us to dwell where we already are. Through ethics, we find our way to that place. As a practice of self-mastery, philosophical training must teach the measure of speech that keeps us in that place in order to imbue learners with the capacity for silence. This sort of speech roots one in one's place, one's polis, and even in one's being. The ability to listen to and participate in the ethical inquiry is the culmination of the attainment of this manner of speech as an attunement to silence—a silence at all times haunted by what it has silenced.

Conclusion

Heidegger openly politicizes many of these themes in his lectures in the years surrounding the Nazi seizure of power. For Heidegger, treating what Plato called a "sickness" involves a pedagogical process. In opposition to the classicist Werner Jaeger's supposedly "humanistic" notion of pedagogy as the "formation of Greek humanity," as rector, Heidegger defines pedagogy as "*the inner binding-fast of human Dasein on the basis of the steadfastness that holds fast* to what fate demands" (*GA* 36–37, 207/158). In Heidegger's words in 1931–32, achieving this steadfastness requires a process of inward self-gathering that is decisively linked to the good:

> In estimating the beauty of a person, everything depends on his *legein*. That he "speaks beautifully" does not mean that he uses brilliant words in the manner of an orator. *Legein* means to gather, to present and reveal something as gathered, and in this way to *show* it to others. Whoever shows something as beautifully gathered is himself beautiful and capable. Only someone who is *inwardly* gathered and connected is capable of such a thing, i.e. someone who possesses that illuminative power of essence which alone makes him fit (*agathatos*) for human existence. (*GA* 34, 198/143)

Silence serves to facilitate a form of inward self-gathering that alone makes people a good fit for human existence. For Heidegger, this fitness is not simply an inborn attribute, but involves a decision, a pedagogical practice, and resoluteness that seek to harness "*the political excitement of the youth*" (*GA* 36–37, 271/206). As Heidegger tells his students in the lecture course he held in the summer of 1934, in the semester after stepping down from the rectorate, this decision is ultimately what makes one a member of the *Volk*. The university and philosophy as a discipline of learning at the modern university are essential to laying the groundwork for this decision at a point when "the world is being reconstructed" (ibid., 271/205). This decision involves gathering themselves in preparation for being part of the gathering of the people. Their university education will play an important role in fostering this decision. As Heidegger concedes, the "student of today will affirm and fulfill the duties of the SA and the Student Union." Yet this outward decision is not enough, especially since the "university has not restructured itself from the new reality and in accordance with its inner law" (*GA* 38, 73/63). The university, in other words, has not sufficiently been coordinated, even if the rector might "appear in an SA-Uniform instead of in the traditional gowns of yesteryear" (ibid., 74/64).

As long as the students are torn between the competing claims of a traditional education system in which the "the university hastens towards its end" and the form of questioning laid out in Heidegger's rectorial address, the university will be at best a site of distraction and scattering (ibid., 75/64). On the one hand, the students are exposed to the business of university philosophy, "the traditional baseless business of philosophy," which "enervates and disappoints." On the other hand, there is "an understanding that places what is obviously accessible in another light and thereby simplifies it according to what is essential" (*GA* 36–37, 271/206). This simplification of what is essential of course involves paring down and removing what is inessential. In opposition to the aimless business of discussion, Heidegger suggests how to train the students into the proper decision and harness their enthusiasm: "Labor camps, militias, settlers, leagues, landscape—seizing beings oneself, taking hold of the soil." This education through physical training and taking hold of the soil stands in opposition to "the boundlessness of the sciences, the unrestrainedness of technology, the limitlessness of the free economy" (ibid., 271/206). In other words, Heidegger reformulates the traditional *völkisch* opposition of scattering and gathering, while proposing a pedagogical practice aimed at inner gathering. This pedagogy seeks to make students "fit for human existence" through the acquisition of measure. Acquiring self-mastery by training the body and the faculty of questioning is the starting point for attaining this measure. Attaining this measure requires renunciation, reticence, and silence acquired through self-mastery. For Heidegger, this self-mastery is developed out of his pedagogical engagement with Greek philosophy.

* * *

The preceding readings of Pythagoras, Plato, and Aristotle have shown that by keeping silent and speaking at the right moment, the Greek male philosopher maintains a stillness and harmony with regard to his surroundings. This stillness is achieved through a process of self-mastery. Although the term "stillness" is used, it should not be understood as a lack of motion, but instead as the harmonizing of one's motions with the motions existent in one's surroundings through a process of attunement. It is thus of great importance to recall that *harmonia* originally refers to a joint, or to fitting together, and that Heidegger's language in the 1930s is dominated by a metaphorics of joining and conjunction (Liddell 1989, 103). In embodying this stillness, one is not absolutely motionless, but attuned to a larger field of motion. Such stillness is intimately linked to the possibility of memory and history—a question that is at the center of Heidegger's concern with idle talk.

As Aristotle writes in his treatise on memory and recollection, "memory does not occur in those who are subject to a lot of movement" (Aristotle 2006, 450a32–33). If memory is an imprint like a signet ring upon the mind, as Aristotle claims (ibid., 450a30–31), it follows that this imprint can only be made upon a stable substratum. The movement of speech,

especially of untimely speech, upsets such stability, and that concern for
stability is at least a portion of the lesson of *Parmenides*, which lapses into
an almost farcical cascade of memory-training exercises, starting at the moment when the young Socrates falls silent. It is also important to remember
that virtuous men are described by Aristotle as stable, which is precisely
what potentially makes them good friends. If philosophical training aims at
the attainment of stillness, it does so with the simultaneous aim of facilitat-
ing memory. In the Greek world, a man who possesses the proper capacity
for silence is a man who also has the capacity to remember.

The role that free-floating language plays in leading to forgetfulness,
even the forgetfulness of being, is a major concern throughout Heidegger's
work. The possibility of merely using a language, of following along with
was has been said, is a major concern for Heidegger throughout the entire
course of his thinking, and is an especially prevalent theme in his early
reading of the *Nicomachean Ethics* (see esp. *GA* 19, 24–27/17–19). In
Heidegger's early reading of Aristotle, he characterizes such empty use
of language as fallenness into the world in which one is carried along by
what is said (*GA* 19, 27/19). According to Heidegger, language used in
this manner is reduced to a repetition of what has been said, a mere passing on of words heard spoken, the thoughtless voicing of words like an
actor who can use them without needing to understand their meaning.
Heidegger succinctly reformulated this concern in a 1952 lecture: "Speaking a language is completely different than using a language. Common
speech uses language" (Heidegger 1968, 87/128). In repeatedly saying
nothing, common or free-floating speech aids in forgetting. Those who
do not use language are the ones who are already capable of listening to
it, while those who do use language in this way are also apt to use it up, to
exhaust it. When read in the light of Heidegger's own affinities to the anti-
Semitic discourses about the dissevering and alienating elements of "world
Jewry," these analyses of idle talk and the utilization of language take on
an entirely different set of resonances. For Heidegger, *völkisch* thinking
would play a role in gathering the people: "The *völkisch* worldview has its
own necessity in the vicinity of the task of a historical gathering" (*GA* 94,
446/324). As a linguistic task, this gathering would significantly involve
silence and would require—like any task of production—significant acts
of exclusion aimed at the essential enemy. Heidegger's lecture courses on
Greek philosophy thus must be read as deeply political pedagogical acts
intended to teach hearers how to better dwell within the proper place.

The lectures in turn were the supplement to the type of physical training in work camps he implemented with great detail as rector. For the Greeks, who made no pretense at equality among different human beings, it was not particularly troubling that the capacity for becoming philosophical involved significant a priori exclusions. For the Greek thinkers analyzed here, a philosophical disposition was both the presupposition and the goal of philosophical training. The same logic underpins the *völkisch* conception of attunement to the people, for one must already be attuned to the people in some manner in order to properly actualize oneself to the people. As Erwin Guido Kolbenheyer puts it in his analysis of language and poetry, the "emotional experience" of the people is the "root, pillar and goal" of our existence (Kolbenheyer 1935, 16). Although he vehemently disagreed with many of the details of Kolbenheyer's thesis, Heidegger's sigetic politics of place, silence, and attunement was nonetheless perfectly at home in this circular logic of exclusion.

The form of silence discussed in this chapter is associated solely with virtuous free Greek men, as opposed to women, slaves, and non-Greeks. This exclusion lies at the root of Western philosophy: the philosopher is who he is by virtue of his power to choose not to speak. Heidegger's entire philosophical endeavor—and perhaps the history of Western philosophy in general—is haunted by this fundamental, violent exclusionary gesture.

6 Being without Measure:
Silencing the Feminine

The classical Greek understanding of silence had very little to do with the dominant modern conceptions of it as the absence of either noise or the spoken word. In the ancient Greek world, silence was a complex phenomenon that followed the contours of a series of exclusions involving gender, social class, ethnicity, and other structures of alterity. Silence registered a Greek male's harmonious relation to his place, demonstrated through his embodied engagement with the world, and was learned through philosophical training. Acquiring such harmony was in a sense the central aim of philosophy for the Greeks.

In the previous chapter, four fundamental aspects of the silence of Greek male self-mastery were identified: silence was shown to involve harmony with one's polis, memory, the proper measure of speech, and truth-saying. With regard to the voice, speech, and language of Greek women, whom the Greeks even regarded as a different race (*genos*), matters were much different (Holmes 2012, 22). Greek men were potential masters of silence. Greek women were mastered by silencing. The silence that corralled and contained their existence was twofold: they were neither to speak nor to be spoken of. This double silencing in turn operated in the service of forgetting, for if a woman lived in a manner that elicited the least amount of speech, she would be all the more easily forgotten. Not surprisingly, this twofold silence was also duplicitous in a highly significant manner, for being too silent was also associated by the Greeks with trickery and deception. Although heroic trickery, shrewdness, and cunning were still recognized in Homeric times, these had ceased to be positive masculine virtues in classical Athens.[1] A duplicitous logic marked the speech and silence of the Greek woman, whose very voice was held to harbor deceptive wiles (see, e.g., Bergren 2008).[2] Her measure was a measureless measure, which necessarily vacillated between two contradictory extremes. On the one hand, she was denied proper measure; on the other, the measure deemed typical of her was excessive. If it "is the nature of excess to turn to its opposite," it was only natural that the measure of women was associated with unpredictable outbursts (Loraux 1995, 243).

Given this curious double logic surrounding the voice of Greek women, a number of contrary qualities are attributed to women in Greek philosophy and tragedy. On the one hand, women are associated with silence and seclusion, with an entire register of darkness contrasting to the clarity and brightness that characterizes the being of men. It is sufficient to reference the Pythagorean table of contraries as reported in Aristotle's *Metaphysics* in order to establish the terrain of this opposition in Greek thought: bounded, light, good, and male, on one side; unbounded, darkness, bad, and female, on the other (*Met.* 986a22–27; Lloyd 1993, 3). Yet despite the long-standing power of these oppositions, the feminine, on the other hand, is also associated with a hyperbolic voice, with violent eruptions, and with uncontrollable speech without bounds—the unbounded *logos* contrasting to the limit achieved by men through the measure. This logic is illustrated in Aristotle's *On the Soul* regarding the extremes of light and sound, where Aristotle shows that what exposes itself in one of the extremes—whether to the extreme of high volume or low volume, brightness or dimness—fails to be what it is, and instead becomes an incomprehensible monstrosity that destroys the senses (Aristotle 1981a, 422a20–26), the bugbear of male paranoia about the being, and therefore the *logos*, of the feminine in ancient Greek philosophy and drama.[3] Yet despite their apparent lack of self-control, silence for women, just as for men, is a matter of moderation, which, according to Nicole Loraux, was "the only virtue that Greek thought agrees to ascribe to women" (Loraux 1998, 18). And whereas the measure for men was moderation of speech, the moderation of women primarily took the form of "obedience to male direction," and "when it does mean more, the allusion is often to sound" (Carson 1995, 126). There was significant fear of women who were *too* quiet (even though ordering a woman to moderate herself might be thought equivalent to yelling, "Be quiet!"). This mixture of the need for control and the fear of seclusion is reflected in a passage from Plato's *Laws* that succinctly captures a number of the contradictory concerns surrounding the voice of women:

On the contrary, half the human race—the female sex, the half which in any case is inclined to be secretive and crafty, because of its weakness—has been left to its own devices because of the misguided indulgence of the legislator. . . . You see, leaving women to do what they like is not just to lose half the battle (as it may seem): a woman's natural potential for virtue is inferior to a man's, so she's proportionately a greater danger, perhaps even twice as great. . . . There's nothing the sex is likely to put up with more reluctantly: women have got used to a life of obscurity and retirement, and any attempt to force them into the open will provoke tremendous resistance from them. (Plato 1997a, 781a–d)[4]

Women are even accused of "getting used to" the very obscurity that is expected of them. As an unruly element vacillating at all times between contradictory qualities, none of which they properly possess, they do not seem to have a place in the polis. If, as Heidegger contends in the *Introduction to Metaphysics*, being for the Greeks first and foremost means being-in-the-polis (*IM*, 117/162), women have no place at all and are essentially *atopos*—if not even, as is the case with Socrates, *atopōtatos*, most out of place.[5]

Since the *logos* of women qua feminine is marked by this strange collusion of opposites, an effective philosophical analysis of the silence of ancient Greek women cannot be achieved by merely negating or reversing the silence of men. Consequently, this analysis will unfold in the tension between two different forms of philosophical *logos* operating simultaneously. On the one hand, it will employ an oppositional argument at the level of assertion to show that the silence of women is beyond measure, disturbs any possible harmony, serves forgetting, and, due to a recurring association of women with trickery, denies women the capacity for straightforward truth-saying. At this level, the silence (and hence the speech) of women will reveal itself to be everything that the speech of man is not. At this level, the divisions will be neat and clean. Unfortunately, however, the analysis cannot stop there, for this logic of oppositions does not allow one to sufficiently pose the question of what it means to be confronted by the irreducible contradictions that mark the silence of Greek women.

Perhaps one can begin to decipher the contours of a manner of analyzing women as a figure of the *chōra*, the "third kind" circumscribed by Plato with great trepidation in the *Timaeus* in a passage that has received much recent attention from feminist scholars,[6] as well as from phenomenology more broadly speaking (e.g., Derrida 1995, 89–127; Casey 1997, 23–50; Sallis

1999): "And there is . . . moreover a third kind—that of the *chōra*—which always is, admitting not of destruction and providing a seat for all that has birth, itself graspable by some bastard reasoning with the aid of insensibility, hardly to be trusted, the very thing we look to when we dream and affirm that it's necessary somehow for everything that is to be in some region and occupy some space, and that what is neither on earth nor somewhere in heaven is nothing" (Plato 2001, 52a8–52b5).

What the "bastard reasoning" of the *chōra* demands is nothing less than the suspension of the principle of noncontradiction in order to try to come to terms with the simultaneous coexistence of opposites. This is a suspension that acknowledges its own impossibility in a speech in which, as Judith Butler puts it in her reading of Luce Irigaray, "all ontological claims are suspended" (Butler 1993, 17). Building upon Irigaray's continued project of cultivating a language of suspended ontology, a language that sways in the space of the ontolinguistic divide to be analyzed in this chapter, the subsequent analysis will argue that the being of Greek women is a *chōral* figure marked by decisive contradictions. This being is, in Irigaray's words, "the simultaneous co-existence of opposites. She is *both one and the other*" (*SW*, 165). As a reflection of the being of women, the speech of women manifested itself as this simultaneous coexistence of opposites. The voice of ancient Greek women is at once a voice of madness and a voice of clarity (Zeitlin 1996, 363); it is at all times both too loud and too quiet;[7] it conceals itself underneath ruses of trickery, but likewise pronounces a hyperbolic though cryptic truth (Bergren 2008, 14–15). The speech of women—and thus their silence—is both all of this and none of this. It is none of this, but it is not nothing.

Though the simultaneous coexistence of these opposites may seem like an impossibility, it is precisely this impossibility that marks the being of women in classical Athens. Irigaray captures the difficulty in a reading of Aristotle: "Theoretically there would be no such thing as woman. She would not exist. The best that can be said is that she does *not exist yet*. Something of her a-specificity might be found in the *betweens* that occur in being, or beings" (*SW*, 167). Seemingly, there would also be no *speech* of women, for it would not yet exist. Yet at this juncture an important distinction occurs: there would also be no *silence* of women. The silence of women is just as impossible as their speech, and this is because women in the eyes of the Greek philosophers exceed their own capacity for self-mastery. Greek women are thus consistently portrayed as exceeding even their own control, as being subject to the vicissitudes of a tempestuous speech that is at times mobilized for the political purposes of the city in necessarily hyperbolic rituals of public mourning and at times reined in for fear of its eruptive force. In short, the Greek woman as woman is, to borrow once again from Irigaray, "*without measure*" (ibid., 342). The voice of the Greek woman is thus situated in the impossible space between the measurelessness of the ideal of absolute silence and the measurelessness of violent eruptions that are incapable of being comprehended.

If *harmonia* is the goal of the silence of male self-mastery, and if the reticence of men serves the role of attuning them to their surroundings, then what is to be made of the *chōral* figure of the woman—the vessel to which all attributes can be assigned, even as all can be denied? Irigaray offers the following (im)possibility: "Now, if everything is taken up with the realization of the *physis, woman has, and will have, no place and thus no existence.* This will be true even in her *privation* of being, which it is the essential task and ceaseless effort of dialectic and dialectic's indispensable intermediaries to bring or bring back to the fullness of the self's possession of substance" (ibid., 166).

But what does it mean to have no place, or to be essentially *atopos?*[8] If all a woman can hope for is to be no worse than her being, "whether for praise or for blame," as Pericles famously remarked,[9] then this is best achieved by being as silent as possible in all regards in order to be all the more easily forgotten. Yet it is precisely this complete silence that violates the measure of *logos*, and such complete silence is at once an extreme and also the measure of the measureless woman.

Yet what does it mean that both Plato and Thucydides associate this forgetting with the being of women? And what is to be made of the association of the being of women with concealment? Forgetting (*lēthē*) is derived from *lanthanō*, "to lie hidden," and Heidegger even goes so far as to translate *lēthē* as "an occurrence of concealment" (*GA* 54, 42/28). This occurrence is not a simple lapse of mind or forgetting of a single subject, but points to something more essential: a monstrous *chōral* register that cannot simply be brought to light through an operation of reason—except, perhaps, through a "bastard reason." In the polis, the feminine is thus not merely forgotten, as if through a simple lapse of mind, but is structurally marked as the forgotten. The feminine is that which is to be forgotten.

In his recovery of the ancient Greek tradition, Heidegger perpetuates an act of silencing that is deeply embedded in Western philosophical discourse.

Manifold figures of silence surround the female voice, but Heidegger remains unresponsive to its silence, even as he dissects the many senses of
silence in the Greek world.

Being without Measure: The Stillest Hour

For the Greeks, the stillest hour is an hour of uncanniness. As "the calm-
est part of the day," according to Aristotle, noon is an unpredictable time,
a time when night gives over to day (Aristotle 1984b: 366a15). It is a time
of transition, precisely at the moment when shadows do not appear. In this
calm interlude, specters, beings without shadows, are most likely to emerge
(Caillois 2003, 124–29; see also *SL*, 222–23). Although calm weather occurs "most often at midnight and midday," earthquakes and violent gusts of
wind are most likely after the noontide stillness, according to the author of
Aristotle's *Problems* (938a23).[10] Stillness and eruptions are so closely linked
that eruptions even seem to require a prior stillness. In Plato's *Phaedrus*,
Phaedrus interrupts Socrates—who throughout the dialogue hints at his
divine possession—precisely at noon, urging him to pause in his speech,
with the words: "Don't you see it's almost exactly noontime when the sun
stands still, as they say?" (Plato 2003, 242a; cf. 259a). What follows in
the afternoon heat is a discourse, not only on madness, but also on the
search for measure and self-control—a dialogue significantly intertwined
with a subtle thematics of silence, especially regarding the proper measure
of speech in rhetoric. In stark contrast to his first speech in *Phaedrus*, the
divinely possessed Socrates speaks here on the edge of madness outside the
polis, out of place, *atopos* (ibid., 229c, 230d). From the stillness of noon,
an eruption of *logos* emerges.

The uncanny nature of the stillest hour relates to the Greeks' larger fear
of the *most silent* silence.[11] Just as they fear what is most still, they also
fear what is most silent, and this fear is made all the more acute given that
silence in classical Athens was often associated with trickery and deception. Throughout the classical Greek era, silence is associated with veiling,
occluding, rendering invisible, and deception.[12] Moreover, women were
strongly associated with regimes of silence in classical Athens, and there
was a "pervasive association between women and deception" (McClure
2001, 5). "You know, according to the men we're capable of all sorts of
mischief," Lysistrata cries in Aristophanes's topsy-turvy eponymous comedy.
"I'd rather be sitting at home like a virtuous maiden, making no trouble

for anyone here, but if anyone annoys me and rifles my nest, they'll find a wasp inside!" (Aristophanes [411 BCE] 1996, 468–71). However, the comic effect of *Lysistrata* is not so much due to its ribald sexual innuendo as to its portrayal of women exercising self-control, lack of self-control being considered to be part of women's nature (ibid., 9–10).[13]

By exaggerating the common conception of women's lack of self-mastery, Aristophanes underscores that the figure of the feminine was associated with a vast discourse and apparatus of tropes of deception that effectively silenced women, even in allowing women to speak and be spoken about, especially in tragedy.[14] To speak of the silence of Athenian women does not mean to say that women in classical Athens were strictly silent in the absolute sense of the term.[15] However, women's ways of speaking and of keeping silent in ancient Athens were sharply distinguished from those of men and related, not so much to "the pitch of the voice, but to the oaths, case endings, and other linguistic features appropriate to women's speech" (McClure 2001, 4). If correct, this provides an intriguing interpretive framework for analyzing the concern about the "shrillness" of feminine voices repeatedly expressed by the author of the Aristotelian *Problems* (Aristotle 1984d, 900a32–b28).

This shrillness can be understood to refer, not only to the sonorous pitch of the voice, but also to the type of speech associated with it: "References in tragedy to 'sharp, high' tones often denote intensity and distress, but not necessarily femininity; and male actors and choruses seem not to have made any thoroughgoing attempts to speak or sing 'like' women (i.e., by adopting a falsetto delivery, or modifying their voices in a systematic way)" (Griffith 2001, 118). What this indicates is that speech, much like silence, involves an entire semiotics of comportment, rather than the voice alone, which is only part of it. Speaking like a woman does not merely require a "shrill" pitch, but the mobilization of an entirely different set of linguistic and even physiognomic resources. There was a refined set of codes that marked what it meant to be silent like a woman, just as the male silence of self-mastery was manifested by a semiotics of physical comportment.

Moreover, what this Aristotelian discussion of shrillness demonstrates is that being silent like a woman was not solely a matter of *being* a woman, for men who lack self-control are considered womanly as well. As Foucault points out in *The Hermeneutics of the Subject*, "the bad moral and intellectual quality of the person who is always fidgeting and making unseemly gestures" is considered effeminate, as is "the man who is effeminate in the sense of being passive in relation to himself, unable to exercise *egkrateia*, mastery or sovereignty, over the self" (Foucault 2005, 344). We find this claim corroborated in Aristotle, who speaks of the softness that "distinguishes the female from the male," which is also characteristic of intemperate men "excessively disposed to amusement" (*NE* 1150b16–18). As the previous chapter demonstrated, it is precisely this sort of amusement from which the ethical man must refrain. There is, it seems, no proper occasion for the feminine voice, even if spoken by a man. And to the extent that a man is not silent like a man, he is like a woman. Yet despite this persistent association of incontinence with femininity, it is necessary to avoid collapsing the gap between what it means to speak *like* a woman and to speak *as* a woman, a difference that harbors an uncanny element.

The uncanny fears, uncontrollable eruptions, violent outbreaks, and conspiratorial whispers provoked by the stillest hour, force unpredictably emerging from calm, are associated with the silence of women. Socrates's wife Xanthippe, we are told, was a woman of this sort, "ill-tempered and quarrelsome to a degree, with a constant flood of feminine tantrums day and night," the *doxa* report (Aulus Gellius [2nd century CE] 1946: 85).[16] It is therefore not surprising that very early in the *Phaedo*, as Socrates is trying to calm his friends and loved ones at the moment of his death, he orders Crito to "have somebody take her home" after she has "cried out and then said just the sort of thing women usually say" (Plato 1998, 60a).[17] Potentially violent female mourning required control and containment, lest it overflow and threaten the polis; but it was often channeled into sanctioned forms of mourning (see, e.g., Loraux 1998).[18] Whereas the soul of the philosopher is threatened in the final moments of the philosopher's life by the womanly voice adopted by Socrates's friends, in the sanctioned mourning rituals, it is the soul of the polis that is at stake. What the author of the Aristotelian *Problems* refers to as the "shrillness" of the female voice disturbs the resonance, jointure, stillness, and fundamental attunement (in Heidegger's phrase) of the polis, and "cities defend the political sphere against behaviors and emotions that threaten its harmony" (ibid., 20). Given their purported lack of self-control and particular audacity, women may be a more dangerous enemy than any found outside the city walls, Nicole Loraux argues.

Just as the silence of men involves the justice and well-being of the Greek polis, so too the silence of women. The polis needs to be silent about this uncanny element, and it needs this silent element likewise to be silent. This silence does not of course preclude friendship between individual men and individual women, for the conjugal relation is precisely such a friendship, but it does raise questions about the possibility of friendship with the *chōral* figure of the feminine as such, which can only be known through a bastard reasoning. Aristotle asks how people can be friends when they are "unaware of how they stand toward each other" (*NE* 1156a).

The Uncanny Mixture: Voiced and Voiceless Silences

VOICED SILENCES

Despite the uncanny fear of the most silent silence, the Greeks nonetheless speak a great deal about many forms of silence. In tragedy, for example, a herald will often announce silence, or a hero or villain may call for silence. Similarly, a rhetorician will speak of how silent he is being, listing the great number of unspeakable acts he will pass over in silence.[19] This is demonstrated by the messenger in the famous scene of disclosure from Sophocles's *Oedipus Rex*. For the messenger, it is not enough to pass over Oedipus's unspeakable deed in silence, for he must first take the additional step of mentioning that he will not speak of it:

> He shouts
> for some one to unbar the doors and show him
> to all the men of Thebes, his father's killer,
> his mother's—no I cannot say the word,
> it is unholy—for he'll cast himself
> out of the land[20]

For this silence to count *as* silence, it must first be announced, it must be marked and traced out, circumscribed within a space of unsayability. For terminological purposes, I will refer to the type of silence in the examples just given as voiced silences. This is a designation that is not intended to be final and rigid, as if in the service of creating a new taxonomy. Instead the term is deployed to set up a juxtaposition with the voiceless silences to be analyzed in the following section. While voiced silences are identified with the masculine virtue of silence, voiceless silences are associated with the duplicitous virtue of silence demanded of women.

Despite the many forms of voiced silence resonating in the Greek world, the actual temporal duration of silence in such cases is not performed.

The orator's silence of omission ("I will not speak of . . . ," "I will not mention . . . ") is understood by the audience as performative and is regarded as a necessary ritual to maintain modesty without the expectation of the actual performance of silence. The power of this rhetorical figure, after all, lies in the fact that the speaker is not at all being silent about the unspeakable acts, but is instead addressing them obliquely through a form of indirect speech, not so much speaking of those acts, but marking them in their unsayability. In the *Menexenus*, Plato's playful mockery of funeral speeches, Socrates performs this type of silence while reciting a speech he says he learned from Aspasia, his female teacher: "And these, in truth, were the deeds of the men who lie here and of others who died for Athens. Many fine words have been spoken about them, but those that remain unsaid are a great deal more numerous and finer still; many days and nights would not suffice for one who sets out to complete the enumeration" (Plato 1997c, 246a–b). Socrates of course will not speak for many days and nights, for that would violate the measure of speech appropriate to a man and to a philosopher, but the gesture toward the many words unsaid at once honors the dead and allows the speaker to maintain the proper measure by circumscribing what he does not say within a measured form of saying.

Aside from the voiced silences of rhetoric, a second major kind of voiced silence occurs in the Greek theater, for in tragedy dramatic silences were treated as "invisible containers" and were generally not portrayed on stage (*SL*, 16). "In surviving Greek tragedy there is scarcely anywhere . . . where the text obliges us to suppose a total silence of more than a few seconds" (Taplin 1972, 57). The ancient Greeks seem to have been very comfortable with silences interwoven with speech, but not with silences that emerge at the cessation of speech—that is, with voiced silences as opposed to voiceless silences. Put yet another way, this means that the Greeks were comfortable with masculine and not feminine silences.

Why is it that the temporal duration of silence is not portrayed on stage? This inability to portray silence reveals a great deal about the being of such silence and about the relation between silence and the voice. What is so strange about such silences for the Greeks? Silvia Montiglio provides a number of clues to answer these questions: "Silence is never neutral in the land of logos. Many of its appearances seem to be variants of a similar sentiment, which could be called the horror of the void. The Greek world is resonant, filled with circulating voices. On the battlefield, in the assembly, in the theater, in the city as a whole, the voice is an organizing principle. Silence threatens this fullness of sound" (*SL*, 289).

In the vociferous world of the Greeks, the voice serves as an organizing principle—the range of the human voice, according to Aristotle, determining the ideal size of both a polis and an army, for if these assemblages grow too large, "who will be the general of such an excessive multitude, or who will be the herald unless he has Stentor's voice?" (Aristotle 1986, 1362b6–7). In a palpable sense, the voice of the herald in the streets and the voice of the general in the field constitute the breath of the city. And if the voice breathes life into the city, then silence marks the "race" that seeks to destroy it, that strange enemy from within. It is thus not without significance that *chōra* is often translated as "void." The capacity for silence marks, punctuates, and structures the male voice, shaping it into proper speech. The incapacity not to remain silent signals a feminine chaos that must in turn be silenced, even if this always overly silent silence "is perhaps the mode of speech that threatens the polis most" (Brault 2009, 204).

VOICELESS SILENCES

In the wake of the work of twentieth-century authors such as Virginia Woolf, Samuel Beckett, and Harold Pinter, we are perhaps not overly disturbed by staged silences (Laurence 1991; Pinter 2009, 22–25). Pinter for his part even distinguishes between silences and pauses, while a performance of Beckett's *Krapp's Last Tape*, to name just one example from Beckett's oeuvre of silence, will begin and end with silences that stretch on for minutes, thus bookending the silences that punctuate the play throughout. J. M. Coetzee, whose novels are structured around the silences of postcolonial violence, even goes so far as to argue that twentieth-century literature's obsession with silence has in fact domesticated such silences, destroying the possibility for them to resonate as silences. "Our ears today are finely attuned to modes of silence," Coetzee writes. "Our craft is all in reading *the other*: gaps, inverses, undersides; the veiled; the dark, the buried, the feminine; alterities. . . . is a mode of reading which, subverting the dominant, is in peril, like all triumphant subversion, of becoming the dominant in turn" (Coetzee 1988, 81). Following Coetzee, it would seem that silence has become a tamed and familiar phenomenon, suggesting that we have ceased to hear silence *as* silence.

While dealing with this brief but enigmatic passage from Aristotle's *Poetics*, it is important to keep in mind what has been demonstrated thus far, namely, that the Greeks do not primarily consider silence (*sigē* or *siōpē*) to be either *alogos* or necessarily soundless. Both words commonly translated as silence lie somewhere within the terrain of language, and both were quite often voiced. If silence is ever without *logos* for the Greeks, it is not the silence of *sigē* or *siōpē*, but a silence that is without sound or voice. This has deep ontological consequences for women, since they are ideally supposed to be soundless, and the only forms of public speech that are sanctioned to them as women are hyperbolic.

In his *Poetics*, Aristotle declares a particular form of silence to be outside the proper purview of what is to be presented on stage in a dramatic work, offering the "man who came from Tegea to Mysia without saying a word" as an example of one of "the unreasonable parts" of a dramatic work that should be left "outside of the actual plot" (Aristotle 1981b, 1460a28–33). Aristotle is referring to Telephus's journey after murdering his kinsmen, Montiglio explains, and Telephus's silence is part of the process of his ritual purification (*SL*, 21).[21] This silence, which is soundless, is distinct from the type of voiced silence that is inscribed with a terrain of *logos*. This voiceless silence is not a silence interwoven with *logos*, but is instead a silence that begins at the cessation of speech. The role of the Greek woman is to live within this form of silence. This is a silence that, strictly speaking, has no place. Despite this mandate of silence, which would seem to circumscribe women within a sphere of control, an uncanny fear surrounds women because of the possibility that their silence contains concealed within it an eruptive force that is *alogos*. That is to say: the silence of women is not essentially *alogos*, but it conceals within it by virtue of its very nature the potentiality for being *alogos*.

If silence is *alogos*, that renders all the more significant the passage from Aristotle's *Politics* that must be regarded as the *locus classicus* for any discussion of the silence of Greek women: "In view of this, one should view each case as the poet did who, speaking of a woman, said, 'Silence brings credit to a,' for this does not apply to a man. And since a child is immature, it is clear that his virtue, too, should be referred not to the child itself but to the [virtue of] his guide, who is mature; and the same applies to the virtue of a slave in relation to his master" (Aristotle 1986, 1260a29–33).[22]

What the passage points to are the violent injunctions that exist around women's speech, such that silence could be considered a *kosmos* to

women—a word that powerfully suggests that, when women keep silent, everything is in its place, *kosmos* being understood according to Ann
Bergren as "the attribute necessary for successful operation" (Bergren 2008,
29). Or, as Irigaray writes: "*Cosmos* should be understood as a gathering-
together and as a functional ordering of the whole by and for the power
of man. *Cosmos* and *logos* being of the same" (Irigaray 1999, 15). This use
of *kosmos* also resonates with Aristotle's cosmic conception of women as
inert matter given shape and form by masculine force (Bianchi 2014, 25).
The silent feminine element is imprinted upon by masculine force, both
in reproduction and in the gendered structure of matter, and a child that
too closely resembles its mother was considered a monstrosity—a term
Aristotle vests with many subtle shades of meaning.

While silence is an ornament for women, a signal of their capacity to be
shaped, ordered, and formed, for men, Aristotle writes, "high-mindedness
is a sort of ornament of the virtues" (*NE* 1124a1). This virtuousness is
embodied in a particular form of reticence, not a reticence that serves to
obscure or obfuscate, but reticence that promotes clarity by paring down
unnecessary speech on unnecessary topics. This is because, as a fragment
from Sophocles reminds us, "concealing is bad and unworthy of a well-born
man."[23] These observations effectively distinguish the forms of male and
female moderation: the feminine moderation with regard to speech that
always stands under the suspicion of deception and the masculine moderation with regard to speech that obligates men to speak freely in certain
circumstances, but also to show restraint in other situations. If the being
of man is in its place via the harmony obtained through moderation as a
result of a silence carried along in the word, then in what way does silence
contribute to keeping women in their place? What, in short, is the place
of women? The place of women is the placeless place of a duplicitously
measureless silence. This placelessness indicates, in Emanuela Bianchi's
words, "a gendered asymmetry in both topology and motility," for there
can be no matter of symmetry with regard to the measureless measure
(Bianchi 2014, 19).

This ontologically impossible place has long been familiar to feminist
philosophy. As Simone de Beauvoir famously writes in *The Second Sex*,
repeating a well-worn passage from Aristotle, "the female is a female by
virtue of a certain *lack* of qualities" (de Beauvoir 2010, 5).[24] Or, to reformulate this phrase to echo Irigaray's words, in Aristotelian metaphysics
and in the Aristotelian polis, even the privation of woman's being is denied

being. Hence, while the silence of men manifests itself as a presence marked by the word, the silence of women is but the absence of an absence. For Aristotle, woman seems to be a lack that cannot make herself known except through the corresponding lack that is silence, or through subservience to her master—although, of course, one must be careful to distinguish between subservient and defiant silence.[25] Moreover, for Aristotle this subservience should even be carried over to the stage, where female characters should not be allowed to speak in an unbecoming manner like males (Aristotle 1981b, 1454a20–25). For the ancient Greeks, women should therefore not only be overlooked, they should also be forgotten, subjected to the type of forgetting that only silence can produce.

As we have seen, silence for the Greeks involves the eyes as much as the mouth, though with regard to men the silence of the eyes operated in the service of the enhancement of memory: only those who could properly listen to Pythagoras and who had trained that listening through a five-year silence could enter the house and see him. This ocular aspect of silence is reversed in the case of women, for not looking at women, or not being forced to look at women is a further manner of keeping silent about them. Moreover, "a silent figure could be present on stage yet remain unseen by the other characters" (*SL*, 189). Through her silence, a woman was effectively rendered invisible. This invisibility is her *kosmos*, and all that she can hope for is to align herself with this *kosmos* through her particular moderation in order to be no better nor worse than her being. Being invisible qua voiceless, she is all the more capable of being easily forgotten.

The silence of women must therefore be distinguished from the silence of the various "others." While the cacophony of slaves and hoi polloi may be annoying and disturbing, as is vividly demonstrated by the drunken slaves "calling in their foreign accents" who rather forcefully disband the erotic male gathering of friends in Plato's *Lysis* (Plato 1997b, 223a),[26] the silence of women represents something much more disturbing and uncanny. Aristotle makes this clear in distinguishing the soul of the slave from the soul of the woman in the *Politics*: "The slave does not have the deliberate part of the soul at all; the woman has it, but it has no authority; and the child has it, but it is not fully developed" (Aristotle 1986, 1260a12–13). What Aristotle is marking out are distinctions with regard to both *logos* and the mind which help bring the uncanny danger of women into focus: unlike the slave, women can deliberate, but they cannot make themselves subservient to their deliberation. This indicates that women are potentially shrewd, possessing a cunning capacity for premeditation that exceeds even their own control. They can possess cunning intelligence as a trick, but not according to the proper measure. They are incapable of the self-mastery that defines a virtuous man, and this applies above all to women as bearers of *logos*. Hence, while the ideal silence of the women is voiceless, when the silence of women becomes voiced it necessarily does so to a hyperbolic degree. It can only attenuate the ontological uncanniness of this necessity, a necessity regarded by Aristotle as an *accidental* necessity—the very combination of contradictory qualities that makes the Greek feminine be such an unthinkable and unbearable monstrosity (Bianchi 2014, 26–51).

At this point it is worth recalling the Heideggerian refrain that has been analyzed in different ways in the previous chapters in order to approach it once again from a difference perspective: "Only what can speak can be silent" (*GA* 19, 15/11). In order to clarify this refrain, it is worth drawing on a distinction made by Jean-François Lyotard: "To be able not to speak is not the same as not to be able to speak. The latter is a deprivation, the former a negation" (Lyotard 1988, 10). According to this distinction, the freeman, as capable of being endowed with a voice (and the *logos* that makes a voice a voice) in the fullest sense, can be deprived of his voice in the preeminent steretic fashion, while women and slaves can only have their speech negated. Women, in short, cannot be deprived of speech in the preeminent form of *sterēsis*. The rhetorical power of this difference is vividly demonstrated by the orator Demosthenes parading out a man silenced through civic exclusion in order to elicit shock from his audience (Demosthenes [360s BCE] 1926, § 92). The significance of this stricken figure is that he represents a man "reduced to the level of a woman or a child" (Redfield 1995, 164). After all, what could be more womanly than a man who cannot speak for himself? Such a loss of voice carries with it a particularly stark horror for the Greek imagination, and is particularly associated with exile.[27] Plato pays witness to this in the *Gorgias* in a comment by Socrates: "And tell me again about Cimon. Tell me: didn't the people he took care of ostracize him, so they wouldn't hear his voice for ten years?" (Plato 2008, 516d7–8). This silence of deprivation must be distinguished from the *chōral* silence of women who cannot be deprived of *logos* because they do not have it in a preeminent sense, even while being voiced to a hyperbolic degree.

Incapable of the type of moderation that is rooted in the proper measure, incapable, in other words, of the moderation of the philosopher and the man, the only possible moderation that can be assigned to women lies beyond the mean as both an excess and a deficiency: complete silence and the occasional sanctioned outburst. Yet it is precisely this complete silence that is beyond the grasp of women, who necessarily lack self-control. This complete silence, in turn, is balanced by the sanctioned injunction to the other extreme, the hyperbolic voice of mourning and tragedy. At best, if a woman avoids these extremes, her speech may occasionally rise to the level of idle chatter. Irigaray describes the significance of this chatter succinctly in her analysis of Plato's cave dwellers:

> They rarely, however, rise above the level of exchanged sensations, of communal daydreams; at best they express opinions on events in the city, or merely pass on the opinions that are making the rounds. Therefore women are incapable of realizing whether some idea—Idea—in fact corresponds to themselves, or whether it is only a more or less passable imitation of men's ideas. Unaware of the value of the names given them by the logos—assuming that some really specific names exist—women would, it seems, not know their definition, their representation, or the relationships with others, and with the All, that are maintained in this way. Women would thus be *without measure*, as a result of being without limits, without proportions that have been established once and for all and that can be referred back to the whole. *They have no proper form.* (*SW*, 342)

At its best, the speech of women can attain the level of a certain type of chatter, the very chatter that an apprentice in philosophy would cease in the earliest stages of training. In fact, the propensity for this very form of chatter might be enough to mark a man as not possessing a philosophical disposition, or even having a physiognomy constitutionally ill-suited for philosophy. Hence, if Greek women are *atopos*, then that is at least in part because their speech carries them away from the matters at hand to which speech refers—those things in the world that anchor being to beings. At its worst, however, the speech and silence of women bear within them monstrous possibilities of eruptive force. Euripides's *Medea* will serve to illustrate this possibility. At its best, the speech of women leads to forgetting; at its worst, it refuses to be forgotten. At once voiceless and hyperbolically voiced, Medea resists the forceful tug of oblivion.

Euripides's *Medea*: Silence as Trickery

Euripides's *Medea* serves as the paradigmatic tragic example for the disturbing and unpredictable, though always shrewdly calculating feminine silence. First at the outset of the play and again toward the middle, we hear Medea planning her murderous plot, her contrivance, trick, or ruse to murder her children, which she plans to enact by "entering silently into the palace where the bed is made" (*Medea*, 40). "In craft and silence I will set about this murder," Medea declares (ibid., 391).

Although uncanny enough on its own, this silence takes on even more conspiratorial aspects as Medea, despite being an outsider "won in a foreign land" by her husband, is able to gain with the greatest of ease silent complicity from the chorus of the women of Corinth—the women *of* Corinth, and not the Corinthian women—well in advance of carrying out her murderous plans (ibid., 256). As she both asks and demands of the chorus, moving between the interrogative and the imperative:

> This much then is the service I would beg from you:
> If I can find the means or devise any scheme
> To pay my husband back for what he has done to me—
> Him and his father-in-law and the girl who married him—
> Just to keep silent. For in other ways a woman
> Is full of fear, defenseless, dreads the sight of cold
> Steel; but, when once she is wronged in the matter of love,
> No other soul can hold so many thoughts of blood. (ibid., 258–66)

And the chorus, that conspiratorial body of women, concedes:

> This I will promise. You are in the right, Medea,
> In paying your husband back. I am not surprised at you
> For being sad.
>   But look! I see our King Creon
> Approaching. He will tell us of some new plan. (ibid., 267–70)

The women of Corinth yield gladly to the foreign woman's command, and their readiness to participate in conspiratorial occlusion is juxtaposed with the robust transparency of Creon, the sovereign male come to make an announcement. Medea, it seems, can only properly speak through her deed, the deed of killing the father's son, and the women of Corinth stand ready to join this silent conspiracy.

As Montiglio skillfully analyzes, the deed of granting silence carried out by the female chorus to a conspiratorial woman despite her foreignness underscores a general fear of women's conspiratorial silences: "Within a society, that of democratic Athens, in which silent seclusion is the condition imposed on women in real life, it is not surprising that women are the experts at conniving silences also on the stage. By representing women who act through secret networks, the tragedians point to the dangers that supposedly lurk behind women's confinement and exclusion from the spheres of public speech . . . they imagine women exchanging confidences that remain dangerously silent for them" (*SL*, 256).

Like the stillest hour, which threatens at any moment to erupt in violent outbreaks, the silence of women contains within it an unpredictable eruptive force. Everything that is contained in the silence most feared by the Greeks is transposed in a great dramatic gesture upon the *chōral* vessel of the woman. The woman is an uncanny figure of silence in the deepest sense of uncanniness as putting oneself out of one's place: the Greek man, and no less the tragic author, does not know where he stands in relation to this silence, nor in relation to its potential to erupt. The man—who if he is a man at all knows when to speak and when to keep silent—has no access to this silence; he can only await its eruption with his own quiet reserve in his sovereignty both hopelessly feeble and boundlessly forceful.

Through the murder of her own children, Medea has brought attention to herself; she has made herself be remembered. Thus, her greatest crime might have been to live in a way that prevented her from being forgotten. It is perhaps for this reason that she must, as Zeitlin shows, disappear at the end of the play in order to affirm that she is not of this world (Zeitlin 1996, 348). As a wanderer on this earth, Medea is above all *atopos* (*SL*, 30–31). Through her defiant speech and no less defiant act, she has disturbed her proper place. She can only be granted a place by not having a place among the human order because she has lived in a way that she will be remembered. She will be remembered, but how will her deed be read? What registers of comprehensibility offer themselves for interpreting her deed? And what can we learn about silence from her incomprehensibility?

Loraux asks precisely how a feminine deed is to be read if feminine nature is marked by such irreducible contradictions. What, in short, can be attributed to the actions of women if they are thought to be beyond even their own control? Loraux offers the following analysis: "Feminine nature is generally marked by excess/lack and is sometimes contained to the extent dictated by the norm, but every *ergon gunaikōn* [womanly action] unfailingly refers to it. Where the deeds of women are concerned, the feminine seems to be a stronger explanatory principle than the category of action" (Loraux 1995, 247). Here the *chōral* element reveals itself in—precisely— its *impenetrability* to male logic. The interpretation always skews toward indexing the deed to the contradictory nature of the feminine. This impenetrability of the deed to logic is central to Gayatri Chakravorty Spivak's groundbreaking essay on the legibility and interpretability of a deed by a woman, "Can the Subaltern Speak?" (Spivak 1988).

Though often misunderstood as a project of recovering lost voices, Spivak in fact speaks against the recovery of lost or unheard voices, for she regards such a recovery not as a matter of cultivating a mere sensitivity to the need for their recovery, but of something perhaps impossible to address: *listening to*, not merely *hearing*, subaltern voices is for Spivak much more akin to a constant process of auto-deconstruction through questioning categorical impositions than it is just a mere matter of recovering lost historical sources by hearing them speak. Such an attempt at listening is also, despite the most vigilant rigor of the listener—a listener who is at all times a translator, even within the same language—both the only possibility for survival of subaltern voices and the agent of their destruction. This possibility of destruction becomes all the more tenuous when the object under analysis is silence. If silence can only be approached through the type of *logos* that first of all makes silence possible, and if such speech must always be aware of the degree of precision appropriate to the matter at hand, the measure of speech surrounding this *chōral* figure must be examined further.

Silenced Voices

While silence for men is decisively associated with the possibility of memory, the story is much different for women. Silence in its various forms carries women off into oblivion in the irreducibly duplicitous meaning of forgetting. After all, the fate of women is a double forgetting: a forgetting that is not even mentioned as forgotten. In contrast to the visible silence of men, the silence of women occurs within a register of invisibility. If Greek tragedy repeatedly dramatizes the overly silent silence of women, or its opposite, the tragic outburst, rendering women visible and audible on stage, and if it does so by speaking about women interminably, this is done because, as Loraux argues, "the tragic genre dramatizes the essential exclusions the city has instituted for the citizens' use" (Loraux 1998, 10). Beyond this dramatic superabundance of silence lies the figure of the *chōra*:

a silence that is always appropriated yet beyond appropriation, always in place yet never quite there, always definable yet beyond any delineating definition. This is a figure that is always silent, yet never not speaking in whispers, or hushed, calm tones that allow one, like Medea, to steal into places in cunning trickery. The role of the feminine voice is to keep silent in the service of forgetting, which ought to be understood, not merely as a form of oblivion, but also as a site of uncanniness.

In his reading of Plato's "Myth of Er," Heidegger offers some illuminating details about this site of forgetting: "The field of concealment is opposed to all *phusis. Lēthē* does not admit any *phuein*, any emerging and coming forth. . . . The place of *lēthē* is that 'where' in which the uncanny dwells in a peculiar exclusivity. The field of *lēthē* is, in a preeminent sense, 'demonic' " (*GA* 54, 176/118–19). It is possible to extrapolate from Heidegger's analysis in order to analyze the forgetting (*lēthē*) surrounding women: this oblivion is not so much a way of treating women, but significantly involves the being of women—with being understood here in the fullest Heideggerian sense.[28] The being of women is uncanny, and the best women can do is keep silent, even if that silence only attenuates their uncanniness. The deed of their silence, and likewise their speech act is, after all, indexed first and foremost to this monstrous being.

Ancient Greek women were expected not only to live silently but in such a way that nothing would be said of them after they had died. In contrast, a virtuous man in classical Athens was accorded an outpouring of public eulogies when he died: "For in none of man's actions is there so much certainty as in his virtuous activities (which are more enduring than even scientific knowledge, and the most honorable of these are the most enduring because those who are blessed live according to them most of all and most continuously; for this seems to be the reason why we do not forget them" (*NE* 1100b13–17).[29]

Monimos, the term that Aristotle uses to describe these enduring virtuous deeds carries a range of meanings, such as being steady, stable, steadfast, having a fixed abode, and being in one's place, applying variously to "fixed stars" and "wine which will keep" (Liddell and Scott 1989, 451). Since he remains in his place after death, the virtuous man does not slip into oblivion even if he dies as reticently as Socrates in the *Phaedo* (Plato 1998, 117e). In contrast, a woman can hope at best for the placelessness of oblivion. If she has lived her life in the most fitting way possible, it will not even be mentioned that she is being forgotten. Silenced in life, she will likewise be silenced in death.

Beyond the ontological implications of this silence, the twofold forgetting that marked the being of women raises more concrete questions
about the possibility of at all meaningfully discussing this silenced silence.
That the forgottenness of women was itself also supposed to be forgotten leaves the state of the source material available for an investigation
into the silence and voice of women in Greek society in a difficult position, Sappho, a unique female authorial voice, notwithstanding (see, e.g.,
Lardinois 2001). "Silent objects in most ancient sources, [women] often
understandably become silent objects in scholarship, which focuses on
male representations of and attitudes toward the female" (Maurizio 2001,
38). If women always already speak from the position of an eternally
deceptive, conniving, and silent figure, then gaining a voice as a woman
requires something much more profound than seizing the reins of sovereign subjectivity, or merely claiming a space for speech as witnessed in
Aristophanes's comedies. What is required is something distinct from the
capacity to simply be able to make utterances, but instead involves the
type of rigorous deconstruction of our position as listeners theorized by
Spivak. In order to even begin to identify the spaces of silence, one must
first be aware of the operation of silencing.

Conclusion: Beyond the Limits of the Measure

Irrespective of whatever sanctioned forms of speech were granted to
Greek women both in public and in private, they were decisively associated
with and relegated to silence. The silence of ancient Greek women is not
only different from the silence of men, it is decidedly other.

In his recovery of a Greek conception of silence, Heidegger's deafness to
the silence of women does not mean that he cannot contribute anything to
an analysis of this silence—indeed, he has much to offer for such an analysis.
It is essential here to refer to Derrida's seminal essay on Heidegger and sexual
difference (Derrida 2007b). Instead of simply observing that Heidegger
overlooks the silence of Greek women, it is also possible to interrogate why
this oversight resulted from deeper, unquestioned investments anchoring
his philosophy. Precisely because Heidegger was so deeply attuned to the
silences of Greek male self-mastery, he was also deeply invested in perpetuating its exclusions. In other words, Heidegger's performances of silence are
always grounded upon a fundamental act of silencing. This obviously has
profound political consequences for Heidegger's thinking.

If, as Heidegger contends, being for the Greeks first and foremost meant being-in-the-polis, then it is worth noting the following silence in Heidegger's description of the polis from his 1935 *Introduction to Metaphysics* in order to interrogate it with regard to both what it shows and what it occludes: "One translates *polis* as state and city-state; this does not capture the entire sense. Rather, *polis* is the name for the site, the Here, within which and as which Being-here is historically. The *polis* is the site of history, the Here *in* which, *out of* which and *for* which history happens. To this site of history belong the gods, the temples, the priests, the celebration, the games, the thinkers, the ruler, the council of elders, the assembly of the people, the armed forces, and the ships."[30] What is the place of the women in this being-with among all of the men and implements of war Heidegger enumerates? If women are not among the visible aspects worth enumerating in the city, then this is because they are, in a very fundamental sense, not in the city. They are not in the city, but that does not automatically mean to say that they are outside of it, and the difference between these two possibilities is not nothing. What lies in that difference is *atopos*.

This state of being *atopos* is perhaps best understood through an analogy with another privative term analyzed by Heidegger in his "Parmenides" lecture course: *apolis*.[31] Heidegger defines *apolis* not as being fully outside or bereft of a polis, but as a way of being in the polis that is out of joint with the being of the polis. Being *a-polis* thus indicates the seemingly paradoxical state of both having and not having a polis, of being deprived of a polis through one's very form of having a polis. This strange dual state not only describes the position of women in the polis, but also illuminates their manner of possessing *logos*. Women possess *logos* in a manner of not-having that is not a full privation, for their very having is a not-having—a relationship best described as steretic. And if what it means to be Greek is significantly related to one's capacity to speak Greek, then the state of women being *alogos* is tantamount to being *atopos*. In her silence, woman is out of place, though not merely by accident, but by virtue of her essence. As a figure of the *chōra*, woman is *atopos*. She is at once more Greek than the other "Others," namely, barbarians and slaves, but she is also less Greek by virtue of always potentially being *alogos* in an entirely unpredictable fashion.

This analysis of Heidegger does not merely involve opening up his closure, but tracing its contours and examining it as a structural blind spot in Heidegger's work. This can only be done by sketching the contours of the terrain within the closure, while also sketching the limits that establish its outside. This is not so much a matter of surveying historical silences, but of *surveying* silence, of traversing a landscape of texts. It goes without saying, yet always bears repeating, that Heidegger's Greek silence is always the silence of a specific elite class of men. Precisely because (and not despite) he was such an attuned listener to the silence of male self-mastery, Heidegger overlooks many forms of silencing and is blissfully blind to the ways in which Greek women were forced to be silent, but also may have chosen to keep silent.[32] My intent is to trace the extent to which he stands firmly outside of a feminist perspective and not to translate him into such a perspective.[33] That Heidegger did not and most likely could not have posed the question of the silence of women represents a moment of prior commitment in his thinking, which must be rigorously deconstructed. It is, to use his own term, an "unrecognized incapacity to decide" (*GA 96*, 174/237). The incapacity to decide is a common term throughout the manuscripts of the 1930s and is closely related to Heidegger's notion of enframing. Enframing imposes an ontological structure upon the world and makes it impossible to pose the question of being and hence to decide the decisive questions of philosophy. Heidegger's philosophy of language is enframed within the classic structure of philosophy as a cultivation of male self-mastery.

Speech and silence cannot simply be read as in contrast to each other; they are always inevitably intertwined. For the ancient Greeks, the masculine stood for the silence brought to bear through the proper measure of the word, which has been the enabling force behind philosophy since its Greek inception, endowing it with its potency. Philosophy has become philosophy by vesting itself with a silence, but equally so with the exclusions wrought by that silence. The feminine, on the other hand, represents the always impossible attempt to forcefully sunder silence from the word. Indeed, the feminine is the site of this violent sundering. Yet if Medea represents the terror associated with silence as trickery, it is worth raising the following question by way of pointing to future directions for the analysis: Does this secretive silence become a virtue with the development of the isolated subject in post-Cartesian philosophy? Would a more complete genealogy of silence find further layers to unearth in the early modern period (see, e.g., Luckyj 2002, 13–41)?

Both capitulating to an aporia of wordlessness and clinging to myths of the potential transparency of speech are equally impossible. Both options—valorizing either silence or representational schemes—do little more than reinscribe the violent founding linguistic gestures of philosophy as phallologocentrism. As the bearer of a philosophical discourse predicated upon a foundational act of violence, it is perhaps not surprising that Heidegger would utilize his philosophy to perpetuate further acts of violence. The more important question is the extent to which this violence is inscribed at the very core of the philosophical endeavor. "Making itself understandable is suicide for philosophy," Heidegger blithely declared as he sought to withdraw from the public sphere (*GA* 65, 435/344). Yet having the power to renounce comprehension and being structurally excluded from comprehension, or from what Hegel would call recognition, are separated by a world of difference. Heidegger's withdrawal is always empowered by this difference. Heidegger's gesture of self-silencing is not only peculiarly masculine, but also classically so. Yet it also announces a false heroics in Heidegger's thinking, for he was always far more comprehensible than he portrayed himself to be. Most important, his affinities were comprehensible, and perhaps nowhere more so than in his attempt in the early 1930s to reinvent himself as a *völkisch* hero of the soil.

7 Land and *Volk*: The Silent Place of the *Black Notebooks*

At the apex of his political career in the summer and winter semesters of 1933–34, Heidegger held two wide-ranging lecture courses under the titles "Basic Questions of Philosophy" and "On the Essence of Truth." The first course is especially conspicuous because of its brevity, accounting for less than one-half to one-third of the length of the printed manuscript of his typical lecture courses.[1] As the editor of the manuscript of the lecture notes, this is partly due to the fact that Heidegger cancelled a number of sessions of the weekly two-hour lecture due to the "extraordinary and unaccustomed duties of the office of the rector" (*GA* 36–37, 299/225). Given the significant burdens placed on his time by the immense administrative task of "Aryanizing" the university and the busy travel schedule he took on in his attempt to position himself in the intellectual vanguard of National Socialism, the truncated length of the lecture course is not surprising. It is also not surprising that in the following semester Heidegger broke with his traditional practice of fastidiously preparing a new lecture course each term and for the most part repeated the content of his winter semester 1931–32 lecture course also titled "The Essence of Truth: On Plato's Cave Allegory and Theaetetus." While much of the 1933–34 lecture course's analysis of Plato mirrors the original version, the latter version nonetheless differs with regard to one significant attribute, which is of particular interest for the topic of silence. Before working through his analysis of Plato's conception of truth in a manner consistent with the earlier version, Heidegger begins the course with an ontologically rich treatment of silence that is completely absent from the earlier version and is seemingly unrelated to the reading of Plato.

Although silence emerges in many places in Heidegger's teaching and writing, this treatment of silence in a seventeen-page section entitled "On Truth and Language" is striking, not only because of its peculiar timing, but also because it ranks as perhaps the most ontologically complex thematic analysis of silence in Heidegger's oeuvre (ibid., 100–116/80–91). It is an especially significant moment in Heidegger's sigetics because, in these few pages, Heidegger overtly announces a reversal of the ontology of silence presented in *Being and Time* and now expressly declares, in his own italics, that the *"capacity for silence is the origin and ground of language"* (ibid., 107/84). With this claim, Heidegger assigns a central role in his thinking to what he deems the capacity for silence. This is a seminal moment in the development and performance of Heidegger's sigetic philosophy, because at the very moment when his public voice as a spokesman for National Socialist university politics was most vocal, that is, at the very moment when he seemed to be least capable of silence, Heidegger chose publicly to rethink the nature of silence. It is illuminating to juxtapose this lecture with the circular Heidegger distributed to the students of Freiburg University at the beginning of the winter semester, declaring in its opening lines that "the National Socialist revolution is bringing a complete upheaval of our German existence," and that "the Führer is the sole future law and reality of the Germans" (*GA* 16, 184–85).[2] Why would Heidegger choose this moment as the appropriate one in which to discuss "the different manners of keeping silent, the multiplicity of its causes and grounds, and . . . the different levels and depths of reticence" (*GA* 36–37, 110/87)? Why, in effect, would he choose to announce that—perhaps—there is not only much that he is not saying, but there are also many ways in which he is not saying it?

Heidegger announces this significant reversal in his philosophy of silence in the initial stages of a new sigetic project, the *Black Notebooks*, whose first volume proclaims: "Yet 'say' it to yourself daily in your taciturnity: be silent about bearing silence" (*GA* 94, 10/8). He intends, he says, to "write out of a great reticence" (ibid., 28/22), implying both a silence about silence and a silence that emerges out of silence. Expressed through steretic non-saying, this taciturn or reticent comportment is produced through the capacity for silence. However, in Heidegger's steretic logic, a space of speech is needed to preserve it as silence. He deals out his speech in small doses to produce the handiwork of thinking, the way a doctor might deal out doses of healing-destructive medicine.

The handiwork of the *Black Notebooks* involves the practice of a "silence which actively keeps silent about itself" (*GA* 97, 484). This silence about silence is derived from Greek male self-mastery and Aristotelian production (*poiēsis*). It is derived only from the Greeks, however, given the failure to overcome the conceptual confines of modern metaphysics, which seeks to reduce everything to presence and absence. Hence the preservation of the place of silence for sigetic practice involves an operation of "silencing over the spoken word of metaphysics" (ibid.) "Silencing over" the language of metaphysics does not mean avoiding it. Much to the contrary, it means employing the language of metaphysics and its machinations intentionally as part of a play with concealment and unconcealment in order to preserve the space of sigetic practice. In other words, the politics of silence practiced in the *Black Notebooks* is not contrary to the public voice of the rector of Freiburg University as a spokesman for National Socialism. That public voice, and all of the snares of the "dictator" of the public realm, enable what Heidegger calls the "freedom" of the handiwork of thinking (ibid., 54). In other words, the public "mask" of Rector Heidegger as the voice of "vulgar National Socialism" enables his deeply antisemitic and ferociously nationalistic private voice espousing "spiritual National Socialism" and a deeply *völkisch* agenda.[3] One can never simply withdraw from the public realm and its dictatorial power, for it is an ontological necessity. Consequently, according to Heidegger's logic, the greatest care for silence requires the greatest violence against language and even—in one of Heidegger's most violent formulations—a "*monstrous rape of the accomplishment* of language" (*GA* 36–37, 104/82).

This inverted relation is rooted in Heidegger's commitment to keeping most silent about what is most essential to him, and "silencing over" preserves his most essential space of sigetic practice in what he refers to as "sites of silence" (*GA* 96, 171/135). These sites of silence are preserved for and by the "concealed Germans" whose "history possesses a power of reticence through which a different form of communication is grounded" (ibid., 31/25). According to Heidegger, these hidden Germans will form a "race of the concealed guardians of stillness" (*GA* 95, 27/21). This is the *völkisch* place of the *Black Notebooks* in a twofold sense of the term "place," both as the soil from which sigetic thinking emerges and as the place of the *Black Notebooks* in Heidegger's thinking.

If the *Black Notebooks* are a work of *völkisch* mythology, Heidegger's phenomenological practice, sigetic philosophy of language, publications, private manuscripts, lecture courses, and the rectorate were all interdependent. In an attempt to "reconnect the most secret ethnic mission of the Germans with the first great beginning" (*GA* 94, 109/80), Heidegger embedded his politics in his philosophy. This raises perhaps the most pressing question about Heidegger's silence: if he cultivated an ethics of silence as a way of concealing this most secret mission, then why did he regard the arrival of National Socialism as allowing for this silence to emerge most fully?

The *Black Notebooks* provide answers to this question because of how they help us understand Heidegger's distinction between so-called spiritual and vulgar National Socialism.[4] What the *Black Notebooks* reveal is that, while Heidegger aligned himself publicly with particular aspects of so-called vulgar National Socialism, including Hitler, he does so in the name of preserving a more "essential" relationship to what he believes Hitler's revolution would enable, namely, an awakening of the Greek-German essence. Heidegger states this politics of strategic alliance explicitly in 1946: "The genuine error of the '1933 rectorate' was not so much that I, like other clever people, did not recognize 'Hitler' in his 'essence,' and that I did not stand alongside them grumbling in the aftermath, in the domain of the lack of will—that is, in the domain of the willing supporters. Rather, the error was that I thought that now would be the time for the [German] people to become inceptive, that is, historical, not with Hitler, but with the awakening of the people to its occidental destiny" (*GA* 97, 98).

Hitler, in other words, was a means to an end; he was a suitable leader, though not essential to the "inner truth and greatness" of the movement. The true project of National Socialism would be the awakening of the German people in the return to its essence and its place through thinking, and this "thinking must necessarily be a fateful dwelling within a singular homeland and a single people" (ibid., 60). Universities would play an essential role in this awakening, not because of their science or academic endeavors, but because they would be places where the likes of Nietzsche, Leibniz, Hölderlin, and Kant could be read again, despite "the German susceptibility to seduction by a foreign entity" (ibid., 47). In 1934, in a wide-ranging lecture course on the philosophy of language, Heidegger makes this link clear to his students, noting a desire "to restructure the university, apparently by moving it into an Allemanic space." But he goes on to express his skepticism about whether the proper groundwork for this transformation has been done, for "just because one speaks of the university's landscape does not mean that the university will change." Indeed, from Heidegger's perspective, this change is unlikely to occur, for "not even 2 percent of the teachers and students speak and understand the language of this landscape" (*GA* 38, 73–74/64). For Heidegger, German thinking has lost its place and can only get back to it through a fundamental attunement rooted in the capacity for silence. Countering the likes of Darré, Kolbenheyer, Grimm, Clauss, and—above all—Alfred Rosenberg, Heidegger sought to portray himself as the philosopher who would translate the voice of the land. Many of Heidegger's academic colleagues were urban bourgeois, and he sought to claim an authenticity in contrast to them based on his humble rural roots.[5]

This place of the Germans and the role of German thinking within it are both so essential to Heidegger that in 1946 he posed this question about the nature of "guilt" in an entry on "justice" (Heidegger's scare quotes): "And if it is 'guilt' we are talking about—is there no 'guilt' when one even today, on his 300th birthday, forces *Leibniz* into oblivion as if nothing had happened there?" (*GA*, 129). Remarks such as these might be brushed aside as the meaningless ramblings of a resentful ex-Nazi if they were not buttressed by a consistent philosophical structure sustained over decades. That thinking is captured by Heidegger's manner of bridging the gap between the two different forms of National Socialism through a peculiar ethical commitment regarding the nature of language as primordially contaminated, or as always already fallen. For Heidegger, the purest vision of National Socialism could only be preserved in the greatest silence, by the greatest din, or the greatest "desolation" (*GA*, 83). He states this in the fourth volume of the *Black Notebooks*: "Nonetheless the *hidden constancy of the workshop* of thinking is not affected by all of this ruination and noise—it is more likely, perhaps, that everything is protected in stillness for a considerable duration" (ibid., 72). What Heidegger—along with the mythical hidden Germans—preserved in silence amid "ruination and noise," that is, amid war and genocide, was his vision of spiritual National Socialism, even while he proffered brutal real-world National Socialism in texts such as the rectorial address and as a university administrator. "The time of the Germans has not yet expired," he writes in 1942. "But the shape of their future history lies in concealment" (ibid., 16). Silence was the medium of this concealment, and it echoed Heidegger's hope for National Socialism expressed in 1933, quoted in chapter 1 above: "*National Socialism* is a genuinely burgeoning power only if it still, behind all of its action and talk, has something to keep silent about—and if it operates with a firm deviousness aimed at future impact" (*GA* 94, 114/84).

Heidegger's sigetics is not simply concerned with some sort of abstract, free-floating, ahistorical speaking of being through a timeless practice of silence. Rather, it is bound to a particular place and a particular time, namely, the southwestern Swabian-Alemannic territory of his day.[6] Placing the *Black Notebooks* in this way serves to underscore the assertion that Heidegger's sigetic practice in its most essential form is not just a general cultivation of silence for the sake of silence, nor can this sigetic practice be transformed and universalized into a general practice of silence. This, I fear, is what happens when Heidegger is valorized as a thinker of silence and letting be. Like many strands of *völkisch* thinking, Heidegger's sigetics is bound to its land, its people, and its history. Sigetics is not simply a general practice of unsayability or a discipline of reticence. After all, as the analysis of the silence of Greek male self-mastery has showed, philosophical silence has never simply been a general cultivation of tact. Applying Heidegger's own principle, the philosopher—more than anyone—must have something to say. Hence there are a particular set of concrete matters that Heidegger chooses to be silent about, and the *Black Notebooks* reveal what these are. In other words, the very things that Heidegger's defenders may conveniently want to be rid of—those pesky "biographical" elements that Heidegger himself conveniently derided—are likewise the very things that are most essential to his thinking, and hence operate most silently within it.

The Capacity for Silence

Analyzing silence in his 1933–34 winter semester lecture course as rector of Freiburg University, Heidegger introduced a new, fundamental term to his thinking: the capacity for silence (*das Schweigenkönnen*), alongside a number of fundamental shifts in his philosophy of language, in a section entitled "The Ability to Keep Silent as the Origin and Ground of Language." In those brief pages, he seeks first to describe the sigetic nature of the capacity for silence by demonstrating how that capacity constitutes the origins of language, and by hinting at the kind of language that can emerge from a space of silence.

Heidegger begins to analyze the claim that silence grounds language in the familiar Aristotelian fashion by acknowledging the circularity of the process, for "we are supposed to speak about keeping silent." Yet even as he poses this question, he draws back, asking instead what it would mean not to speak about keeping silent. What form of silence would it presuppose if one were to preserve silence in a wordless reverence? Is it not possible that "one could sell oneself short all too cheaply and relegate keeping silent, as a dark 'mystical' thing, to the so-called emotional premonition and intimation of its essence" (*GA* 36–37, 107/85)? Hence, Heidegger concludes, we will speak about silence but not believe that "with the help of a 'definition' we have come to grips with keeping silent." Silence can be defined and can be rendered legible to a certain degree through speech. This speech, moreover, is not contrary to silence, even if it is the interruption of silence. At this point Heidegger turns to a question that is of particular importance to him from the late 1920s on: the status of language in distinguishing the human being from other animals. Whereas he distinguishes in *The Fundamental Concepts of Metaphysics* between the animal as poor in world and the human as world-forming, here he draws the distinction based on the animal's incapacity for silence.[7]

At first Heidegger seems to suggest that, if the animal does not have to or simply cannot speak, and if it is constantly silent, it must be "prepared for and capable of speaking to a much a higher degree, because it can keep silent more—indeed, constantly" (*GA* 36–37, 107/85). But something even more fundamental distinguishes the human from the animal, namely, that, even though silence is the origin and ground of language, animals have no capacity to speak. Humans, those creatures who have a deficient capacity for silence because they do in fact speak, and do so constantly and resoundingly, are the only creatures able to keep silent as a capacity for silence. Hence, Heidegger concludes: "Human language arises from the inability to keep silent, and consequently from a lack of constraint. The *miracle* of language is therefore based on a *failure*" (ibid., 108/85). According to Heidegger, animals are incapable of this failure.

The rationale of this strange "miracle" is found in a sentence quoted repeatedly in this book: "Only what can speak can be silent" (*GA* 19, 15/11). The capacity for silence thus emerges as a complex, manifold concept along the distinction between muteness and silence. On the one hand, the capacity for silence can be meaningfully applied to analyze particular instances of silence. This does mean that every act of silence is equal, however, for "a mute is unable to keep silent, even though he says nothing" (*GA* 36–37, 86/109). Nonvocalization is insufficient to determine the distinction between muteness and the capacity for silence. Moreover, something else must be known, namely, whether or not the speaker is empowered to choose silence. The secret, spiritual Germans come into their own as the people empowered to choose silence. The capacity for silence as an act or deed requires this prior sanctioning of the possibility of choosing silence as an arrangement, attunement, or structure that distinguishes it from muteness. "Keeping silent is rather, at the very least, the not-talking of someone who can talk. As we said before, it is a definite, exceptional way of being able to talk" (ibid., 109/86). In the fourth volume of the *Black Notebooks,* Heidegger states this even more succinctly: "The reticent one is talkative" (*GA* 97, 484).

The *Black Notebooks* preserve Heidegger's peculiar performance of this form of not-talking as an exceptional way of being able to talk. They are the performance of a willfully chosen silence whose medium is the word. Layered over with manifold registers of silence, they are perhaps most important, not for what they do say, but for what they do not say and the manner in which they do not say it. Moreover, they fill a gap in Heidegger's work, which he discusses in his critique of his treatment of silence in *Being and Time*, where he states that he "did not see what really has to follow from this starting point: keeping silent is not just an ultimate possibility of discourse, but discourse and language arise from keeping silent" (*GA* 36–37, 110/86). This observation is significant for a number of reasons. Beyond announcing a decisive reversal of a critical element of his own conception of language in *Being and Time*, it also provides significant hints about how silence operates in Heidegger's work. If "discourse and language arise from keeping silent," and keeping silent requires one to have something to say, this means that speech and silence are co-constitutive. Yet what is perhaps most telling about this passage is Heidegger's reticence about silence expressed through his play with concealment. Although he announces that he has "gone back over" and "worked through" the "different manners of keeping silent, the multiplicity of its causes and grounds," he will not rehearse these manifold registers of silence at the moment. Instead, he will only communicate as much as "is needed for the advancement of our questioning." The *Black Notebooks* are not only the continuation of that questioning, they also provide the space for the performance of the very silence that is being questioned. They are the extended performance of a "silence that actively keeps silent about itself" (*GA* 97, 484). This does not make them unique, for almost any text in the Heideggerian oeuvre, especially the event manuscripts from the 1930s, applies some degree of this sigetic principle. The *Black Notebooks* constitute the most intense application of this principle, and we should not seek to banish them from a philosophical consideration of Heidegger's work simply because of their abhorrent politics—even if doing so is a seemingly justifiable act of professional self-preservation. Scholars have long heralded the path of Heidegger's thinking, the movement inherent to it, and the pleasures of a thinking that is, in its words, under way. One cannot simply seek to back out from this path if it ends up in a place one is no longer comfortable with.

Coincidentally enough, Heidegger regarded himself as living in the essential landscape of thinking, that is, in a particularly propitious space for the production of silence. It is a matter of little importance to decide whether this landscape brought thinking forth within him, like Plato's Ion, connected to the gods through a chain of inspiration, or whether Heidegger, as a thinker, found his way to this landscape. Regardless of the nature of the cause-effect relationship, the landscape of the Black Forest enables and produces the "highest form of saying," endowing the rare listening ear with the capacity for silence. Heidegger's *völkisch* ontology of language involves vesting oneself with this silence as an endowment bestowed upon only a select few listeners who possess a particular power of attunement that emerges from the soil and conditions of "world-wide historical destiny of Germanity" (ibid.). If the harmonious silence of ancient Greek men emerged out of an attunement to *logos*, in Heidegger's sigetics, landscape replaces the role of *logos*, or at least supplements it. This landscape is not nature in general, but the particular landscape of a particular people—in this case the landscape and people of the Black Forest.

Remaining in the Provinces

Although the black of the *Black Notebooks* is not the black of the Black Forest, the reader may be forgiven for associating the two. Given the interdependence of place, landscape, *Volk*, and language, the complexities of Heidegger's politics of silence are perhaps best captured in a text about the place and rootedness of Heidegger's thinking: the 1933 text published under the title "Creative Landscape: Why Do I Stay in the Provinces?" This brief text is significant, not only for the manifold senses of silence that Heidegger skillfully manipulates within the space of a few pages, but also because it was written at a time when Heidegger had already developed a highly refined attunement to the power of silence.

For the moment I will set aside any debate about the historical veracity of the incident Heidegger narrates in "Creative Landscape," for the question has been dealt with capably elsewhere (e.g., Safranski 1998, 210–90; Farías 1991, 162–68; Faye 2009, 46–49).[8] More important than the veracity of these events is the role of the text in Heidegger's cultivation of his public persona. The text ostensibly serves as Heidegger's justification for turning down a second call to a university chair in Berlin University in 1933, after an initial call in 1930. Heidegger's biographers have carefully detailed the philosopher's flirtations with various posts in Berlin and Munich, including his behind-the-scenes politicking for the leadership of an ideological training academy for university instructors (*Dozentenakademie*) intended to mold the spirit of National Socialist academics as the capstone of their *Habilitation* (the German second doctorate). Opinions about Heidegger in Berlin and throughout the different levels of the National Socialist administration of cultural politics varied, ranging from those of staunch defenders such as Minister of Science, Education, and National Culture Bernhard Rust to charges of mental illness and questions about his dedication to Nazi ideology. His work was being described disparagingly in unsolicited attacks sent to Rust, as "Talmudic-Kabbalist" in nature and suspiciously popular among "Jews, half-Jews and representatives of a neo-scholastic, distinctly Catholic worldview."[9] Once again, such historical questions are not of primary interest for us now, but suffice it to note that, upon turning down the initial 1930 offer, on account of not feeling "sufficiently equipped" for the job, Heidegger did not, as Rüdiger Safranski writes, "make any triumphant programmatic 'declaration in favor of the province'" (Safranski 1998, 211). However, Heidegger's response to the 1933 call involves precisely such a declaration of the value of provincial life, which he portrays first and foremost as a silent life, and one that permitted his "taking shelter in the bustle of calculation" (*GA* 97, 17).

Before we broach "Creative Landscape," it is essential to take note of the way Heidegger carefully disseminated the text as a radio lecture. As the editorial notes on it report, it was broadcast on the radio in Berlin, then twice more on the Freiburger Sender and Südfunk radio stations, and subsequently published in the culture section of *Der Alemanne*, the National Socialist political propaganda organ of Upper Baden, in 1934 (*GA* 13, 246). In it, Heidegger describes his "work-world," his hut, and the people surrounding it, high in the Black Forest. This "creative landscape," with its soaring hawks, sloping meadows, and splendid skies, is not a landscape that Heidegger observes likes some passing tourist, but one that he "experiences in its hourly changes, day and night, in the great comings and goings of the seasons" (CL, 9/27).

Given Heidegger's dissemination of the text through official party organs, it is perhaps not surprising that "Creative Landscape" is one of
Heidegger's most overtly *völkisch* texts. Whether or not there was direct
influence, it echoes a number of themes from the chapter "Soul and
Landscape: Northern and Mediterranean Land" in Ludwig Ferdinand
Clauss's *Die nordische Seele* (The Nordic Soul) and from Walther Darré's
musings on the "creative" nature of the "Nordic race" (Clauss 1940,
19–25; Darré 1940, 277–308). Darré depicts the German peasantry as
the most noble class of the Nordic race and a model for reeducating the
"big-city mind" (Darré 1940, 282). Clauss is more interested in how the
Nordic soul has been formed by the landscape, which "is not something
the soul comes upon, something finished, rather, it is something the soul
forms by means of the racially determined gesture of its vision" (Clauss
1940, 19). The landscape, in other words, is not simply something that is
there, but instead something created through being looked upon by those
with the proper vision. "All vision out into the world," Clauss writes,
"is creative" (ibid., 106).[10] In this vision the Nordic soul "infuses" the
material of the terrain with its imprint, "but not every terrain offers the
same possibilities" (ibid., 19). The Nordic race, with the characteristic
distance, reticence, and measure that Clauss attributes to it, arises through
a unique interaction between racial and environmental traits. While
Heidegger strips this narrative of its direct racial component in this particular text, his pastoral scene relies upon and gestures toward the more
overtly racist depictions of the German peasantry and landscape. Moreover, the goal of the text is for him to announce his place as a thinker
within a political movement deeply skeptical of the purportedly idle
activities of professional philosophers. If Darré describes the nature of the
peasant as implicitly philosophical, Heidegger tries to position himself
as the philosophical translator of the peasant-philosopher. It is for this
reason that Heidegger specifically places, not only himself as a person,
but also his philosophical work in the landscape, in contrast to those
who, as he remarks, "engage in idle talk about the '*Volk*' in a 'pseudo-
philosophy' that has suddenly become overzealously '*völkisch*'" (*GA* 94,
291/213). Much like Heidegger's critique of Erwin Guido Kolbenheyer,
remarks like this should not be regarded as antagonistic to the *völkisch*
movement, but instead as part of Heidegger's political strategy to put
himself at the vanguard of the movement.

Creative Landscape

In "Creative Landscape," Heidegger seeks to portray his philosophical work, not as a labor that breaks into this creative landscape, but as a work that comes to be in and through a harmony with the movements of the landscape. Of the act of writing, he says that the "struggle to mold something into language is like the resistance of the towering firs against the storm" (CL, 10/28). Such striving for expression through the "handicraft of writing" is not foreign to the peasant world, quietly moving outside the hut of this solitary thinker, for it takes place "right in the midst of the peasants' work" (LH, 344/262; CL, 10/28). And Heidegger himself, too, belongs right in the midst of this work. He is perfectly in sync with the rhythms of the peasants' daily toil, for his work is "*of the same sort*" (CL, 10/28). These rhythms are illustrated in Heidegger's essay "The Origin of the Work of Art" in the example of the peasant woman's shoes, which "vibrate with the silent call of the earth, its silent gift of the ripening grain, its unexplained self-refusal in the wintry field" (Heidegger 1994b, 19/14). In the description of the work-world, it is Heidegger's words, and not the shoes, that yield to the silent call of the earth, these words bending gently in response to it.

These themes of rhythmicity, synchronization, and silence evoke a proximity "rooted in the immediate belonging together with the farmers" (CL, 10/28). This immediacy, moreover, is portrayed as an immediacy of silence. Indeed, as Heidegger tells us, during breaks from his work—work that as of late forces him to travel so much and participate in so much of the endless chatter of "conferences, lecture trips, committee meetings and my teaching work down here in Freiburg"—he sits with the peasants in the house of one of his neighbors (ibid., 11/28). They sit either around the fire or the table, with Heidegger granted the seat of honor in this modest household: the crucifix corner. "*For the most part*," Heidegger writes laconically, "we do not speak" (ibid., 10/28). This is perhaps only fitting given his account of the silence of his forefathers: "My father was a quiet man. My grandfather was even quieter and a cobbler" (*GA* 97, 50). Perhaps Heidegger was trying to reverse this regression by being even quieter than his grandfather. In any case, the scene is one of silence, of what Derrida has rather critically referred to as the homosocial space of *Miteinanderschweigen*, being together in (masculine) silence (Derrida 1997, 49–74). "We smoke our pipes *in silence*," Heidegger writes. These themes seem to be

standard ones for this *völkisch* genre. In a work published by the winners
of the third annual vocational competition of German students published
in conjunction with Heinrich Himmler's Racial Heritage Foundation
(Anenerbe), the winning student team plays with a similar set of themes in
depicting the Alemannic peasants of the region. They describe a domestic
scene where it "sometimes become 'as quiet as a mouse.'" In this silence,
"the 80-year-old grandfather puffs a few more times on his pipe" before
beginning a story (Vohburger 1940, 60–61).[11] Notably, Heidegger does not
question this silence as a space of boredom, a deep-seated boredom perhaps
more acutely that of the women and children than that of the men. It is
worth contrasting Heidegger's depiction of the peasant silence with Herta
Müller's account of her childhood among the Swabian settlers in Romania:
"This isolated Banat-Swabian dump, a very remote village. Then there was
the infinitely cold silence in this village. Farmers really don't talk very much.
. . . The disdain for the city . . . it was unbearable" (Müller 2010, 19). What
was unbearable to Müller was the oppressive silence Heidegger valorizes
and was complicit in creating through the exclusions of this purportedly
harmonious gathering together in silence. We have seen how deeply these
exclusions are embedded in Heidegger's thinking about silence.

For the moment, however, let us stick to what Heidegger would like us
to see in this scene. In the immediacy of this proximity, gathered together
in the weariness of a day's work under the sign of God, the men sit silently,
smoking away their silence, the silence of the smoke twisting its way around
the cross above the head of the honored guest, this silence ringing out
against the silence of the unmentioned children squirming, fidgeting in
boredom, the silence—slightly broken—of the women shuffling. "Perhaps,"
Heidegger tells us, "a word falls" (CL, 10/28). This word is not spoken or
offered up. It does not cross someone's lips. It is not stated or announced.
It is not inserted or interjected. The word simply falls, as if no one in particular were responsible for its issuance. The word is about the world of
work. It reports on the goings-on: "that a marten broke into the hen-house
last night, that one of the cows will probably calve in the morning, that
someone's uncle suffered a stroke, that the weather will soon 'turn'" (ibid.).
Such are the words that fall in this space of masculine communal silence.
In his *völkisch* "classic" *Volk ohne Raum* (People without Space), Hans
Grimm describes a similar reticence in his own pastoral scenes: "Whoever
speaks in the village speaks mostly about farm labor and daily work and has
to hold his tongue a bit." In such a space, where "all have cattle and land

and know the necessities of the village and the valley," Grimm writes, "the chatty know-it-all is made contemptible" (Grimm 1932, 18–19). Given the peasant's proclivity for—in Darré's words—knowing how "to get the job done the right way," there is little need for excess verbiage in this space of belonging (Darré 1940, 283).

What is to be made of these strange reports that fall into this silent place, these strange rumors, these messages requiring no response, which, had they "fallen" among other people, a people itself fallen, would be relegated to the realm of pernicious idle talk? This silence, this immediacy out of which and into which these words of the peasants "fall," gains depth when read in its *völkisch* context. Notably, a word about the work of the philosopher does not fall into this space. We do not hear anything of Heidegger's work, nothing along the lines of: "One of my articles is going to come out in the local Nazi paper tomorrow." Or, "Let me tell you how I got all the Jews out of the university." There is no reciprocity of exchange in this common work-world where Heidegger carries out his handiwork of writing. Why is Heidegger silent about his work to these stolid peasants? The answer is as simple as Heidegger would have us believe the peasants themselves are: the peasants—much like the Greeks in prior chapters—do not need to hear about dwelling closer to being since they already do just that, and Heidegger's words could be nothing but a violent modification of what they already experience in and as their very being. These peasants, in short, dwell in silence. It is worth recalling Darré's conclusion at this point: "Genuine peasantry is therefore also always philosophically disposed and every peasant is by nature a philosopher" (ibid., 293). The peasants, who contain within themselves a characteristic silence, are impervious to idle talk; it is not that their words speak what is essential, but more so that what is essential emerges from their words. Here Heidegger indulges most overtly in the type of Germanic *völkisch* mythology that he usually reserves for the Greeks; here his affinities to a set of discourses openly proffered by the regime are laid bare. Here he once again echoes the work of Grimm. When an outsider seeks to inquire into the history of Grimm's stylized village in *Volk ohne Raum*, Grimm reminds his readers that "here there's nobody to spill the beans" (Grimm 1932, 25).

Meanwhile, in this calm world of "rootedness in the Alemannian-Swabian soil," a rumor is circulating, this time with its origins in the local newspaper (CL, 11/28). It seems that Heidegger has been called from the city, the city of "pleasure palaces," where "one can easily be as lonely as almost nowhere else" (ibid., 11–12/28–29). The city would perhaps be another "refuge for wenches and Jews," as Heidegger wrote to his brother in July 1933.[12] Heidegger has not only been called from this city, but called to the city. Once again, it must be reiterated that the actual veracity of this story is not of immediate interest for the analysis of the story's operation. We will treat the story for the moment as mythology, personal mythology, as the work of a public figure carefully crafting his image around a particular form of silence bound to the soil of southwest Germany. We need not treat the text as anything other than a refined piece of public relations, a contribution to the crafting of a persona, a philosophical "Checkers speech," in order to understand its operation.

A seventy-five-year-old farmer, an "old friend," we are told, has read about the call in the paper. He has heard the rumor. He knows that Berlin—that Berlin of Walter Benjamin's childhood, Bertolt Brecht's whores, and Alfred Döblin's (but also Hitler's) ruthless thugs—is calling, and the farmer finds it necessary to let a word fall about this. In Heidegger's laconic words, this old man "heard about the call from Berlin" (CL, 12/29). The German resonates with a sly ambiguity that opens up a double reading. *Ruf*, while on the one hand meaning "call," referring to the call a professor gets when being summoned to a university chair, also means "reputation." The friend, therefore, has read about the call to Berlin, but he has also read about the reputation of Berlin. And he has heard about them both from the newspaper. This friend knows what kind of place Berlin is, and there is little doubt that this *Berliner Ruf* is a bad thing. Berlin is the place of the "the city man, the ape of civilization" (*GA* 29–30, 7/5; cf. Derrida 2011, 96). Alfred Döblin portrays the world of the city man in *Berlin Alexanderplatz*, a work the Nazis disparagingly referred to as "Asphalt Literature" [Fishburn 2008, 44–48]). In a scene contrasting with that of Heidegger silently smoking his pipe in the crucifix corner, Döblin depicts how his protagonist Franz Biberkopf sits down to smoke and drink with his cronies, all fellow small-time criminals, at a late-night Berlin establishment: "When Franz came in, there was a big row going on and a lot of loud talk and swearing. . . . When lovely eyes begin to wink, when full glasses gleam and clink, there comes once more, once more, the call to drink" (Döblin 2004, 64).

The call to drink again and again in this place without limit, this place of loud talk and swearing, in this place of noise and anonymity—such is the *Berliner Ruf*. No word falls between these men because there is no space for the words to fall. Words are hurled, pummeled, and pounded out like thick beer glasses slammed onto the table—or so we are to imagine it resonating in the peasant's reaction to the *Berliner Ruf.* The city is the place of the thug, the whore, *the Jew* (Mosse 1981, 22–23). Grimm reflects on the fate of village boys who set out to find their way by migrating to the city. Sure, "there's a different kind of money there, and girls," and "they will get richer in opportunities for pleasure, they will get the chance to properly celebrate for a few hours every workday," but that is all "a different kind of life" (Grimm 1932, 18). With his summons to the capital announced in the papers, Heidegger stands on the threshold of losing himself in this other life.

What is playing out in this suspicion of Berlin is Heidegger's staged performance of a tension between rootedness and groundlessness. Everything involving this call, Heidegger will have us believe, including its medium of announcement and rejection, is pulling him toward a groundlessness, away from his Alemannian-Swabian rootedness, that soil from which the savior of the occidental essence will emerge. It is especially significant that a newspaper reports Heidegger's call, that he seemingly had not found it necessary to tell his peasant friend himself. The newspaper and its message are contributing to pulling Heidegger away from his rootedness. When Fritz Heidegger sent his brother Martin a thought piece from a newspaper reporting on Martin's potential relocation away from the Black Forest, Martin replied: "I helped it find its way to a trash can. Such things are certainly not decided in the paper."[13] The warning in *Being and Time* about the danger of idle talk embodied by such papers helps to explain this reaction: "Idle talk is constituted by such gossiping and passing the word along—a process by which its initial lack of grounds becomes aggravated to complete groundlessness. And indeed this idle talk is not confined to vocal gossip, but even spreads to what we write, where it takes the form of 'meaningless writing'" (*BT,* 168–69/163).

The newspaper had passed the word along, and the peasant friend picked it up. Is Heidegger combating meaningless writing with his own meaningless writing and idle chatter? Is there no authentic saying to respond to what is said inauthentically? Heidegger warns us about the power of such publications: "In the public world one can be made a 'celebrity' overnight by the newspapers and journals. That always remains the surest way to have one's ownmost intentions get misinterpreted and quickly and thoroughly forgotten" (CL, 11/28). However, as Avital Ronell points out, Heidegger resorted to precisely such a journal in an attempt to obscure his political past posthumously. Referring to Heidegger's interview with the German magazine *Der Spiegel*, which Heidegger granted on the condition that it only be published after his death, Ronell writes: "In other words, is Heidegger's last word, made to be articulated after his death, a woundingly ironic utterance made against the grain of his thinking (what does it mean for Heidegger to intend to tell the truth in a newspaper?), or will his afterwordly in-the-world discourse force a rethinking of language's housing projects?" (Ronell 1989, 14). Is Heidegger employing the same irony in this text, a text channeled to various newspapers and radios? Must we begin rethinking his work at a much earlier point?

The questions must remain open for now, because our peasant, ensconced in his world of black and white, is waiting on his answer. Doubtless he is a patient soul. After all, he has not been raised in the great "unbridled rat race" that is the modern urban world (*GA* 94, 339/247). In the many senses of the phrase, this originary dweller is of another time, not the least of which is the time of myth. "What," Heidegger asks, "would he say?" (CL, 12/29). The tone of the narrative is enough for us, given a sufficient familiarity with the *völkisch* trope of the peasant, to already guess that he will not "say" anything, and that Heidegger will have us believe that what he thereby says by saying nothing is not nothing. Indeed, the friend says both nothing and something. Heidegger, who often laces his philosophical texts with a heightened sense of suspense and tension sustained over an entire semester, falls flat as a dramatist in his mytho-poetic attempt at autobiography.[14] The scenery in this drama is kitsch, the characters, including Heidegger himself, are one-dimensional, and the dialogue little more than the forced silence of a clumsy author. But for now in this micro-drama of autobiography staged for the ears of an entire regime, the moment of the peasant's silent speech is upon us. As Heidegger narrates the moment of climax: "Slowly he fixed the sure gaze of his clear eyes on mine, and keeping his mouth tightly shut, he thoughtfully put his faithful hand on my shoulder. Ever so slightly he *shook* his head. That meant: absolutely *no!*" (CL, 13/29). "The Alemanne does not speak very much, he thinks things over," write the prize-winning Nazi student group of the Wintersweiler villagers (Vohburger 1940, 58). "The Nordic man's deepest form of 'pouring his heart out' is expressed in turning red and in a glint or a cloud in the eye, in the position of his eyelids, in a soft trembling or quivering of his lips, his nostrils, or in falling silent, in a faltering of speech" (Clauss 1940, 35). Heidegger's benevolent peasant has spoken in exactly the manner his readers would have expected, with a silent gesture.

As the newspapers swirl around and the specter of idle chatter begins to ensnare the *Herr Professor*, only the silent gesture—a gesture ever so slight, nothing more than a barely perceptible shake of the head and a firm hand—can draw our philosopher back into the world of rootedness, back onto the forest path. This hand, this gentle but firm hand, this hand of the friend whose voice does not speak, must softly pull Heidegger back. Perhaps this peasant is the voice heard in the enigmatic passage in *Being and Time* where Heidegger refers to the "voice of the friend whom every Dasein carries with it" (*BT*, 163/158).[15] In any case, he would like us to see the following in this scene: the peasant communicates silently and immediately in the proximity of a being-with that needs no words. Heidegger is threatened with essential distortion, tempted to flee from his own deepest being-with by the siren call of the city, with its pleasure palaces, whores, and rowdy drinking sessions. In the terminology of *Being and Time*, words would be a modification of this originary situation. The newspaper had announced the summons, but the sure hand of the silent friend draws the son of the provinces back in. It only takes one glance into his sure, clear eyes. This is why we stay in the provinces. This is the silence and space in which Heidegger's politics is embedded, the "lost native country of thought," as Derrida rather derisively puts it (Derrida 1982, 27). Heidegger expresses as much after the war in the fourth volume of the *Black Notebooks*:

> The premonition is becoming ever clearer to me that our homeland, the heart of the southwestern German country, has the fate of being the historical birthplace of the occidental essence. That may sound strange, but it has no other way of being; for it is a land that is at once endowed with spirit and earthly beauty. It shelters invisible wealth for the temperament, preserves the deepest poetry and the highest form of saying. But we must first discover this birthplace and awaken from occidental thinking without remaining bound to what an aberrant time has left behind and seemingly, yet not actually, uprooted. (Freedom). (*GA* 97, 54)

We risk overlooking the philosophical significance of what would otherwise be easily dismissed as merely biographical observations if we regard the *Black Notebooks* as nothing more than diaries, as jottings, notes, reminders, or autobiographical sketches. The *Black Notebooks* serve as the reservoir for the unsaid in Heidegger's work. Heidegger's thinking is essentially bound to a particular place, and this place is particularly propitious for the entirety of the so-called occidental essence. This essence bears within it a particular silence.

The *Black Notebooks* as the Performance of Silence

The *Black Notebooks* have been criticized for being sketchy, poorly written, and seemingly preparatory in nature. With time, however, the reader begins to recognize, not so much a guiding thread throughout them, but a web of terms or a fabric woven together within their pages. At times this fabric is held together with great cohesiveness, while at times it seems intentionally to unravel. This fabric binds together within it many different tentative alliances of words, with a number of fundamental terms emerging repeatedly at critical junctures and then often disappearing without warning. The weft and warp of this fabric is silence. Even in their most direct, obtuse, and offensive moments, Heidegger still holds something in reserve. He announces this in the fourth volume: "I only trust in one thing: that we have been given the gift of knowing more than we say. Otherwise, the word has no weight" (*GA* 97, 57). Silence will return heft to the word, not just any kind of silence, but the particular sigetic silence found in the *Black Notebooks*.

In the earliest entries of the first volume of the *Black Notebooks,* Heidegger stages a conversation with himself as he considers entering the "situation" (*GA* 94, 7/7). Silence is at the center of many of the questions he poses to himself. Pondering how a man comes to himself, for example, Heidegger asks: "Must he not have kept silent for a long time in order once again to find the force and power of language and to be borne along by it?" (ibid., 6/6). "Must the great lone path be ventured, silently—into Da-sein, where beings become more fully beings?" (ibid., 7/7). Remaining silent about silence is the fundamental mode of attunement that sets the ground for listening, a listening that must be learned anew by those attuned to its voice. This listening is not for all, but for the "futural ones," solitary ones, and the rare listeners—a *Volk* within the *Volk*, perhaps. Heidegger describes the listening attained by these solitary few in a characteristic passage: "*Originary silence* as *further* silence in and out of the pre-sentiment of language. But that silence is not inactive—rather, the initially open listening into (beings)" (ibid., 78/59).

The few, solitary and silent ones listen into something quite specific, which Heidegger refers to as the emergency. As an ontological term, the emergency is at best tangentially related to any actual incidents of destruction, including Europe's destruction in World War II.[16] For Heidegger, listening to the call within the emergency is the only essential political task, for it is useless to "try and improve any aspect whatever of that which lies on the surface, instead of bringing into salience the most extreme and broadest emergency: the decay of being" (*GA* 94, 88/67). Sigetic politics at this level does not involve making adjustments to what has already come to be, but instead involves an essential questioning rooted in an attuned listening that speaks through a silent saying in tune with this listening.

> But how to experience this plight? Is it necessary that many, the many, experience it? No—that is even impossible. The "situation"—not what passes for that today, but the place of the track of the essence of being—should and can be known only to a few, and they must be silent if they are to act in the power of this knowledge. . . . Because nothing escapes contemporary people, because they have a facile and correct answer for everything, whereby they throttle everything as already having been, the essential must therefore remain in silence now and for the future—but all the harder and all the clearer may be what is said in the power of that silence. (*GA* 94, 88/67)

Heidegger's ontological politics is a politics of decomposition. More precisely, it is a politics of hastening the decomposition of that which is already in a state of putrefaction brought about by a public sphere that devours everything by simplifying it. In order to take power in this situation, one must be silent—not by withholding the word, but by speaking silently. Those with knowledge of the essence of being are in the throes of a struggle with the "vulgar" public sphere. They cannot simply withdraw and preserve their authenticity in silence, but instead must be "relentless in the firm goal, malleable and changing in the ways and weapons" (ibid., 111/81). Seemingly in need of a pep talk, Heidegger pumps up his resolve just a few pages later with sayings suitable for motivational posters in a Nazi military barracks: "No flight, no weariness, always on the attack. Not to have full powers, but to *be* the power!" (ibid., 116/85). Whereas he had initially hoped that World War II would bring about the "purification of being from its deepest disorder" (*GA* 96, 238/187), later, in the midst of the war, he thought that Europe must harvest and attenuate the power of decomposition so as to make "essential decisions" (ibid., 141/110).

What Heidegger calls the "tyranny of the self-evident" (*GA* 36–37, 99/79), that is, the tendency of the masses to draw facile, muddled equivalences, has degraded a host of spent, used-up, worn-out words, leading to a "regime of the devastation of language" (*GA* 96, 221/174). The listening few hold back in a silence that will not shrink from expressing itself through false, apparent equivalences for the sake of the many who cannot and should not understand what is held in reserve in silence. Indeed, it may be the task of the listening few to proffer idle chatter as a way of preserving the essential saying. "Who considers the possibility," Heidegger asks, "that a word is necessary so that a silence would be possible?" (*GA* 96, 215/169). After all, one cannot escape the public sphere by withdrawing from it, for it is a structural necessity of human existence. A language that necessarily fails does not preserve itself by keeping silent, yet it can at least influence the particular formation of its failure by controlling the way it speaks. This is how Heidegger would like us to understand, not only his voice as rector, but also his voice of reckoning in the *Black Notebooks*: the necessarily elusive attempt to control a discourse that seeks to write the story of its own failure.

This complex play between failure, the essential word, and the deed of silence is illustrated in a particularly dense passage from the third volume of the *Notebooks*. There Heidegger describes a hierarchical process of returning the handiwork of thinking to a form of speaking in which being "achieves the highest loyalty to its own essence." Philosophy of language only serves to push the word further astray and further to distort the essential saying. Silence plays a particularly important role in rescuing the word, and thereby the question of being: "The first 'act' of this rescue consists in the capacity for silence, the second in learning to hear the rare conversation, the third in the attempt to hint at the essential word. However, any effort in this direction becomes ensnared in the vicinity of the things that have recently been written and spoken; and even if this effort does rise above this ensnarement, it remains in the grips of the common distortion of the essence of language" (*GA* 95, 288–89/225).

The word always fails in what it intends to say, and even restoring its essential occurrence in the three-step process Heidegger describes is insufficient to rescue it. This is because the word has always already been abandoned, falling victim to the chatter of things already spoken—the material for so many hasty comparisons. The originary contamination of language justifies a performative ambivalence for Heidegger that links together the poles in his inverted politics of language. Heidegger the politician and university administrator enables Heidegger the thinker of the essential homeland. The silence of the essential homeland will be most safely preserved if it does not make itself conspicuous as silence. The *Black Notebooks* safeguard the "inconspicuous, nameless element of *being-historical thinking*," making possible the most originary questioning in Heidegger's work.

Yet, once again, even at this high level of abstraction, *völkisch* precedents can be found for Heidegger's sigetic thinking. Clauss, the *völkisch* thinker with whom Heidegger has the most in common, identifies a similar aporia in the Nordic soul: "When the soul speaks, then, well!, it is no longer the soul that speaks. Yet if the Nordic man were to speak in the hour of his most profound inspiration, his words, when heard from the outside, would often seem to say something completely different from what they mean for him on the inside. Then he envelopes himself as it were in words in order to avoid the word that burns all too deeply in his soul" (Clauss 1940, 35).

In Clauss's portrayal, the Nordic soul requires a form of chatter to preserve its most intimate form of speech. To preserve this intimacy, the Nordic soul produces a space of preservation through an outpouring of speech. This speech guards the word that cannot be said, and this entire interchange requires a landscape in which speech and silence can resonate. While there are certainly many ways in which Heidegger differs from Clauss, there are nonetheless a deep set of affinities that unite them. The fact that Heidegger both reveals and occludes those affinities is built into the operation of Heidegger's sigetic politics. Silence binds those affinities together.

After the Holocaust . . .

Perhaps the most fitting conclusion would be to turn briefly to another Heideggerian literary flourish in the short autobiographical text "The Pathway," his 1949 paean to the landscape around his hometown of Meßkirch. The text has become so central to the postwar rehabilitation of Heidegger as a thinker of letting-be and peaceful dwelling together with nature that the town of Meßkirch has even marked out the actual path as part of its meager yet earnest efforts at marketing the local Heidegger product.

The text is overlaid temporally with layers of remembrance as Heidegger strolls down the path while the landscape awakens childhood memories, with the bench evoking memories of the books that he set down there during many "clumsy attempts at deciphering them as a young man," and the bell tower tolling in the distance evoking memories of rubbing his hands raw as a child pulling the ropes of the bells (PW, 87/69). Heidegger worries about the "gigantic energies of atomic power" and about

endless work for its own sake that "only creates a nullity." Both of these
phenomena are among the many things that threaten what he calls "the
simple" (ibid., 89/70–71). "The simple conserves what abides and what
is great," Heidegger writes. This simple also speaks in a language of the
"unspoken" and we are in danger of "losing our sense of hearing for its
language" (ibid., 89/70).

Up to this point, these are familiar themes already brought out in the
reading of "Creative Landscape." However, with the bell in the church
tower tolling the eleventh hour, Heidegger brings these themes into a
peculiar convergence with something even more troubling: "With its final
toll the stillness becomes even stiller. It reaches to those who were sacrificed
before their time in two world wars. The simple has become simpler" (ibid.,
90/71). What could it possibly mean to say that the simple has become
simpler through two world wars? Is it nothing more than an infelicitous
slip of the philosopher-poet's pen? Read on its own, the line might seem
harmless, yet the *Black Notebooks* begin to open up moments such as these
to their own unspoken commitments, especially when read in the light of
Heidegger's *völkisch* contemporaries. Given this conjuncture of affinities, it
is necessary to interpret this in terms of Heidegger's essential people being
rid of their inessential enemy, their essential complication. After all, if the
German essence and space were cluttered with an enemy—Jews—who
threatened their very essence, then it would simplify things to be rid of that
enemy. I do not see any reason to offer Heidegger a generous interpretation of these lines, especially based on his own sigetic principles and overt
expressions of antisemitism.

It was long thought that Heidegger was silent about the Holocaust, aside
from his sparse remarks on the lack of death in the concentration camps
quoted in the opening pages of this book.[17] The fourth volume of the
Black Notebooks shatters this assumption. Heidegger not only frequently
addresses the Holocaust, often in ellipses, allusions, and asides touching
on such terms as guilt and desolation, he also proffers a disturbing vision
of the Holocaust, which would require its own separate book.

If one collects together these many comments, one sees that it is not so
much the case that Heidegger approves of the Holocaust. His approach
to it is somewhat different and perhaps even more disturbing. The Holocaust for Heidegger is simply a matter of ethical indifference. It merely
involves counting, masses, numbers, and the monstrosity of the gigantic.
Heidegger mentions the Holocaust to the extent that it involves him or is

the immediate reason for his annoyance under denazification, but other than that, he seems perfectly content to overlook the Holocaust as a matter of insignificant ethical concern. All mass death—whether through war or genocide—is the same in Heidegger's logic, for it is all based on the same fundamental decision, a decisionless decision to forget being fostered within a space of technological domination of sameness. Indeed, National Socialism only matters to Heidegger after the war to the extent that its unmatched desolation may in fact have silently preserved some part of the secret essence of the Germans for future generations. As a result of National Socialism, the simple became simpler for Heidegger, while his silences become more silent. This book has been an attempt to make those silences speak.

Epilogue

Philosophy and Totalitarianism

In his enigmatic retelling of the biblical story of Abraham in *Fear and Trembling*, Kierkegaard warns us that we have lost the ability to comprehend the Abraham story because we have become accustomed to reading it backwards. We interpret the story based on its ending, starting with God sending an angel to revoke his order to Abraham to kill his son Isaac, with the angel arriving at precisely the moment when Abraham resolutely places the knife to his son's throat (Kierkegaard 1983, 59–63). By interpreting the story with the knowledge that Abraham was not ultimately compelled to carry out God's order to sacrifice Isaac, we domesticate Abraham and make him palatable. Only by reading the story from the beginning, Kierkegaard contends, and only by accompanying Abraham in the silence of his three-day journey through the desert as he grapples with the gravity of the task ahead of him, and withholds his intentions in silence, can we begin to recover a sense of the terror conveyed by the story. Kierkegaard sought to recover that terror for his readers.

Echoing Kierkegaard's concern about reading backwards with the outcome of the story already in mind, I would suggest that Heidegger's role in the crimes of National Socialism is often misunderstood due to our tendency to read the story backwards. Heidegger might seem a minor figure when measured on the scale of the crimes of the Holocaust; when measured, for example, on the scale of the machinery of death at Auschwitz, where twenty thousand people could be gassed and incinerated every twenty-four hours,[1] or against the gruesome mass shooting at Babi Yar in Ukraine, where approximately 33,771 of Kiev's Jews were murdered in September 1941 (Berkhoff 2008, 291–92). To diminish Heidegger's Nazi role based on such reasoning would be to read the story backwards, however, notwithstanding that the denazification commission that dealt with his case was by all accounts well disposed toward him (Ott 1993, 318). Summarizing the impact of the first few months of Nazi rule, Saul Friedländer describes the importance of figures such as Heidegger in administrative roles in institutions such as universities: "As the first months of 1933 went by, Hitler must have seen that he could count on the genuine support of church and university; whatever opposition may have existed, it would not be expressed as long as direct institutional interests and basic dogmatic tenets were not threatened. The concrete situation of the Jews was a litmus test for how far any genuine moral principle could be silenced; although the situation was to become more complex later on, during this early period the result of the test was clear" (Friedländer 1998, 60).

In fact, Heidegger exemplifies the Nazi regime's enforcement of conformity (*Gleichschaltung*), inasmuch as he helped steer an important German institution through the first major administrative act of antisemitism, the so-called restoration of the civil services called "Aryanization." This is not only Heidegger's personal legacy, but also his philosophical legacy. Although he cast himself in the postwar years as one of the members of the university whose "genuine moral principle" was silenced by Nazism, he was actually among those perpetrating the silencing. The Freiburg economist Adolf Lampe says that, as rector, Heidegger "defended his positions with fanatical and terroristic intolerance and summoned the political force of the party to his defense."[2]

When assessing Heidegger's place in the history of National Socialist crimes, it is important to keep in mind a few important factors. With the publication of *Being and Time* in 1927, Heidegger quickly rose to fame. After the Nazis came to power in January 1933, that fame afforded Heidegger a great amount of power, which could have been used to achieve many different ends. The Nazis were acutely concerned with public relations, especially when dealing with prominent figures such as Heidegger (Koonz 2003, 69–102). In the archives, one encounters continual references to Heidegger's fame and his importance to the international reputation of German science. It is clear that this fame led to him being treated with the proverbial white gloves by the regime for fear of being regarded abroad as mistreating prominent individuals.[3] Heidegger was most egregiously complicit at the very moment when it was least necessary to be complicit. We read the story backwards if we expect to find the full murderous apparatus of a genocidal authoritarian state in place during the time of Heidegger's so-called "political adventure."[4] Heidegger helped to build that dictatorial state, engaging with it as a thinker, as a *völkisch* devotee, and as a university administrator implementing racist decrees beyond the letter of the law. In 1933, Heidegger was a full professor of philosophy, and hence an anointed member of the elite. From that position of significant privilege, he mobilized the social capital granted to him as a philosopher, professor, and university administrator to advocate for the Nazi revolution. When read through the lens of Heidegger's elaborate performance of silence, all of these biographical details of Heidegger's life take on philosophical significance. Within Heidegger's ethics of silence, all action is both political and philosophical.

In addition to recognizing Heidegger's eminent public stature, one should also keep in mind that a great amount of resistance was still possible in the era of *Gleichschaltung*. Many of the deans, departmental chairs, and directors of the medical clinics of Freiburg University did indeed express strong resistance and serious concerns to the rector's office about the dismissal of experts. In numerous letters addressed to the rector, these administrators and professors objected to the aggressive Nazification of the university enacted by Heidegger, and specifically to the purging of expertise from the university. They did not suffer any negative consequences.[5] To cite another example, the files on the major book burning staged by the National Socialist Student Federation in May 1933, known as the "Action against the Un-German Spirit," contain many scathing letters of protest.[6] Had he been so inclined, Heidegger's unique international stature and "Aryan" credentials would have allowed him significant leeway available to few other Germans at the time, for 1933 was not 1943. Even in Heidegger's own perverse telling of the story, it took courage to be a Nazi in 1933, since it would have been "more comfortable to stand aside" (*GA* 16, 375). Heidegger did not regret this courage after the war, but instead boldly boasted of it, portraying 1933 as a decisive moment and himself as a decisive man of action. For Heidegger, silence was one of those actions. In one of his many entries in the fourth volume of the *Black Notebooks*, labeled "The Error of 1933," Heidegger describes the need to act: "But keeping away—merely doing so and standing by and hunkering down in the past, all of that would have been impossible even then" (*GA* 97, 98). Heidegger is not describing an impossibility based on outer compulsion, but one based on inner compulsion. The period of *Gleichschaltung* was not equivalent to a thoroughly authoritarian state actively crushing any form of dissent, while simultaneously carrying out an unprecedented process of genocide. One should therefore avoid reading Heidegger's story backwards, but instead become accustomed to treating him, at the very least, as one would treat a figure such as Carl Schmitt, namely, as an avowed Nazi thinker whose intellectual prowess served the ends of a genocidal authoritarian regime. Heidegger was a thinker with conviction, and the skill with which he has crafted his postwar image should not distract us from a reasoned consideration of his place in the history of National Socialism, nor in the history of Western philosophy.

Instead of reading Heidegger backwards, we should turn to the early twentieth century to begin to trace out the *völkisch* lineage of many of Heidegger's terms, especially in supposedly apolitical postwar texts. For example, the word "thing," one of the fundamental terms in Heidegger's postwar terminology, is only a few degrees removed from the Nazi-era revival of Germanic mythology. As part of an official party program to build outdoor theaters (*Thingstätte*), the party revived *Thing* as an antiquated spelling of the word *Ding* to designate the gathering places constructed for neo-Germanic rituals (Stommer 1985; Eichberg and Jones 1977). This does not mean to say that Heidegger is necessarily perpetuating National Socialism by other means in the 1950s when he then places notion of the thing at the center of his thinking, but he is nonetheless expressing a set of affinities to a well-established language. One could also explore further *völkisch* resonances in words such as "emergency" and "machination," both of which were used to describe the supposed Jewish threat and conspiracy against the German people in the 1920s and into the Nazi era. Indeed, if Heidegger was a somewhat unorthodox *völkisch* thinker in the 1930s, given his focus on the Greek element, one might say that in the 1950s, he is a much more orthodox Germanic *völkisch* thinker in his readings of Stefan George, Friedrich Hölderlin, and Johan Peter Hebel. *On the Way to Language*, for example, follows a rather straightforward set of *völkisch* themes about landscape, the German language, gathering, and silence. One might also pursue a similar set of links through the influential postwar essay "Building Dwelling Thinking" (Heidegger 1971), which follows many of the same etymological reflections on the German word for building (*bauen*) that Walther Darré followed in his prewar lucubrations on the Nordic peasantry (*Bauerntum*). Moreover, one could also consider exploring Heidegger's turn to Hölderlin as the element that links his philosophy

of language, reading of the Greeks, and *völkisch* valorization of the landscape. A more detailed examination of these terminological and thematic
affinities might raise very troubling questions about some of the very texts
that have most firmly established Heidegger's immense postwar reputation, especially outside of the discipline of philosophy. For example, Hans
Grimm found a significant postwar audience for his screed decrying the
"silence" imposed upon the Germans and denouncing the "collective guilt
artificially attributed to our tortured people" (Grimm 1950, 47). Without
reducing Heidegger to Grimm, it is worth noting the extent to which both
authors follow a similar career arc from Weimar Germany through National
Socialism to a phase of rehabilitation in postwar West German democracy.
We might conveniently seek to banish *völkisch* writers from the canon, but
matters are perhaps not so simple with Heidegger as they are with Grimm,
a second-rate writer at best. Yet Heidegger should not be rehabilitated
simply for the high quality of his thinking while Grimm is banished for
his authorial mediocrity—for that is the very temptation that has all too
often clouded philosophers' judgment about Heidegger. Echoing Jean-Luc
Nancy, the immense heritage of "Heidegger's thought cannot simply be
struck from our history" (Nancy 2017, 61). If that is the case, then the
discipline of philosophy must untangle the affinities embedded in that
history. This process of disentanglement cannot take place from some site
of purported moral purity, but rather from the standpoint of a discipline
still entangled not only in Heidegger, but also in what made Heidegger
possible. Indeed, the gesture of banishing Heidegger is often enacted to
evade questions about one's own standpoint and one's own discipline.

   Returning specifically to the topic of silence, it is also important to
consider Heidegger's self-perception as demonstrated in his own accounts
of his political past. As outlandish as it might sound, Heidegger—much
like Grimm—would like to present himself as being silenced by National
Socialism.[7] In other words, Heidegger regarded himself as a victim of National Socialism. In his public postwar accounts of his involvement with
National Socialism, Heidegger portrays himself as first being swept along
naïvely by the nationalist zeitgeist, then eventually realizing the brutality
of the regime, and thereafter taking steps to distance himself from the regime. From this point on, Heidegger portrays himself as being forced into
a silent form of resistance as a so-called inner emigrant—or so he would
have us believe. This should come as no great surprise given the persistence
of Nazi networks after the war and the proliferation of aid organizations

dedicated to serving so-called victims of "internment," culminating in the notorious aid organization for former SS officers known as "Silent Assistance for Prisoners of War and Interned Persons" (Schröm 2002). Yet even if it stretches the bounds of credulity in comparison with these violent forms of silencing, Heidegger would like us to believe that he too was silenced by National Socialist violence as the movement abandoned its spiritual mission of *völkisch* regeneration. In other words, it stands to reason that Heidegger maintained a fidelity to the "inner truth and greatness of National Socialism," and that he continued to express his affinities to the movement through his philosophical work. Simultaneously, he skillfully navigated the perceptions of the public sphere and actively sought to have his name "cleansed" and his teaching responsibilities at the university restored to him. In other words, the dramatically altered political conditions of postwar West Germany made it necessary to cloak these affinities in different forms of silence. Heidegger was not alone in this. When Carl Schmitt and Ernst Jünger began to regroup to consider possibilities for a new journal in the late 1940s, they rekindled "conversations in the security of silence" (Laak 2002; Morat 2012). Heidegger's postwar philosophy should be read as the staging ground for one of these conversations. Heidegger's postwar thinking on space and place, which has been influential in fields such as architecture, art history, and the philosophy of technology, is embedded in *völkisch* affinities and is significant for tracing the afterlife of *völkisch* thinking.

The *Black Notebooks* serve to illuminate many of the unspoken assumptions central to this conversation. This is because they hold steadfast to Heidegger's portrayal of himself as being silenced, but owing to their preservation of Heidegger's antisemitism, they also significantly revise the narrative about what exactly was silenced in Heidegger's thinking. In this narrative, Heidegger repeatedly reinforces the notion that he was in the vanguard—solitary, unheard, unswaying—of a movement of essentially spiritual National Socialism. With war and genocide raging throughout Europe, Heidegger somehow feels that this in some way is all about him. He feels himself to be at the center of this world-historical moment as the only one who can see through it to what it reveals about the essence of humanity and the entanglement of the so-called Occident in technologically enabled destruction. More important, however, Heidegger sees himself as a victim of this destruction. He regards himself as victimized by National Socialism, and eventually by the Americans, by the Soviets, and by the

French under the postwar occupation government. The fourth volume of the *Black Notebooks* is replete with this narrative of victimization. "The Germans," Heidegger writes, "now stand in the shadow of the betrayal of their own essence that they have perpetrated against themselves" (*GA* 97, 84). His sense of personal victimization reaches its peak when he worries, in a letter to his brother Fritz written in December 1945, that he might be forced to give a deposition in French to the occupation authorities: "The 'gracious' treatment by the French has not turned out well for me. My own people are upset. I am being shot at again. I cannot get away from these negotiations. Whether the hearing in Hüfingen is enough, I do not know. . . . Perhaps I must once again be silent for ten years; for I refuse to appear in the French language, where I cannot speak among my own people."[8]

For Heidegger the height of victimization consisted in being forced to give an account of himself in front of foreign authorities in the language of those authorities. For a former Nazi bureaucrat who Aryanized Freiburg University with exemplary alacrity, sending many Jewish faculty members into uncertain futures in uncertain languages and uncertain places, the "imposition" of giving a French-language deposition is farcically mild. At the very moment when hundreds of thousands of survivors of concentration camps lingered in displaced persons camps negotiating difficult multilingual bureaucracies in order to remain alive and secure their potential safe passage home (if they still had one), Heidegger regards it as an affront to be confronted with the possibility of giving a deposition in a foreign language to account for his complicity in National Socialist crimes. This is perhaps not surprising in a thinker who considered German the essential language of thinking, because of the "special inner relationship of the German language with that of the Greeks and with their thought" (*GA* 16, 679/331).

At another somewhat more philosophical level, Heidegger is also concerned with a moment of world-historical destruction that seeks to destroy his thinking, whether by eliminating the conditions of possibility for producing listeners, or by a more maniacal attempt to silence him. If Heidegger could feel that the second, independent denazification commission convened by Freiburg University was again "shooting at him," after the overly "genteel" treatment of the French denazification commission, this is because he believed that he had been "shot at" all along as a genuine victim of National Socialist crimes. The world, leveled off by the sameness of endlessly reproducible technological rationality, sought to silence the thinking of being, the unique, "inconspicuous, nameless element." The inconspicuous, nameless thinking of being would dissolve into a public sphere that would take on planetary dimensions with the occupation of Germany and the subsumption of Germany into an American-Bolshevist planetary regime of sameness: "How despicable is the helpless groveling under the shadowing carried out by the planetary terror of the world public sphere, in comparison with which the massive brutality of 'National Socialism' is entirely harmless, even despite the undeniable palpability of the desolation that it *participated* in wreaking" (*GA* 97, 87).

National Socialism lost its way and devolved into little more than Americanism, Bolshevism, even "world Jewry" (Trawny 2015b, 78). Heidegger alone stood at the helm piloting a ship without passengers on its way to a place where the necessary listeners did not yet exist, but would perhaps one day sprout from the soil, or reemerge in soldiers returning from the front. These former soldiers, for Heidegger, were the great "spiritual youth" who "made sacrificial offerings which one is silent about" (*GA* 97, 136). "I trust in only one thing," Heidegger writes after the war, "that in the future we will be bestowed with the power to once again know more than we say. Otherwise the word will remain without weight" (*GA* 97, 57). Evidently Heidegger alone knew the measure of that weight.

In surveying the literature on the *Black Notebooks*, I am surprised at how often Heidegger's lies get repeated and how many scholars make the mistake of taking Heidegger at his word, especially regarding his rectorate. Two basic errors should be stricken from the record. First, Heidegger did not avoid implementing anti-Jewish measures as rector; rather, he implemented them with great vigor. Second, Heidegger's involvement with National Socialism did not end with rectorate in 1934. He continued his negotiations regarding the *Dozentenakademie* until 1935, and in the same year, the Ministry of Culture proposed his name as dean in Freiburg, a suggestion rejected by the then rector, Eduard Kern, since Heidegger "had completely forfeited the trust of his Freiburg colleagues during his rectorate."[9] Even his position after 1935, and as a professor designated as "politically reliable" in 1942, was a negotiated, highly political one. A philosopher who could mobilize a phone call from Il Duce to Goebbels, via the Italian ambassador, in order to intervene on his behalf for the publication of an essay does not cut a convincing figure as someone who "devoted himself exclusively to his philosophical studies" after 1934, as his own denazification judgment reports.[10]

Heidegger scholarship needs to distance itself from Heidegger's portrayals of the rectorate for the simple reason that Heidegger was an inveterate liar.

He had no qualms about outright fabrication. His apologia "Rectorate: Facts and Thoughts" would be better titled "Rectorate: Facts and Lies." This tendency to lie should not be confused with some sort of philosophical play with concealment and unconcealment, but instead emerges out of something much less philosophically sophisticated: the simple fact that ex-Nazis tended to lie out of self-preservation. "In German collective memory, a standard narrative describes the process of denazification, recurring in a stylized version in many autobiographies" (Jarausch 2006, 47). Heidegger provides a version of this stylized narrative, including the typical obfuscation and diminishing of his ideological commitment, casting it instead in terms of necessity and coercion. This was only exacerbated by what Lutz Niethammer calls the "bystander factory," a rushed, summary process of judgment that had little interest in genuine denazification—whatever that might have meant (Niethammer 1982). Among the four occupation zones, the southwestern French zone was regarded as the most lax (Jarausch 2006, 53), as Heidegger recognized and effectively used to his advantage during his first denazification procedure at the hands of the French occupation forces, when the young lieutenant Edgar Morin took a special interest in his case (Ott 1993, 329–30). Heidegger, the declared category B bystander, was churned out of the "bystander factory" with a willing blindness to his lies. This was aided by the fact that, as Ott documents, "relatively little evidence was adduced from the files of the rector's office" during his second denazification by Freiburg University's independent commission (ibid., 318). While the professors on Heidegger's denazification commission may have felt particularly interested in the Heidegger case, they were far more interested in protecting the perceived sanctity of the German professoriate and the independence of the university. Indeed, from their perspective, Heidegger's greatest crimes had little to do with anti-Jewish policy, but rather with how Heidegger violated their sense of dignity as professors by encouraging Nazi student groups to challenge the traditionally top-heavy power structure of German universities. The relative leniency of even the second, somewhat more rigorous denazification commission furnished the necessary alibis for rehabilitating Heidegger's postwar reputation. The trajectory of this story is a typical one for denazification.

In some strands of Heidegger scholarship, however, it is often the very people who call for treating the "personal" as irrelevant in philosophical analysis who have recourse to Heidegger's personal account. This goes something along these lines, echoing Heidegger's own dismissal of Aristotle's

biography: It does not matter that Heidegger was a Nazi because we are
doing philosophy. Yet even if it did matter, Heidegger was not really a very
committed Nazi, nor a very good one, nor one for very long. We know
this because Heidegger himself tells us so. According to this reasoning, the
disavowal of the personal is justified through recourse to the personal. I
would suggest that those who seek to renounce attention to the persona
of the philosopher should at least not rely on the person himself as their
source about that person's life. This would seem to be an obvious consequence of their own philosophical commitments about the irrelevance of
the person. Those who disparage the introduction of biographical elements
into philosophical analysis should be willing to consult other sources and
reject the importance of the philosopher's personality by first fully recognizing the philosopher's actions (Rorty 1990, 21). My suspicion is that
the unwillingness to confront the historical facts is grounded in an insufficient renunciation of the personal and ultimately motivated by a fear of
what it would mean to confront Heidegger's complicity without reading
backwards.

There are further philosophical reasons for not taking Heidegger at his
word. As *Heidegger's Fascist Affinities* has shown, Heidegger's thinking is
structured around a play with concealment and unconcealment. In fact,
for Heidegger, that play is central to the very task of philosophizing, and
no less to the task of politics. Moreover, according to his inversion of language, the more essential something is to his thinking, the more intense,
subtle, and multilayered that play is. This is at the core of the "insidious
ambiguity" that Heidegger places at the center of his thinking. One might
take this insidious ambiguity as a motive for dismissing Heidegger in the
manner of Emmanuel Faye (2009). There is something very tempting
and justifiable about this response, and this book has surely amplified that
tendency. In the wake of the *Black Notebooks*, there has been a renewed
call to banish Heidegger, be done with him, eject him from the realm of
thinkers. Yet if Heidegger represents some kind of threat, if we risk being
tainted by exposure to his work, as Richard Wolin would have it, then
that is because the elements that made Heidegger possible may still be
embedded in the discipline of philosophy. Carrying out this excavation
work risks raising far more troubling questions about how the humanities
can and have responded to totalitarian regimes than we would raise if we
simply banished Heidegger from the domain of philosophy. Indeed, just
when the Right is attacking the values and institutions of liberal education,

one trembles at the possibility of feeding into these narratives by highlighting the humanities' role in fostering National Socialism. It seems to be a much safer gesture simply to banish Heidegger and return to defending the humanistic values of a liberal arts education.

Banishing Heidegger from the realm of philosophy is easily justified and offers a certain sense of satisfaction. Some take this tendency a step further and use Heidegger's insidious ambiguity to object to the entirety of postmodernism—a broad and malleable grab-bag term that can accommodate a variable range of entities and political exigencies. Derrida, the figure who has been a guiding hand throughout this analysis, has long been a target of such attacks. Doubtless, Derrida's own play with a purportedly insidious ambiguity has been the source of the vehemently polarizing reaction his work has long caused among philosophers. But in contrast to Heidegger, Derrida's ambiguity is anchored by a deeply Levinasian ethical commitment to the Other. Derrida's work is open-ended, revisable, and rooted in an ethical care that is foreign, not only to Heidegger's personality, but also to his thinking. Heidegger, in contrast, is not only a thinker of place, but a thinker of *a* place. He is not only a thinker of silence as a free-floating universal concept, but a thinker of *a* silence. As ambiguous as the performance of his thinking might be, it is unambiguously rooted in the soil of a fixed place, and this accounts for its insidious element.

"Whoever thinks greatly must err greatly," Heidegger writes with a self-serving flourish of grandiosity (*GA* 13, 81). The statement sanctions a convenient indifference to the actual content of those errors, if not even a heroic celebration of their greatness. Moreover, this assertion facilitates establishing a spurious relation between erring greatly and thinking greatly, implying that thinking greatly requires erring greatly and that the actual content of the errors committed in the course of developing this thinking are a justifiable means to an end. Heidegger erred greatly and we perhaps do not yet know how greatly. One might be tempted to say that it does not matter. I have recourse to Derrida one final time: "We cannot understand what Europe is and has been during this century, what Nazism is and has been, and so on, without interrogating what made Heidegger's discourse possible" (Derrida 1987, 178). If Derrida is correct, then evading this story means evading something central to the nature of Western philosophy, and hence to the nature of the thinking in whose midst we still stand. Heidegger was not simply an unmoored individual, but a product of German configurations and confluences, of a set of historical currents that intersected with particular intensity in his life and work. He was a product, in many ways, of a world we still live in and with.

After all, are we so certain that our institutions, disciplines, and ways of thinking will withstand the onslaught of another *Gleichschaltung*? Will Western philosophy in its present disciplinary iteration within the structures of the modern neoliberal university serve as a source of resistance? Or might it already lie within a configuration of complicity? German universities in 1933 faced a particular conglomerate of pressures, including those pressures created by highly enthusiastic Nazi student groups and by a vanguard of professors with nationalist and antisemitic leanings. The combination of these two forces helped to radicalize universities both from above and below. Yet despite whatever pressure German universities faced, they were spared one deep vulnerability of the neoliberal university: German students could not make demands based on their status as *customers*. The neoliberal logic of the satisfied student-customer may be the greatest threat to universities in the United States. Tracing the history of German universities in the era of enforced conformity may help teach some valuable lessons about the possible threats facing universities, but it can only take us so far. Examining Heidegger as typifying both *Gleichschaltung* and postwar *völkisch* affinities may help us understand how the humanities respond both positively and negatively to political pressure, and about thinking, writing, and teaching as forms of complicity.

Heidegger's defenders call him naïve and politically inexperienced, but to think that we can simply call him naïve and wash our hands of the whole "political adventure" and restore clarity would itself be naïve. Heidegger's detractors seek to banish him from the discipline out of a naïve assurance in the purity of that gesture—as if one actually knows what one is banishing. This book has moved between these two poles guided by the firm commitment that we must at least know what we are defending or rejecting. This lies buried beneath manifold strata of silence, and the excavations begun here may only have begun to scratch the surface.

Notes

Prologue

1. On *Gleichschaltung*, see Fritzsche 1998.

2. Martin Heidegger to Fritz Heidegger, April 13, 1933, in *HA*, 35.

3. For an introduction to the stumbling-stone project, see Dörte Franke's 2008 documentary *Stolperstein* on the artist Günter Demnig; historical information on the victims memorialized by stumbling blocks in Freiburg can be found in Meckel 2006.

4. For a defense of Heidegger's statement and elucidation of this concept of perishing, see Agamben 1999, 73–86; for a discussion of the "absolute insanity of these words," see Faye 2009, 304–5.

5. Arendt reports on a protest action in the form of collective suicide at the French internment camp in Gurs, to which many of Freiburg's Jews who had fled to France were deported.

6. Martin Heidegger to Fritz Heidegger, April 13, 1933, in *HA*, 35.

7. Holocaust histories often mention Heidegger as exemplifying early academic enthusiasm for the Nazi revolution. See Koonz 2003, esp. 50–54; Friedländer 1998, 41–72; Ericksen 2012, 92.

8. Fritz Heidegger to Martin Heidegger, March 30, 1930, in *HA*, 16.

9. "Der Philosoph Heidegger in die NSDAP eingetreten [The Philosopher Heidegger Joins the NSDAP]," in *Der Alemanne: Kampfblatt der Nationalsozialisten Oberbadens* 121, 3 (May 3, 1933), reprinted in Schneeberger 1962, 23.

Chapter 1

1. Mosse 1981; Puschner 2001; Tourlamain 2014; on Heidegger's place in the so-called conservative revolution, see Morat 2007, 35–50.

2. Leo 2016; the occasion for Leo's reflections was a conference on the *Black Notebooks* held at University of Siegen on April 22–25, 2015.

3. Weinreich 1946 is a notable exception.

4. Hausmann 2011; Heiber 1991.

5. Contra Emmanuel Faye, who writes that "the very principles of philosophy are abolished" in Heidegger (Faye 2009, 316).

6. For a range of perspectives on Heidegger's purported political silence, see Bernstein 1992, 79–141; Derrida 1990, 145–48; de Beistegui 1998, 146–62; Krell 1992, 138–41; Rockmore 1997, 202–3.

7. For this approach I am indebted to Babich 1992.

8. On the controversial history of Heidegger's willingness to include the phrase in postwar editions of the text, see *IM*, xv–xvii; see also Ireland 2014.

9. I borrow the term "critical phenomenology" from Guenther 2013: xi–xxx.

10. For more on this ambiguity, see the section "Ambiguity in the Essence of Philosophy (Metaphysics)" in *GA* 29–30, 14–36/11–24; Derrida 1989, 1993.

11. Martin Heidegger to Fritz Heidegger, May 4, 1933, in *HA*, 36.

12. Many of Heidegger's addresses and speeches can be found in three main sources: Schneeberger's self-published document collection *Nachlese zu Heidegger* contains an especially comprehensive collection of periodical publications by and about Heidegger, especially from Nazi propaganda organs. For official documents and selections from Heidegger's correspondence, see *GA* 16 and Denker and Zaborowski 2009.

13. The prevalence of references to Heidegger's purported naïveté indicates the extent to which his own narrative is still decisive. Heidegger establishes this narrative in *GA* 16, 384. On this supposed naïveté, see Mehring 2016, 291; Grondin 2010, 40; Hemming 2016, 113; Rockmore 1997, 262.

14. On Heidegger's relationship to the public sphere during National Socialism, see Trawny 2014, 25–35; on the relation between "the they" and politics, see Dostal 1994, 517–55; on the links between "the they" and Heidegger's concept of the *Volk*, see Phillips 2005, 17–21.

15. Martin Heidegger to Fritz Heidegger, March 2, 1932, in *HA*, 26.

16. On the paradoxical relationship to technology among German *völkisch* thinkers, see Herf 1984.

17. See "Der Philosoph Heidegger in die NSDAP eingetreten," in Schneeberger 1962, 23.

18. Although in this passage Heidegger identifies his 1934 lecture course "Logic as the Question of the Essence of Language" as explicitly related to his sigetics, silence emerges more directly as a topic of explicit analysis in *GA* 36–

37; on Heidegger's sigetics, see Vallega-Neu 2013, 119–45; see also Gonzalez 2008, 358–91; Ziarek 2013, 149–56.

19. Gillespie 2000, 140–66, draws the link between Aristotle and Heidegger's politics as rooted in a restoration of prudence as the privileging of praxis over theoretical knowledge, but does not address the topic of language.

20. On the idea of a Nazi "morality," see Koonz 2003; Aly 2014, 205–18; Levinas 1990.

21. One potential objection to this approach might be what Mehring calls the "iceberg thesis": "Defenders of the 'iceberg thesis' read Heidegger's marginal statements as so to speak the tip of the iceberg. As a result the borders between a philologically strict manner of reading and hermeneutic speculation and insinuation become fluid" (Mehring 2016, 295).

22. I deal with the concept of the mask in detail in Knowles 2015: 93–117; on the phrase "secret spiritual Germany," see Kisiel 2009: 145–54; Polt 2013: 63–85; for the use of the phrase "secret Germany" among the members of the George-Kreis in the 1920s, see Raulff 2009 and Norton 2002.

23. *BT*, 129/125; Wolin 2016, 49–53 is symptomatic of a reading that mistakenly reduces "the they" to an absolute, deeming it "so disproportionately negative that we are seemingly left with no immanent prospects for realizing our authentic natures in the domain of ontic life as such." He thus accuses Heidegger of a "*radical devaluation of the life-world.*"

24. Nancy 2017, 24, puts the question quite succinctly: "One can ask: did the configuration of thought go in search of the anti-Semitic motif, or was it, conversely, the antisemitism that suggested a part of the configuration? It is difficult, no doubt impossible, to decide this question."

25. Translated by Richard Polt.

26. Hence I disagree with statements such as Zaborowski's that "in contrast to Carl Schmitt, for example, antisemitism did not play a *philosophical* role for Heidegger" (Zaborowski 2016, 429).

27. Antisemitic statements also abound, of course, in his private correspondence. For some of the more flagrant examples, see Trawny 2015b, 18–37.

28. For a detailed reconstruction of this event based on the Freiburg University Archives, see Knowles 2018.

29. Heidegger uses the term "handicraft" repeatedly to describe the style of the *Black Notebooks* (*GA* 94, 159, 291, 365, 390, 397, 399, 401, 407; *GA* 95, 9, 104; *GA* 96, 64, 69; *GA* 97, 22, 71–81, 97, 115–19, 125, 167–91, 284, 308, 333, 347, 449, 479, 503, 508).

30. For a detailed reading of the passage, see Fritsche 1999, 124–41.

31. Martin Heidegger to Fritz Heidegger, April 1946, in *HA*, 137.

32. The files of the Bundesarchiv Berlin-Lichterfelde (BArch NS15/209) do not confirm Heidegger's claim (*GA* 16, 392) that he was under surveillance by the Nazi Security Service. They only show him to have been under the routine observation of the Reich Surveillance Office under Alfred Rosenberg to which every professor was subject.

33. Martin Heidegger to Fritz Heidegger, February 23, 1942, in *HA*, 81.

34. Martin Heidegger to Fritz Heidegger, January 18, 1945, in *HA*, 119.

35. Heidegger to Kurt Bauch, May 1, 1942, in Heidegger and Bauch 2010, 79.

36. Martin Heidegger to Fritz Heidegger, November 15, 1944, in *HA*, 112.

37. Bundesarchiv Berlin-Lichterfelde, BArch NS15/209.

38. The relevant documentation is available in Heidegger's personnel file at the Hauptstaatsarchiv Stuttgart, file EA 3/150, Bü 835; cf. Heidegger's many false claims in *GA* 16, 393.

39. Martin Heidegger to Fritz Heidegger, September 7, 1941, in *HA*, 77; Cf. *GA* 16, 393.

40. Martin Heidegger to Fritz Heidegger, January 12, 1945, in *HA*, 116; Heidegger's correspondence with his friend the art historian Kurt Bauch, who joined the Nazi party in Freiburg on the same day as Heidegger, offers perhaps the most revealing insight into his state of mind from 1934 to 1945.

41. Bundesarchiv Berlin-Lichterfelde, BArch R4901/12444. Leaman and Simon 1992, 261–92, reproduces portions of this report.

42. The context of Heidegger's philhellenism is revealed quite masterfully in Bambach 2003. On Heidegger's Heraclitus and Parmenides lectures, see Ramet 2012.

43. Even prior to the publication of the *Black Notebooks*, Robert Bernasconi persuasively argued against the notion that Heidegger's lecture courses can be regarded as a critique of National Socialist racial ideology (Bernasconi 2000, 50–67).

44. Martin Heidegger to Kurt Bauch April 15, 1945, in Bauch and Heidegger 2010, 102; Speck 2015, 169–90.

45. Martin Heidegger to Fritz Heidegger, July 23, 1945, in *HA*, 127; cf. *GA* 97, 83.

46. Thurnher 2016 persuasively argues against the common assumption that Heidegger's "private National Socialism" was somehow less radical than the goals of the party.

47. Martin Heidegger to Fritz Heidegger, July 23,1945, in *HA*, 127.

48. For the most detailed analysis of Heidegger's denazification process, see Ott 1993.

49. Martin Heidegger to Fritz Heidegger, September 21, 1949, in Homolka and Heidegger 2016, 142; for a scathing analysis of this decision to describe himself as a "fellow-traveler of being," see Thomä 2016.

50. Martin Heidegger to Fritz Heidegger, July 23, 1945, in *HA*, 126.

51. Martin Heidegger to Fritz Heidegger, December 17, 1945, in *HA* 132.

52. Martin Heidegger to Fritz Heidegger, August 9, 1945, in *HA* 129.

53. Martin Heidegger to Fritz Heidegger, September 21, 1949, in *HA*, 141.

54. This is diametrically opposed to the attempt to rehabilitate Heidegger's silence after the publication of the *Black Notebooks* in Marafioti 2016.

55. On Jaspers and *Existenzphilosophie*, see *GA* 97, 22, 91, 199, 208–9; Sartre, Heidegger writes in 1946, is "extremely intelligent, even greater than his intelligence is his authorial talent, even greater than that is his aptitude for presenting himself as original, even greater than that is the concealment of sources, and even greater than that is the *miscomprehension* of *Being and Time*, 'On the Essence of Ground,' 'What Is Metaphysics,' and the Kant book. Everything is still stuck in the standpoint of the Cartesian consciousness, despite the calls for 'freedom,' 'concretion,' and 'existence'" (*GA* 97, 166).

56. Martin Heidegger to Fritz Heidegger, September 21, 1949, in *HA*, 42.

57. Writing of Heidegger's "postmortem suicide," Reinhard Mehring complains of a "marketing decision" that led the Heidegger family and the publisher of the *Heidegger Gesamtausgabe* to "switch to marketing Heidegger as a politically scandalous author, rather than as a great 'thinker'" (Mehring 2016, 298; see, too, Krell 2016, 310). On the textual history of the *Black Notebooks*, see *GA* 94, 530–32, editor's epilogue. Heidegger preserved the *Black Notebooks* and edited them over the decades before they were deposited in the Deutsches Literaturarchiv Marbach in the mid-1970s. He intended both their content and existence to be kept secret until they could be published as the capstone to his complete works. However, since the publication of the *Gesamtausgabe*, begun in the 1970s, has progressed more slowly than planned, and given the nature of the material they contain, the administrators of the Heidegger estate decided to break with the original mandate and publish the *Black Notebooks* in 2014, earlier than had been intended.

58. Martin Heidegger to Fritz Heidegger, July 31, 1945, in *HA*, 129.

59. In a number of angry passages written around the time of his denazification proceedings, Heidegger refers obliquely to Jaspers's work on guilt (*GA* 97, 99, 129–35, 146, 172, 260, 333, 461, 523).

60. The scholarly and journalistic literature on the *Black Notebooks* is already quite extensive. The first edited volume to appear in English is Farin and Malpas 2016, followed by Trawny and Mitchell 2017. In German, see Gander and Striet 2016; Heinz and Kellerer 2016; Trawny and Mitchell 2015. See also the essays in *HA*.

61. Typical of this is Friedrich-Wilhelm von Herrmann's attack, in Herrmann 2016, 92, on Trawny's *Myth of the Jewish World Conspiracy*. Jean Grondin's assertion that "as a patriot Heidegger was totally blinded by Hitler" (Grondin 2016, 235), portraying him as a naïve bumpkin bewitched by Nazi antisemitic rhetoric and propaganda, is equally troubling and unconvincing.

62. The classic example of this strategy is Dreyfus 1991.

63. Vallega-Neu 2015 offers the most thorough analysis of Heidegger's sigetics.

64. Martin Heidegger to Elisabeth Blochmann, September 19, 1933, in *GA* 16, 168.

Chapter 2

1. On the links between Heidegger and Clauss see Faye 2009, 18–38, and on the völkisch movement more broadly, Faye 2009, 141–42. Cf. Alice Yaeger Kaplan's analysis of French intellectuals drawn to fascism in Kaplan 1986.

2. Heidegger's talent for self-representation is thoroughly analyzed in Mehring 1992.

3. See Weingart 1995, albeit based on a dubious notion of resistance, on Clauss's life.

4. Cf. the chapter "Der Antisemitismus der NSDAP" in Huber 1933, 90–96, and Bartels 1919.

5. On Heidegger's place in the völkisch movements of the early twentieth century, see Bambach 2003 and Sluga 1993; see also the classic intellectual histories of Mosse 1981; Herf 1974; Stern 1974.

6. Gilman 2017 begins this work of linking Heidegger's antisemitism to common tropes of the time.

7. On Schmidt's biography, see Leaman and Simon 1994. For a useful overview of philosophy in National Socialism, see Sieg 2013.

8. See Bauch 1917b for a more detailed statement of his antisemitic philosophy of language; for an analysis of Bauch's work and context, see also Sieg 1991 and 2004.

9. Sieg 2013, 136, documents Nicolai Hartmann's comment on the "Jewification" of the journal Kant-Studien.

10. Krois reprints the report from the *Frankfurter Zeitung* as an appendix to his essay.

11. Translated in Bambach 2003, 53; original citation: www.zeit.de/1989/52 /die-verjudung-des-deutschen-geistes.

12. Heidegger also uses the term *volklich* in the concurrent *Black Notebooks* in GA 94, 109–10/80, 123–25/90–92, 140/103, 157/115.

13. For a description of this pageantry, see Sluga 1993, 1–4.

14. For an analysis of the political implications of Heidegger's use of "Dasein" in connection with national or historical groups, see Kisiel 2002, 135–57.

15. On the role of translation in Heidegger's thought, see Sallis 2002, 1–21.

16. On the relation between nearness and language, see Ziarek 1994; for a critique of the limitations of Heidegger's early conception of space and proximity, see Mitchell 2010, 1–14.

17. Heidegger, of course, ought to be regarded as contributing to the ruination of language under National Socialism. Perhaps the finest analysis of this transformation is found in Klemperer 2006.

Chapter 3

1. On St. Augustine, see Dahlstrom 2009 and 2010; on Eckhart, see Caputo 1986 and Schürmann 1973. Derrida 2008, 73–81, focuses his own reading of Kierkegaard's *Fear and Trembling* on the question of silence.

2. It is perhaps for this reason that the literature on Heidegger and language often tends to focus on Heidegger's later work, especially *On the Way to Language* and the Hölderlin lectures, and not on *Being and Time*; see Aler 1972; Dahlstrom 2013; Dastur 2013; Sallis 1970.

3. On the connection between Husserl and Aristotle in Heidegger's early thinking, see his 1963 autobiographical text "My Way to Phenomenology," in Heidegger 1972.

4. For an analysis of the Aristotelian origins of this operation of *logos*, see Baracchi 2008, 56–58.

5. See Aristotle 1981b, 1457a5–10, and 1963, 16b25ff.; Kisiel 1995, 178, underscores the importance of assertion (*apophansis*) as related to silence: "Most importantly, apophansis is a garrulous language in which the punctuations of silence ultimately play no role."

6. On the primacy of vision in *Being and Time*, see McNeill 1999, 17–55.

7. For other references to §34, see LH, 318/243; *GA* 36/7, 110/86–7.

8. This tendency is even stronger in *GA* 19, 87/60, where Heidegger associ-

ates *logos* with taking apart, even declaring that "[w]hat is intermingled is separated out 'by our taking it apart'. Such *diarein* is the basic function of *logos*; in discourse, *logos* takes things apart"; in 1931, Heidegger declared his analysis of language in *GA* 19 to be "unsatisfactory" (*GA* 33, 5/2).

9. The same goes for his usage of *legein* (*BT*, 25/24, 33/31, 34/32, 44/44).

10. For more detailed analyses see Brogan 2013; Dastur 2002; Schalow 1995.

11. On this twofold notion of being in Heidegger's work, see Brogan 2005.

Chapter 4

1. See the editor's epilogue in *GA* 29–30, 540–41/372.

2. On the overlap between Heidegger and Jewish thought, see Zarader 2006; Gordon 2003; Düttmann 2000.

3. On Aristotle's aporetic "system," see Wieland 1962, 29–33.

4. Heidegger's approach to the manifold meanings of being was of course deeply influenced by Brentano 1960; for an analysis of Brentano's influence on Heidegger, see Volpi 1978.

5. I draw this understanding of *ēthos* from Baracchi 2008.

6. See Aristotle 1963, 12b16–13a17; *Met.* 1022b22–1023a7; *Physics* 191b33–193b22. For a more traditional analysis of these passages, see Anton 1957.

7. In "Vom Wesen und Begriff der phusis: Aristoteles, Physik B, 1" ("On the Essence and Concept of phusis in Physics B, 1") (Heidegger 1976d, 295–301/225–30).8. As Heidegger stresses (*GA* 33, 65/54), this conception of *adunaton* is utilized in the formulation of the principle of noncontradiction by Aristotle in *Met.* 1005b29–30.

9. Heidegger is referring to Aristotle, *Physics* 221b12–14.

10. I disassociate myself from Heidegger's disparaging references to disabilities.

11. Adorno 1964 identifies the concept of authenticity as central in Heidegger's politics.

12. Hitler's understanding of selection was drawn in part from Lenz 1927.

13. E.g., Martin Heidegger to Fritz Heidegger, March 2, 1932, in *HA*, 26.

14. Martin Heidegger to Kurt Bauch, May 1, 1942, in Bauch and Heidegger 2010, 78.

Chapter 5

1. These themes are already prominent in the earliest volume of the *Black*

Notebooks, where Heidegger speaks of the "measurelessness of the groundless" (*GA* 94, 216/158).

2. Regarding the Other in the construction of Greek self-identity, see Chanter 2011.

3. Foucault also deals with the questions of truth-saying and silence in Foucault 2001 and Foucault 2008.

4. Aulus Gellius employs the Latin *tacere* to describe this silence; cf. Foucault 2005, 413–17.

5. Foucault is especially intrigued by the silencing of writing in Foucault 2005, 414; the link between silence and reading for the Greeks is well known. For an analysis of the vocal nature of reading see Svenbro 1993, 161–86.

6. Hans Blumenberg traces the history of the translation of curiosity into sinfulness in the early Christian tradition in Blumenberg 1985, 285–308.

7. This transformation of ritual forms of silence is significantly linked what Marcel Detienne calls the "gradual secularization of speech" that started around the time of the Pythagoreans (Detienne 1996, 15).

8. On the role of rectitude as the proper philosophical posture, see Cavarero 2016.

9. See, e.g., the influential essays collected in Allen 1965. On the role of the theory of the forms in Plato's metaphysics, see Meinwald 1992, 365–96.

10. *Parmenides* has long been regarded as the source of much of Neoplatonic thought (see Dodds 1928, 129–42; cf. Gadamer 1999a and b), and as a source of negative theology, but these are questions I must leave aside here, with no intent to depreciate such approaches.

11. The tutorial is published along with various student protocols in *GA* 83, 25–37.

12. On the importance of this aspect of mild coercion bringing Socrates back, see Baracchi 2002: 40–42.

13. In Plato's *Phaedrus*, the written word has structural similarities to Heidegger's conception of idle talk, for "once something is written down, every speech is whirled about every which way, picked up as well by those who understand as by those who have no business reading it" (272e). This has been analyzed quite brilliantly in Derrida 2004.

14. "It is a lack of education not to know of what things one should seek a demonstration and of what he should not."

15. In his later thinking of the event, Derrida captures the essence of this aporia in Derrida 2007a.

16. Baracchi 2008, 57; see also Brogan 2005, 79–81.

17. Sallis is explicitly referring to Plato's discussion of the good as beyond being in the *Republic* 509b.

18. This is what Heidegger calls "what is momentarily concrete, which as such can always be otherwise" (*GA* 19, 164/112–13); see also Heidegger's discussion of *orthotēs, eu*, and *orthos logos* at *GA* 19, 149–51/103–4; cf. Cavarero 2016, 52–55

19. For a detailed analysis of *phronēsis*, see Aubenque 2007.

20. The association of physical traits with character dispositions is also pervasive in Aristotle, and it cannot be forgotten that Plato was a great connoisseur of boys' noses.

21. I borrow this elegant distinction between *mobilized* and *vested* terms from Malabou 2011, 5.

22. Plato describes a similar injunction in the *Laws* (Plato 1997a, 934e–935a).

23. On the *bios xenikos*, see Arendt 1981, 53.

Chapter 6

1. As Montiglio (*SL*, 51) notes, in Homeric epics *hēsuchia* is not a heroic virtue, and is the "enemy of glory"; on the link between *hēsuchia* and *sōphrosunē* in the development of the polis, see Vernant 1982, 86.

2. Bergren draws on the seminal work by Detienne and Vernant 1978.

3. On the feminine as monstrosity in Aristotle's cosmology and biology, see Bianchi 2014, 3–5.

4. For a commentary on this passage, see Zeitlin 1996, 369–74. Cf. also Aristotle's discussion of the potentially unbridled sexual passion of pubescent girls, who "have much need of surveillance," in the *History of Animals* (Aristotle 1984a, 581a12–22).

5. Wendy Brown (1994) bases her interpretation of Plato's playful employment of certain feminine traits in the figure of Socrates in part on the *Phaedrus*.

6. See Bianchi 2014, 85–114; Grosz 1995, 111–34; Hill 2011; Kristeva 1984; on Greek women as *chōra*, see Loraux 1998, 73–77.

7. This is the central argument of Loraux 1998.

8. For a detailed analysis of Aristotle's conception of *phusis, topos* and women with reference to Irigaray, see Hill 2011, 11–91.

9. Analyses of gender in ancient Greece almost all quote this statement by Pericles, cited in Thucydides, *History of the Peloponnesian War* 2.45; reproduced here from the translation in Schaps 1977, 323. For an especially subtle approach

to the consequences of this conception of feminine *phusis*, see Loraux 1995, 227–48.

10. On earthquakes, see Aristotle 1984b, 367a22–23; on violent winds, 366a13–19.

11. On the stillest hour, see also Irigaray 2001, 62–67. It is an auspicious hour for Nietzsche's Zarathustra (Nietzsche 1983, 145–47).

12. Classical Athens lacked the positive sense of trickery associated with Homeric heroes like Odysseus (*SL*, 252–88).

13. See also Lysistrata's explanation for keeping silent under the threat of her husband's violence at 515–40.

14. Foucault 1990, 27, documents how silence can be the product of a vast array of discourses that talk interminably.

15. Cambiano 1995, 113, notes that evidence exists that there were women in Plato's Academy, Epicurus's school, and among the Cynics, though he says that "it is difficult to establish whether they also taught or wrote."

16. It is perhaps worth noting in passing that the *doxa* report the same of Heidegger's wife Elfriede, often blaming her for Heidegger's radicalism.

17. On the significance of this passage, see Loraux 1995, 149–50.

18. See also Vernant 1982, 64, 76–77.

19. See *SL*, on injunctions of silence, 13–17; on calls for silence, 167–73; and on the rhetorical figure of occultation, 116–57.

20. Sophocles 1960, 1287–97; see also Clay 1982, 277–98.

21. The play does not survive.

22. Aristotle is quoting from Sophocles's *Ajax*.

23. Sophocles, fr. 76, quoted and translated in *SL*, 281.

24. De Beauvoir is referring to a passage from Aristotle 1943, 728a18–21: "Further, a boy actually resembles a woman in physique, and a woman is as it were an infertile male; the female, in fact, is female on account of an inability of a sort, viz., it lacks the power to concoct semen out of the final state of the nourishment (this is either blood, or its counterpart in bloodless animals) because of the coldness of its nature." Cf. *SW*, 160–67. For an extended analysis of the passage, see Bianchi 2014, 51–57.

25. Glenn 1997 seeks to recover a history of defiant silence as speech. She draws in part on Audre Lorde's essay "The Transformation of Silence into Language and Action," in Lorde 1984, 40–44. On defiant silences, see also Constable 2005; on silence as a form of resistance, see Gaventa 1982.

26. In *Lysistrata* (461), Aristophanes plays with the common assumption that both women and slaves have a proclivity for drunkenness.

27. See Foucault's reading of exile as silencing based on a passage from Euripides's *The Phoenecian Women* in Foucault 2001, 28–29; cf. Montiglio 2005, 30–37.

28. On *phusis* as being, see Heidegger 1976e; cf. Hill 2001, 18–39.

29. On *mnēmosunē*, cf. GA 34, 295/210.

30. *IM* 117/162; cf. GA 54, 133–143/89–97; for analysis of Heidegger's concept of the polis, see Fried 2000, 138–42.

31. Heidegger (GA 54, 134–139/90–94) draws the term from Sophocles's *Antigone* and employs it in the context of discussion of *dikē* (right, justice)

32. For a subtle analysis of various linguistic strategies employed through the "muted" voice of women in different cultures, see Gal 1991, 175–203.

33. For an attempt to describe Heidegger as employing a "feminine" voice, see Graybeal 1990.

Chapter 7

1. "Die Grundfrage der Philosophie" takes up only 80 pages in GA 36–37. By way of comparison, his lecture courses in the three prior semesters are 197 (GA 35), 322 (GA 34), and 224 (GA 33) pages long.

2. Cf. Heidegger's remarks to himself at the beginning of the summer semester 1933 that the students were too "spiritually immature" for the "revolution *within* the university" (GA 94, 116/85).

3. On the distinction between "spiritual" and "vulgar" National Socialism, see Trawny 2015b, 16–17; Thurnher 2016, 380–83.

4. I deal with this in detail in my essay "Heidegger's Nazi Conscience." For references to vulgar National Socialism, see GA 94, 99, 104. On spiritual National Socialism, see GA 94, 135–36. For a discussion of the relation between the two, see GA 94, 532–33.

5. Although it would go beyond the scope of this work, Heidegger's class antagonisms vis-à-vis his colleagues played a critical role in his treatment of the professoriate as rector. These antagonisms and the grudges they engendered in turn influenced how those very same professors on the university's independent denazification commission dealt with the "Heidegger case."

6. Krell concedes this in his review of the fourth volume of the *Black Notebooks*, but dismisses it as a matter without philosophical significance (Krell 2016, 328–29).

7. Heidegger's most extensive treatment of the question can be found in GA

29–30, 261/176–273/185. For a more recent treatment of philosophy's attempt to deny *logos* to animals, see Seshradi 2012.

8. The relevant documentation can found in Heidegger's personnel file in the Hauptstaatsarchiv Stuttgart, file EA 3/150, Bü 835.

9. Geheimes Staatsarchiv Preußischer Kulturbesitz, *HA*, Rep. 76 IVa, Nr. 71.

10. It is worth recalling how the language of creativity was addressed in Kolbenheyer 1935.

11. The book is attributed to a student team specializing in cultural studies from the Karlsruhe Pedagogical Institute. Wintersweiler is in deep southwest Germany, south of Freiburg, and close to the French and Swiss borders.

12. Martin Heidegger to Fritz Heidegger, April 27, 1933, in *HA*, 29.

13. Martin Heidegger to Fritz Heidegger, December 18, 1931, in *HA*, 21.

14. For a critique of Heidegger as a dramatist, see Hyland 2015, 341–57.

15. Derrida 1993 examines this passing reference to the friend at length.

16. For more on the emergency, see Polt 2006.

17. See Lang 1996; Derrida 1990. Cf. also Paul Celan's reaction to Heidegger's silence in Lyon 2006, 159–73. Notice that it persists even in Nancy 2017, 51, where he speaks of "the stubborn silence of Heidegger on the camps." Nancy does admit that that portion of the book was written prior to reading *GA* 97, but it is nonetheless a testament to the power of the narrative of Heidegger's silence.

Epilogue

1. Auschwitz reached this capacity by the summer of 1944; see Piper 1994, 174.

2. Adolf Lampe to the rector of Freiburg University, October 6, 1945, Universitätsarchiv Freiburg, file C67/2817.

3. In one of the more controversial sections of *Eichmann in Jerusalem*, Hannah Arendt criticizes Jewish acceptance of the category of the "prominent" figure as implicit acceptance of the idea that certain lives were more worthy than others (Arendt 1963, 131–34).

4. Lacoue-Labarthe 1990 employs the phrase in an ironic sense. See also Lacoue-Labarthe 1998, 290–91.

5. In Freiburg the letters of protest tended to come primarily from the Faculty of Law and the directors of the university's medical clinics: Universitätsarchiv Freiburg, file B1/3986.

6. Bundesarchiv Berlin-Lichterfelde, file BArch NS38/2418.

7. For a decisive rebuttal of this self-portrayal, see Morat 2012.

8. Martin Heidegger to Fritz Heidegger, December 1, 1945, in *HA*, 131.

9. Bundesarchiv Berlin-Lichterfelde, file BArch R4901/1796.

10. Quoted in Ott 1993, 326; for a detailed analysis of Heidegger's denazification, see Seeman 2002, 112–31.

References

Archives and Archival Material
Bundesarchiv Berlin-Lichterfelde: Series R4901, R8088, NS15, NS 38.
Hauptstaatsarchiv Stuttgart: EA 3/150, Bü 835.
Geheimes Staatsarchiv Preußischer Kulturbesitz: HA, Rep. 76 IVa, Nr. 71.
Universitätsarchiv Freiburg: Series B1, C67.

Primary and Secondary Material
Adorno, Theodor. 1973. *Jargon of Authenticity*. Translated by Knut Tarnowski and
    Frederic Will. Evanston, IL: Northwestern University Press.
Agamben, Giorgio. 1999. *Remnants of Auschwitz: The Witness and the Archive*.
    Translated by Daniel Heller-Roazen. New York: Zone Books.
Albanis, Elisabeth. 2009. "Anleitung zum Hass: Theodor Fritschs antisemitisches
    Geschichtsbild." In *Antisemitische Geschichtsbilder*, ed. Werner Bergmann and
    Ulrich Sieg, 167–91. Essen: Klartext.
Aler, Jan. 1972. "Heidegger's Conception of Language in *Being and Time*." In
    On Heidegger and Language, ed. Joseph J. Kockelmans, 33–64. Evanston, IL:
    Northwestern University Press.
Allen, Reginald E. 1965. *Studies in Plato's Metaphysics*. New York: Humanities
    Press.
Aly, Götz. 2014. *Why the Germans? Why the Jews? Envy, Race Hatred, and the
    Prehistory of the Holocaust*. Translated by Jefferson S. Chase. New York: Met-
    ropolitan Books.
Améry, Jean. 1999. *On Suicide: A Discourse on Voluntary Death*. Translated by
    John D. Barlow. Bloomington: Indiana University Press.

Anton, John Peter. 1957. *Aristotle's Theory of Contrariety*. London: Routledge and Paul.

Arendt, Hannah. 1963. *Eichmann in Jerusalem: A Report on the Banality of Evil*. New York: Penguin.

———. 1981. *The Life of the Mind*. New York: Harcourt Brace Jovanovich.

———. 1994. "We Refugees." In *Altogether Elsewhere: Writers on Exile*, ed. Marc Robinson. Boston: Faber and Faber.

Aristophanes. [411 BCE] 1996. *Lysistrata*. Translated by Jeffrey Henderson. In *Three Plays by Aristophanes: Staging Women*, ed. Jeffrey Henderson. New York: Routledge.

Aristotle. 1943. *Generation of Animals*. Translated by A. L. Peck. Cambridge, MA: Harvard University Press.

———. 1963. *Aristotle's "Categories" and "De Interpretatione."* Translated by J. L. Ackrill. Oxford: Clarendon Press.

———. 1966. *Metaphysics*. Translated by Hippocrates G. Apostle. Bloomington: Indiana University Press.

———. 1980. *Physics*. Translated by Hippocrates G. Apostle. Grinnell, IA: Peripatetic Press.

———. 1981a. *On the Soul*. Translated by Hippocrates G. Apostle. Grinnell, IA: Peripatetic Press.

———. 1981b. *Poetics*. Translated by Hippocrates G. Apostle. Grinnell, IA: Peripatetic Press.

———. 1984a. *The History of Animals*. In *The Complete Works of Aristotle: The Revised Oxford Translation*, vol. 1, ed. Jonathan Barnes. Princeton, NJ: Princeton University Press.

———. 1984b. *Meteorology*. In *The Complete Works of Aristotle: The Revised Oxford Translation*, vol. 1, ed. Jonathan Barnes. Princeton, NJ: Princeton University Press.

———. 1984c. *The Nicomachean Ethics*. Translated by Hippocrates G. Apostle. Grinnell, IA: Peripatetic Press.

———. 1984d. *Problems*. Translated by E. S. Forster. In *The Complete Works of Aristotle: The Revised Oxford Translation*, vol. 2, ed. Jonathan Barnes. Princeton, NJ: Princeton University Press.

———. 1986. *Politics*. Translated by Hippocrates G. Apostle. Grinnell, IA: Peripatetic Press.

———. 2006. *Aristotle on Memory*. Translated and edited by Richard Sorabji. Chicago: University of Chicago Press.

Aubenque, Pierre. 2007. *Der Begriff der Klugheit bei Aristoteles*. Translated by Nicolai Sinai and Ulrich Johannes Schneider. Hamburg: Meiner.

Aulus Gellius. [2nd century CE] 1795. *The Attic Nights of Aulus Gellius*. Translated by William Beloe. London: Printed for J. Johnson.

———. 1946. *The Attic Nights of Aulus Gellius*. Translated by John Carew Rolfe. Cambridge, MA: Harvard University Press.

Babich, Babette. 1992. "Questioning Heidegger's Silence: A Postmodern Topology." In *Ethics and Danger: Essays on Heidegger and Continental Thought*, ed. Arleen B. Dallery, Charles E. Scott, and P. Holley Roberts, 83–106. Albany: State University of New York Press.

Bajohr, Frank, and Dieter Pohl. 2008. *Massenmord und schlechtes Gewissen: Die deutsche Bevölkerung, die NS-Führung und der Holocaust*. Frankfurt: Fischer.

Bambach, Charles R. 2003. *Heidegger's Roots: Nietzsche, National Socialism, and the Greeks*. Ithaca, NY: Cornell University Press.

Baracchi, Claudia. 2002. *Of Myth, Life, and War in Plato's Republic*. Bloomington: Indiana University Press.

———. 2008. *Aristotle's Ethics as First Philosophy*. Cambridge: Cambridge University Press.

———. 2013. "A Vibrant Silence: Heidegger and the End of Philosophy." In *Being Shaken: Ontology and the Event*, ed. Michael Marder and Santiago Zabala, 92–121. New York: Palgrave Macmillan.

Bartels, Adolf. 1919. *Der deutsche Verfall: Vortrag, gehalten am 21. Januar 1913 zu Berlin: mit einem Nachwort: Der Zusammenbruch*. Zeitz: Sis.

Battersby, Christine. 1989. *Gender and Genius: Towards a Feminist Aesthetics*. Bloomington: Indiana University Press.

Bauch, Bruno. 1917a. "Lesebrief" *Der Panther: Deutsche Monatsschrift für Politik und Volkstum* 4 (6): 742–46.

———. 1917b. "Vom Begriff der Nation: Ein Kapitel zur Geschichtsphilosophie." *Kant-Studien* 21 (1): 139–62.

Bauch, Kurt, and Martin Heidegger. 2010. *Briefwechsel 1932–1975*, ed. Almuth Heidegger and Alfred Denker. Freiburg: Karl Alber.

Beauvoir, Simone de. 2010. *The Second Sex*. Translated by Constance Borde and Sheila Malovany-Chevallier. New York: Knopf.

Bergmann, Werner. 1999. "Völkischer Antisemitismus im Kaiserreich." In *Handbuch zur "Völkischen Bewegung" 1871–1918*, ed. Uwe Puschner, Walter Schmitz, and Justus H. Ulbricht, 449–63. Munich: K. G. Saur.

Bergren, Ann. 2008. "Language and the Female in Early Greek Thought." In

Weaving Truth: Essays on Language and the Female in Greek Thought, 13–42. Cambridge, MA: Harvard University Press.

Berkhoff, Karel. 2008. "Dina Pronicheva's Story of Surviving the Babi Yar Massacre: German, Jewish, Soviet, Russian and Ukrainian Records." In *The Shoah in Ukraine: History, Testimony, Memorialization*, ed. Ray Brandon and Wendy Lower, 291–317. Bloomington: Indiana University Press.

Bernasconi, Robert. 2000. "Heidegger's Alleged Challenge to the Nazi Concepts of Race." In *Appropriating Heidegger*, ed. James E. Faulconer and Mark A. Wrathall, 50–67. Cambridge: Cambridge University Press.

———. 2017. "Another Eisenmenger? On the Alleged Originality of Heidegger's Antisemitism." In *Heidegger's "Black Notebooks": Responses to Anti-Semitism*, ed. Andrew J. Mitchell and Peter Trawny, 168–85. New York: Columbia University Press.

Bernstein, Richard J. 1992. "Heidegger's Silence? *Ēthos* and Technology." In Bernstein, *The New Constellation: The Ethical-Political Horizons of Modernity/ Postmodernity*, 79–141. Cambridge, MA: MIT Press.

Beistegui, Miguel de. 1998. *Heidegger and the Political: Dystopias*. New York: Routledge.

Bialas, Wolfgang, and Anson Rabinbach. 2007. "Introduction." In *Nazi Germany and the Humanities: How Academics Embraced Nazism*, ed. Wolfgang Bialas and Anson Rabinbach, vii–lii. London: Oneworld Publications.

Bianchi, Emanuela. 2014. *The Feminine Symptom: Aleatory Matter in the Aristotelian Cosmos*. New York: Fordham University Press.

Blumenberg, Hans. 1985. *The Legitimacy of the Modern Age*. Translated by Robert M. Wallace. Cambridge, MA: MIT Press.

Böschenstein-Schäfer, Renate. 1962. "Zur Geschichte des Wortes 'zersetzen.'" *Zeitschrift für deutsche Wortforschung* 18 (1): 40–80.

Brault, Pascale-Anne. 2009. "Playing the Cassandra: Prophecies of the Feminine in the *Polis* and Beyond." In *Bound by the City: Greek Tragedy, Sexual Difference, and the Formation of the Polis*, ed. Denise Eileen McCoskey and Emily Zakin, 197–220. Albany: State University of New York Press.

Brentano, Franz Clemens. 1960. *Von der mannigfachen Bedeutung des Seienden nach Aristoteles*. Hildesheim: Olms.

Brogan, Walter. 2005. *Heidegger and Aristotle: The Twofoldness of Being*. Albany: State University of New York Press.

———. 2013. "Listening to the Silence: Reticence and the Call of Conscience in Heidegger's Philosophy." In *Heidegger and Language*, ed. Jeffrey Powell, 32–45. Bloomington: Indiana University Press.

Brown, Wendy. 1994. "'Supposing Truth were a Woman . . .': Plato's Subversion of Masculine Discourse." In *Feminist Interpretations of Plato*, ed. Nancy Tuana, 157–80. University Park: Pennsylvania State University Press.

Butler, Judith. 1993. *Bodies That Matter: On the Discursive Limits of "Sex."* New York: Routledge.

Caillois, Roger. 2003. "The Noon Complex." In *The Edge of Surrealism: A Roger Caillois Reader*. Translated by Claudine Frank. Durham, NC: Duke University Press.

Cambiano, Giuseppe. 1995. "Becoming an Adult." In *The Greeks*, ed. Jean-Pierre Vernant, 86–119. Chicago: University of Chicago Press.

Caputo, John D. 1986. *The Mystical Element in Heidegger's Thought*. New York: Fordham University Press.

Carson, Anne. 1995. "The Gender of Sound." In Carson, *Glass, Irony, and God*, 119–42. New York: New Directions.

Casey, Edward S. 1997. *The Fate of Place: A Philosophical History*. Berkeley: University of California Press.

Cavarero, Adriana. 2016. *Inclinations: A Critique of Rectitude*. Translated by Amanda Minervini and Adam Sitze. Stanford, CA: Stanford University Press.

Cesare, Donatella di. 2015. *Heidegger, die Juden, die Shoah*. Frankfurt: Klostermann.

Chanter, Tina. 2011. *Whose Antigone? The Tragic Marginalization of Slavery*. Albany: State University of New York Press.

Clauss, Ludwig Ferdinand. [1932] 1940. *Die nordische Seele: Eine Einführung in die Rassenseelenkunde*. Munich: Lehmann.

Clay, Diskin. 1982. "Unspeakable Words in Greek Tragedy." *American Journal of Philology* 103 (3): 277–98.

Coetzee, J. M. 1988. *White Writing: On the Culture of Letters in South Africa*. New Haven, CT: Yale University Press.

Constable, Marianne. 2005. *Just Silences: The Limits and Possibilities of Modern Law*. Princeton, NJ: Princeton University Press.

Dagerman, Stig. [1947] 2011. *German Autumn*. Translated by Robin Fulton Macpherson. Minneapolis: University of Minnesota Press.

Dahlstrom, Daniel. 2009. "Temptation, Self-Possession, and Resoluteness." *Research in Phenomenology* 39 (2): 248–65.

———. 2010. "Truth and Confession: Confession and Existential Analysis." In *A Companion to Heidegger's Phenomenology of Religious Life*, ed. S. J. McGrath and Andrej Wiercinski, 263–84. Amsterdam: Rodopi.

———. 2013. "Heidegger's Ontological Analysis of Language." In *Heidegger and Language*, ed. Jeffrey Powell, 13–31. Bloomington: Indiana University Press.

Dahms, Hans-Joachim. 2009. "Philosophie." In *Die Rolle der Geisteswissenschaften im Dritten Reich 1933–45*, ed. Frank Rutger Hausmann, 193–228. Berlin: De Gruyter.

Darré, Richard Walther. [1929] 1940. *Das Bauerntum als Lebensquell der nordischen Rasse*. Munich: Lehmann.

———. [1930] 1937. *Neuadel aus Blut und Boden*. Berlin: Spaeth and Linde.

———. 1941. "Unser Weg." In Darré, *Um Blut und Boden: Reden und Aufsätze*, 69–106. Munich: Zentralverlag der NSDAP.

Dastur, Françoise. 2002. "The Call of Conscience: the Most Intimate Alterity." In *Heidegger and Practical Philosophy*, ed. François Raffoul and David Pettigrew, 87–98. Albany: State University of New York Press.

———. 2013. "Heidegger and the Question of the 'Essence' of Language." In *Heidegger and Language*, ed. Jeffrey Powell, 224–39. Bloomington: Indiana University Press.

Davis, Bret W. 2007. *Heidegger and the Will: On the Way to "Gelassenheit."* Evanston, IL: Northwestern University Press.

Demosthenes. [360s BCE] 1926. "Against Midias." In *Demosthenes, with an English Translation*. Translated by A. T. Murray. Cambridge, MA: Harvard University Press.

Denker, Alfred, and Holger Zaborowski, eds. 2009. *Heidegger-Jahrbuch 4: Heidegger und der Nationalsozialismus I: Dokumente*. Freiburg: Alber.

Derrida, Jacques. 1982. "Différance." In *Margins of Philosophy*, 1–28. Translated by Alan Bass. Chicago: University of Chicago Press.

———. 1987. "On Reading Heidegger." *Research in Phenomenology* 17 (1): 171–88.

———. 1989. *Of Spirit: Heidegger and the Question*. Translated by Geoffrey Bennington and Rachel Bowlby. Chicago: University of Chicago Press.

———. 1990. "Heidegger's Silence." In *Martin Heidegger and National Socialism: Questions and Answers*, ed. Günther Neske and Emil Kettering, 145–48. New York: Paragon House.

———. 1993. "Heidegger's Ear: Philopolemology (Geschlecht IV)." In *Reading Heidegger: Commemorations*, ed. John Sallis, 163–220. Bloomington: Indiana University Press.

———. 1995. "Khōra." In Derrida, *On the Name*, 89–127. Translated by Ian McLeod. Stanford, CA: Stanford University Press,

———. 1997. *Politics of Friendship*. Translated by George Collins. New York: Verso.

———. 2004. "Plato's Pharmacy." In *Dissemination*, 67–186. Translated by Barbara Johnson. London: Continuum.

———. 2005. "Derrida's Response to Catherine Malabou." In *Augustine and Postmodernism: Confessions and Circumfession*, ed. John D. Caputo and Michael J. Scanlon, 138–43. Bloomington: Indiana University Press.

———. 2007a. "A Certain Impossible Possibility of Saying the Event." *Critical Inquiry* 33 (1): 441–61.

———. 2007b. "*Geschlecht* I: Sexual Difference, Ontological Difference." Translated by Ruben Bevezdivin and Elizabeth Rottenberg. In Derrida, *Psyche: Inventions of the Other*, vol. 1, ed. Peggy Kamuf and Elizabeth Rottenberg, 7–26. Stanford, CA: Stanford University Press.

———. 2008. *The Gift of Death and Literature in Secret*. Translated by David Wills. Chicago: University of Chicago Press.

———. 2011. *The Beast and the Sovereign*. Volume 2. Translated by Geoffrey Bennington Chicago: University of Chicago Press.

Detienne, Marcel. *The Masters of Truth in Archaic Greece*. Translated by Janet Lloyd. New York: Zone Books, 1996.

Detienne, Marcel, and Jean-Pierre Vernant. 1978. *Cunning Intelligence in Greek Culture and Society*. Translated by Janet Lloyd. Atlantic Highlands, NJ: Harvester Press Humanities Press.

Diogenes Laërtius. [2nd/3rd centuries CE] 1950. *Lives of Eminent Philosophers*. Volume 2. Translated by Robert Drew Hicks. Cambridge, MA: Harvard University Press.

Döblin, Alfred. 2004. *Berlin Alexanderplatz: The Story of Franz Biberkopf*. Translated by Eugene Jolas. New York: Continuum.

Dodds, Eric R. 1928. "The Parmenides of Plato and the Origin of the Neoplatonic 'One.'" *Classical Quarterly* 22 (3/4): 129–42.

Dostal, Robert. 1985. "Beyond Being: Heidegger's Plato." *Journal of the History of Philosophy* 23 (1): 71–98.

———. 1994. "The Public and the People: Heidegger's Illiberal Politics." *Review of Metaphysics* 47 (3): 517–55.

Dreyfus, Hubert. 1991. *Being-in-the-World: A Commentary on Heidegger's Being and Time, Division I*. Cambridge, MA: MIT Press.

Düttmann, Alexander García. 2000. *The Gift of Language: Memory and Promise in Adorno, Benjamin, Heidegger and Rosenzweig*. London: Athlone Press.

Eichberg, Henning, and Robert A. Jones. 1977. "The Nazi Thingspiel: Theater for the Masses in Fascism and Proletarian Culture." *New German Critique* 11 (2): 133–50.

Ericksen, Robert P. 2012. *Complicity in the Holocaust: Churches and Universities in Nazi Germany*. Cambridge: Cambridge University Press.

Euripides. *Medea*. 1955. In *Euripides I*, ed. David Grene and Richmond Lattimore. Translated by Rex Warner. Chicago: University of Chicago Press.

Farías, Victor. 1991. *Heidegger and Nazism*. Philadelphia: Temple University Press.

Farin, Ingo, and Jeff Malpas, eds. 2016. *Reading Heidegger's "Black Notebooks 1931–1941."* Cambridge, MA: MIT Press.

Faye, Emmanuel. 2009. *Heidegger: The Introduction of Nazism into Philosophy in Light of the Unpublished Seminars of 1933–1935*. Translated by Michael B. Smith. New Haven, CT: Yale University Press.

Figal, Günter. 2000. "Refraining from Dialectic: Heidegger's Interpretation of Plato in the *Sophist* Lectures (1924/25)." In *Interrogating the Tradition: Hermeneutics and the History of Philosophy*, ed. Charles E. Scott and John Sallis, 95–110. Albany: State University of New York Press.

Foucault, Michel. 1990. *The History of Sexuality*. Volume 1. Translated by Robert Hurley. New York: Vintage Books.

———. 2001. *Fearless Speech*. Los Angeles: Semiotext(e).

———. 2005. *The Hermeneutics of the Subject: Lectures at the Collège de France, 1981–82*. Translated by Graham Burchell. New York: Palgrave Macmillan.

———. 2008. *The Courage of Truth: The Government of Self and Others II: Lectures at the Collège de France, 1983–1984*. Translated by Graham Burchell. New York: Palgrave Macmillan.

Franke, Dörte. 2008. *Stolperstein*. New York: Indigo Productions. DVD.

Frei, Norbert. 1996. *Vergangenheitspolitik: Die Anfänge der Bundesrepublik und die NS-Vergangenheit*. Munich: Beck.

Fried, Gregory. 2000. *Heidegger's Polemos: From Being to Politics*. New Haven, CT: Yale University Press.

Friedländer, Saul. 1998. *Nazi Germany and the Jews: The Years of Persecution, 1933–1939*. New York: HarperCollins.

Fritsch, Theodor. 1939. *Handbuch der Judenfrage: Die wichtigsten Tatsachen zur Beurteilung des jüdischen Volkes*. Leipzig: Hammer.

Fritsche, Johannes. 1999. *Historical Destiny and National Socialism in Heidegger's "Being and Time."* Berkeley: University of California Press.

Fritzsche, Peter. 1998. *Germans into Nazis*. Cambridge, MA: Harvard University Press.

Gadamer, Hans-Georg. 1999a. "Parmenides oder das Diesseits des Seins." In Gadamer, *Gesammelte Werke*, 7: 3–31. Tübingen: Mohr Siebeck.

———. 1999b. "Der platonische 'Parmenides' und seine Nachwirkung." In Gadamer, *Gesammelte Werke*, 7: 313–27. Tübingen: Mohr Siebeck.

Gal, Susan. 1991. "Between Speech and Silence: The Problematics of Research on Language and Gender." In *Gender at the Crossroads of Knowledge: Feminist Anthropology in the Postmodern Era*, ed. Micaela di Leonardo, 175–203. Berkeley: University of California Press.

Gander, Hans-Helmuth, and Magnus Striet, eds. 2016. *Heideggers Weg in die Moderne: Eine Verortung der "Schwarzen Hefte."* Frankfurt: Vittorio Klostermann.

Gaventa, John. 1982. *Power and Powerlessness: Quiescence and Rebellion in an Appalachian Valley*. Urbana: University of Illinois Press.

Gillespie, Michael Allen. 2000. "Martin Heidegger's Aristotelian National Socialism." *Political Theory* 28 (2): 140–66.

Gilman, Sander. 2017. "Cosmopolitan Jews vs. Jewish Nomads: Sources of a Trope in Heidegger's *Black Notebooks*." In *Heidegger's "Black Notebooks": Responses to Anti-Semitism*, ed. Andrew J. Mitchell and Peter Trawny, 18–35. New York: Columbia University Press.

Glenn, Cheryl. 1997. *Rhetoric Retold: Regendering the Tradition from Antiquity through the Renaissance*. Carbondale: Southern Illinois University Press.

Goebbels, Joseph. 1929. *Das kleine abc des Nationalsozialisten*. Berlin: Kampf.

Gonzalez, Francisco J. 2008. "And the Rest is *Sigetik*: Silencing Logic and Dialectic in Heidegger's *Beiträge zur Philosophie*." *Research in Phenomenology* 38 (3): 358–91.

———. 2009. *Plato and Heidegger: A Question of Dialogue*. University Park: Pennsylvania State University Press.

Gordon, Peter Eli. 2003. *Rosenzweig and Heidegger: Between Judaism and German Philosophy*. Berkeley: University of California Press.

Graybeal, Jean. 1990. *Language and "the Feminine" in Nietzsche and Heidegger*. Bloomington: Indiana University Press.

Griffith, Mark. 2001. "Antigone and Her Sister(s): Embodying Women," In *Making Silence Speak: Women's Voices in Greek Literature and Society*, ed. André Lardinois and Laura McClure, 117–36. Princeton, NJ: Princeton University Press.

Grimm, Hans. 1932. *Volk ohne Raum*. Munich: Albert Langen, 1932.

———. 1950. *Erzbischofschrif: Antwort eines Deutschen*. Göttingen: Plesse.

Grondin, Jean. 2016. "Warum ich Heidegger in schwieriger Zeit treu bleibe." In *Heidegger und der Antisemitismus: Positionen im Widerstreit, mit Briefen von Martin und Fritz Heidegger*, ed. Walter Homolka and Arnulf Heidegger, 232–41. Freiburg: Herder.

Grosz, Elizabeth. 1995. *Space, Time, and Perversion: Essays on the Politics of Bodies.* New York: Routledge.

Grün, Bernd. 2010. *Der Rektor als Führer: Die Universität Freiburg von 1933 bis 1945.* Freiburg: Alber.

Grunsky, Hans. 1937. *Der Einbruch des Judentums in die Philosophie.* Berlin: Junker and Dünnhaupt, 1937.

Guenther, Lisa. 2013. *Solitary Confinement: Social Death and Its Afterlives.* Minneapolis: Minnesota University Press.

Hausmann, Frank-Rutger. 2011. *Die Geisteswissenschaften im "Dritten Reich."* Frankfurt: Klostermann.

Heiber, Helmut. 1991. *Universität unterm Hakenkreuz.* Munich: Saur.

Heidegger, Arnulf. 2016. "Vorwort." In *Heidegger und der Antisemitismus: Positionen im Widerstreit, mit Briefen von Martin und Fritz Heidegger,* ed. Walter Homolka und Arnulf Heidegger, 11–13. Freiburg: Herder.

Heidegger, Martin. 1968. *What Is Called Thinking?* Translated by J. Glenn Gray. New York: Harper and Row.

———. 1971. "Building Dwelling Thinking." In *Poetry, Language, Thought,* trans. Albert Hofstadter. New York: Harper and Row.

———. 1972. "My Way to Phenomenology." In Heidegger, *On Time and Being,* 74–82. Translated by Joan Stambaugh. New York: Harper and Row.

———. 1976a. "Brief über den Humanismus." In Heidegger, *Gesamtausgabe,* vol. 9, *Wegmarken,* 313–64. Frankfurt: Klostermann.

———. [1935] 1976b. *Einführung in die Metaphysik.* Tübingen: Niemeyer.

———. 1976c. "Vom Wesen der Wahrheit." In Heidegger, *Gesamtausgabe,* vol. 9, Wegmarken, 177–202. Frankfurt: Klostermann.

———. 1976d. "Vom Wesen und Begriff der *phusis*: Aristoteles, *Physik* B, 1." In Heidegger, *Gesamtausgabe,* vol. 9, *Wegmarken,* 239–302. Frankfurt: Klostermann.

———. 1976e. "Was ist Metaphysik?" In Heidegger, *Gesamtausgabe,* vol. 9, *Wegmarken,* 103–22. Frankfurt: Klostermann.

———. [1927] 1979. *Sein und Zeit.* Tübingen: Niemeyer.

———. 1981a. *Aristoteles, "Metaphysik" Theta 1–3: Von Wesen und Wirklichkeit der Kraft.* Vol. 33 of Heidegger, *Gesamtausgabe.* Frankfurt: Klostermann.

———. 1981b. "The Pathway." In *Heidegger the Man and the Thinker.* ed. Thomas Sheehan, 69–72. Chicago: Precedent.

———. 1981c. "Why Do I Stay in the Provinces?" In *Heidegger the Man and the Thinker.* ed. Thomas Sheehan, 27–30. Chicago: Precedent.

———. 1982a. *Identität und Differenz.* Pfullingen: Neske.

———. 1982b. *On the Way to Language*. Translated by Peter D. Hertz. San Francisco: Harper and Row.

———. 1982c. *Parmenides*. Vol. 54 of Heidegger, *Gesamtausgabe*. Frankfurt: Klostermann.

———. [1959] 1982d. *Unterwegs zur Sprache*. Pfullingen: Neske.

———. 1983a. *Aus der Erfahrung des Denkens*. Vol. 13 of Heidegger, *Gesamtausgabe*. Frankfurt: Klostermann.

———. 1983b. "Der Feldweg." In Heidegger, *Gesamtausgabe*, vol. 13, *Aus der Erfahrung des Denkens*, 87–90. Frankfurt: Klostermann.

———. 1983c. *Die Grundbegriffe der Metaphysik: Welt, Endlichkeit, Einsamkeit*. Vols. 29–30 of *Gesamtausgabe*. Frankfurt: Klostermann.

———. 1987. *Nietzsche*. Vols. 3 and 4. Translated by David Farrell Krell. New York: Harper and Row.

———. 1988. *Vom Wesen der Wahrheit: Zu Platons Höhlengleichnis und Theätet*. Vol. 34 of *Gesamtausgabe*. Frankfurt: Klostermann.

———. 1989. *Beiträge zur Philosophie (Vom Ereignis)*. Vol. 65 of *Gesamtausgabe*. Frankfurt: Klostermann.

———. 1992a. *Parmenides*. Translated by Richard Rojcewicz and André Schuwer. Bloomington: Indiana University Press.

———. 1992b. *Platon: "Sophistes."* Vol. 19 of *Gesamtausgabe*. Frankfurt: Klostermann.

———. 1993a. "On the Essence and Concept of *phusis* in *Physics* B, 1." In *Pathmarks*, 183–230. Translated by William McNeill. Cambridge: Cambridge University Press.

———. 1993b. "The Self-Assertion of the German University." In *The Heidegger Controversy: A Critical Reader*, ed. Richard Wolin, 29–40. Translated by William S. Lewis. Cambridge, MA: MIT Press.

———. 1994a. "Die Zeit des Weltbildes." In Heidegger, *Holzwege*, 75–114. Frankfurt: Klostermann.

———. 1994b. "Der Ursprung des Kunstwerkes." In Heidegger, *Holzwege*, 1–74. Frankfurt: Klostermann.

———. 1995a. *Aristotle's "Metaphysics" Theta 1–3: On the Essence and Actuality of Force*. Translated by Walter Brogan and Peter Warnek. Bloomington: Indiana University Press.

———. 1995b. *The Fundamental Concepts of Metaphysics: World, Finitude, Solitude*. Translated by William McNeill. Bloomington: Indiana University Press.

———. 1995c. *Phänomenologie des religiösen Lebens*. Vol. 60 of Heidegger, *Gesamtausgabe*. Frankfurt: Klostermann.

————. 1997a. *Plato's "Sophist."* Translated by Richard Rojcewicz and André Schuwer. Bloomington: Indiana University Press.

————. 1997b. *Was Heißt Denken?* Tübingen: Niemeyer.

————. 1998a. *Logik als die Frage nach dem Wesen der Sprache.* Vol. 38 of Heidegger, *Gesamtausgabe.* Frankfurt: Klostermann.

————. 1998b. "What is Metaphysics?" In *Pathmarks*, ed. William McNeill, 82–96. Translated by David Farrell Krell. Cambridge: Cambridge University Press.

————. 2000a. *Introduction to Metaphysics.* Translated by Gregory Fried and Richard Polt. New Haven, CT: Yale University Press.

————. 2000b. *Reden und andere Zeugnisse eines Lebensweges, 1910–1976.* Vol. 16 of Heidegger, *Gesamtausgabe.* Frankfurt: Klostermann.

————. 2000c. "Die Selbstbehauptung der deutschen Universität." In *Reden und andere Zeugnisse eines Lebensweges, 1910–1976.* Vol. 16 of Heidegger, *Gesamtausgabe*, 107–17. Frankfurt: Klostermann.

————. 2000d. "Spiegel-Gespräch mit Martin Heidegger." In *Reden und andere Zeugnisse eines Lebensweges, 1910–1976.* Vol. 16 of *Gesamtausgabe*, 652–83. Frankfurt: Klostermann.

————. 2001. *Sein und Wahrheit.* Vols. 36–37 of Heidegger, *Gesamtausgabe.* Frankfurt: Klostermann.

————. 2002a. "The Age of the World Picture." In Heidegger, *Off the Beaten Track*, ed. Julian Young, 57–72. Cambridge: Cambridge University Press.

————. 2002b. *The Essence of Truth: On Plato's Cave Allegory and Theaetetus.* Translated by Ted Sadler. New York: Continuum.

————. 2002c. *Grundbegriffe der aristotelischen Philosophie.* Vol. 18 of Heidegger, *Gesamtausgabe.* Frankfurt: Klostermann.

————. 2002d. "The Origin of the Work of Art." In Heidegger, *Off the Beaten Track*, ed. Julian Young and Kenneth Haynes, 1–56. Cambridge: Cambridge University Press.

————. 2002e. "Schöpferische Landschaft: Warum bleiben wir in der Provinz?" In *Aus der Erfahrung des Denkens.* Vol. 13 of Heidegger, *Gesamtausgabe*, 9–13. Frankfurt: Klostermann.

————. 2005. *Bremer und Freiburger Vorträge.* Vol. 79 of Heidegger, *Gesamtausgabe.* Frankfurt: Klostermann.

————. 2008. *Nietzsche I and II.* Stuttgart: Klett-Cotta.

————. 2009a. *Logic as the Question of the Essence of Language.* Translated by Wanda Gregory Torres and Yvonne Unna. Albany: State University of New York Press.

———. 2009b. "*Der Spiegel* Interview with Martin Heidegger." In *The Heidegger Reader*, ed. Günter Figal, 313–33. Translated by Jerome Veith. Bloomington: Indiana University Press.

———. [1996] 2010a. *Being and Time: A Translation of "Sein und Zeit."* Translated by Joan Stambaugh. Albany: State University of New York Press.

———. 2010b. *Being and Truth*. Translated by Gregory Fried and Richard Polt. Bloomington: Indiana University Press.

———. 2010c. *The Phenomenology of Religious Life*. Translated by Matthias Fritsch and Jennifer Anna Gosetti-Ferencei. Bloomington: Indiana University Press.

———. 2012a. *Bremen and Freiburg Lectures: Insight in That Which Is and Basic Principles of Thinking*. Translated by Andrew J. Mitchell. Bloomington: Indiana University Press.

———. 2012b. *Contributions to Philosophy (of the Event)*. Translated by Richard Rojcewicz and Daniela Vallega-Neu. Bloomington: Indiana University Press.

———. 2012c. *Seminare: Platon, Aristoteles, Augustinus*. Vol. 83 of Heidegger, *Gesamtausgabe*. Frankfurt: Klostermann.

———. 2014a. *Überlegungen II–VI (Schwarze Hefte 1931–1938)*. Vol. 94 of Heidegger, *Gesamtausgabe*. Frankfurt: Klostermann.

———. 2014b. *Überlegungen VII–XI (Schwarze Hefte 1938/9)*. Vol. 95 of Heidegger, *Gesamtausgabe*. Frankfurt: Klostermann.

———. 2014c. *Überlegungen XII–LXV (Schwarze Hefte 1939–41)*. Vol. 96 of Heidegger, *Gesamtausgabe*. Frankfurt: Klostermann.

———. 2015. *Anmerkungen I–V (Schwarze Hefte 1942–48)*. Vol. 97 of Heidegger, *Gesamtausgabe*. Frankfurt: Klostermann.

———. 2016. *Ponderings II–VI, Black Notebooks 1931–1938*. Translated by Richard Rojcewicz. Bloomington: Indiana University Press.

———. 2017a. *Ponderings VII–XI, Black Notebooks 1938–1939*. Translated by Richard Rojcewicz. Bloomington: Indiana University Press.

———. 2017b. *Ponderings XII–XV, Black Notebooks 1939–1941*. Translated by Richard Rojcewicz. Bloomington: Indiana University Press.

Heinz, Marion, and Sidonie Kellerer, eds. 2016. *Martin Heideggers "Schwarze Hefte": Eine philosophisch-politische Debatte*. Frankfurt: Suhrkamp.

Held, Klaus. 2016. "Heidegger und das Politische." In *Heidegger und der Antisemitismus: Positionen im Widerstreit, mit Briefen von Martin und Fritz Heidegger*, ed. Walter Homolka and Arnulf Heidegger, 257–69. Freiburg: Herder.

Hemming, Laurence Paul. 2016. "The Existence of the *Black Notebooks* in the Background." In *Reading Heidegger's "Black Notebooks 1931–1941*," ed. Ingo Farin and Jeff Malpas, 109–26. Cambridge, MA: MIT Press.

Herrmann, Friedrich-Wilhelm von. "The Role of Martin Heidegger's *Notebooks* within the Context of His Oeuvre." In *Reading Heidegger's "Black Notebooks 1931–1941,"* ed. Ingo Farin and Jeff Malpas, 89–94. Cambridge, MA: MIT Press.

Herf, Jeffrey. 1984. *Reactionary Modernism: Technology, Culture, and Politics in Weimar and the Third Reich.* Cambridge: Cambridge University Press.

———. 2006. *The Jewish Enemy: Nazi Propaganda during World War II and the Holocaust.* Cambridge, MA: Harvard University Press.

Hill, Rebecca. 2011. *The Interval: Relation and Becoming in Irigaray, Aristotle, and Bergson.* New York: Fordham University Press.

Hitler, Adolf. [1925] 2016. *Hitler, Mein Kampf: Eine kritische Edition*, ed. Christian Hartmann, Thomas Vordermayer, Othmar Plöckinger, Roman Töppel, Edith Raim, Pascal Trees, Angelika Reizle, and Martina Seewald-Mooser. Munich: Institut für Zeitgeschichte.

Hölderlin, Friedrich. 1967. "Patmos." In *Poems and Fragments*, ed. and trans. Michael Hamburger, 483–97. London: Anvil Press Poetry.

Holmes, Brooke. 2012. *Gender: Antiquity and Its Legacy.* Oxford: Oxford University Press.

Homolka, Walter, and Arnulf Heidegger, eds. 2016. *Heidegger und der Antisemitismus: Positionen im Widerstreit, mit Briefen von Martin und Fritz Heidegger.* Freiburg: Herder.

Huber, Engelbert. 1933. *Das ist Nationalsozialismus: Organisation und Weltanschauung der NSDAP.* Stuttgart: Union Deutsche Verlagsgesellschaft.

Hyland, Drew A. 2015. "Heidegger's (Dramatic?) Dialogues." *Research in Phenomenology* 45 (3): 341–57.

Iamblichus. [3rd/4th centuries CE] 1818. *The Life of Pythagoras.* Translated by Thomas Taylor. London: Watkins.

Ireland, Julia A. 2014. "Naming *phusis* and the 'Inner Truth of National Socialism.'" *Research in Phenomenology* 44 (3): 315–46.

Irigaray, Luce. 1985. *Speculum of the Other Woman.* Translated by Gillian C. Gill. Ithaca, NY: Cornell University Press.

———. 1999. *The Forgetting of Air in Martin Heidegger.* Translated by Mary Beth Mader. Austin: University of Texas Press.

———. 2001. "To Conceive Silence." In Irigaray, *To Be Two.* Translated by Monique Rhodes and Marco Cocito-Mono. New York: Routledge.

Irwin, Terence. 1990. *Aristotle's First Principles.* Oxford: Clarendon.

Jarausch, Konrad Hugo. 2006. *After Hitler: Recivilizing Germans, 1945–1995.* Oxford: Oxford University Press.

Jaspers, Karl. 2001. *The Question of German Guilt*. Translated by E. B. Ashton. New York: Fordham University Press.

Kaplan, Alice Yaeger. 1986. *Reproductions of Banality: Fascism, Literature, and French Intellectual Life*. Minneapolis: University of Minnesota Press.

Kierkegaard, Søren. 1983. *Fear and Trembling and Repetition*. Translated by Howard V. Hong and Edna H. Hong. Princeton, NJ: Princeton University Press.

Kisiel, Theodore. 1995. "The Genetic Difference in Reading *Being and Time*." *American Catholic Philosophical Quarterly* 69 (2): 171–87.

———. 2002. "In the Middle of Heidegger's Three Concepts of the Political." In *Heidegger and Practical Philosophy*, ed. François Raffoul and David Pettigrew, 135–57. Albany: State University of New York Press.

———. 2009. "The Siting of Hölderlin's 'Geheimes Deutschland' in Heidegger's Poetizing of the Political." In *Heidegger und der Nationalsozialismus II: Interpretationen*, Heidegger-Jahrbuch 5, ed. Alfred Denker and Holger Zaborowski, 145–54. Freiburg: Alber.

Klemperer, Victor. 2006. *The Language of the Third Reich: LTI, Lingua Tertii Imperii: A Philologist's Notebook*. London: Continuum.

Knowles, Adam. 2015a. "The Gender of Silence: Irigaray on the Measureless Measure." *Journal of Speculative Philosophy* 29 (3): 302–13.

———. 2015b. "A Genealogy of Silence: *Chōra* and the Placelessness of Greek Women." *philoSOPHIA: A Journal of Continental Feminism* 5 (1): 1–24.

———. 2015c. "Heidegger's Mask: Silence, Politics and the Banality of Evil in the *Black Notebooks*." *Gatherings: The Annual Journal of the Heidegger Circle* 5: 93–117.

———. 2018. "Martin Heidegger's Nazi Conscience." In *Probing the Limits of Categorization: The Bystander in Holocaust History*, ed. Christina Morina and Krijn Thijs. New York: Berghahn.

Kolbenheyer, Erwin Guido. 1935. *Lebenswert und Lebenswirkung der Dichtkunst in einem Volke*. Munich: Langen and Müller.

Koonz, Claudia. 2003. *The Nazi Conscience*. Cambridge, MA: Belknap.

Kracauer, Siegfried. 1995. "The Cult of Distraction." In *The Mass Ornament: Weimar Essays*, 323–30. Cambridge, MA: Harvard University Press.

Krell, David Farrell. 1992. *Daimon Life: Heidegger and Life-Philosophy*. Bloomington: Indiana University Press, 1992.

———. 2015. *Ecstasy, Catastrophe: Heidegger from "Being and Time" to the "Black Notebooks."* Albany: State University of New York Press.

———. 2016. "Troubled Brows: Heidegger's *Black Notebooks*, 1942–48." *Research in Phenomenology* 46 (2): 309–35.

Kristeva, Julia. 1984. *Revolution in Poetic Language.* Translated by Margaret Waller. New York: Columbia University Press.

Krois, John Michael. 2002. "Warum fand keine Davoser Debatte zwischen Cassirer und Heidegger statt?" In *Cassirer–Heidegger: 70 Jahre Davoser Disputation,* ed. Dominic Kaegi and Enno Rudolph, 234–45. Hamburg: Meiner.

Laak, Dirk van. 2002. *Gespräche in der Sicherheit des Schweigens: Carl Schmitt in der politischen Geistesgeschichte der frühen Bundesrepublik.* Berlin: De Gruyter.

Lacoue-Labarthe, Philippe. 1990. *Heidegger, Art and Politics.* Translated by Chris Turner. Oxford: Blackwell.

———. 1998. *Typography: Mimesis, Philosophy, Politics.* Translated by Christopher Fynsk. Stanford, CA: Stanford University Press.

Lang, Berel. 1996. *Heidegger's Silence.* Ithaca, NY: Cornell University Press.

Lardinois, André. 2001. "Keening Sappho: Female Speech in Sappho's Poetry." In *Making Silence Speak: Women's Voices in Greek Literature and Society,* ed. André Lardinois and Laura McClure. Princeton, NJ: Princeton University Press.

Lardinois, André, and Laura McClure, eds. 2001. *Making Silence Speak: Women's Voices in Greek Literature and Society.* Princeton, NJ: Princeton University Press.

Laurence, Patricia Ondek. 1991. *The Reading of Silence: Virginia Woolf in the English Tradition.* Stanford, CA: Stanford University Press.

Leaman, George, and Gerd Simon. 1992. "Deutsche Philosophen aus der Sicht des Sicherheitsdienstes des Reichsführers SS." In *Jahrbuch für Soziologiegeschichte 1991,* ed. Carsten Klingemann, Michael Neumann, Karl-Siegbert Rehberg, Ilja Srubar, and Erhard Stölting. Opladen: Leske and Budrich.

———. 1994. "Kant-Studien im Dritten Reich," *Kant-Studien* 85 (4): 443–69.

Lenz, Fritz. 1927. *Menschliche Auslese und Rassenhygiene (Eugenik).* Vol. 2 of *Menschliche Erblichkeitslehre und Rassenhygiene,* ed. Erwin Baur, Fritz Lenz, and Eugen Fischer. Munich: Lehmann.

Leo, Per. 2016. "Über Nationalsozialismus sprechen: Ein Verkomplizierungsversuch." *Merkur* 70 (827): 29–41.

Levinas, Emmanuel. 1990. "Reflections on the Philosophy of Hitlerism." *Critical Inquiry* 17 (1): 63–71.

Liddell, Henry George, and Robert Scott. 1989. *A Lexicon Abridged from Liddell and Scott's Greek-English Lexicon.* Oxford: Clarendon.

Lloyd, Genevieve. 1993. *Man of Reason: "Male" and "Female" in Western Philosophy.* London: Routledge.

Loraux, Nicole. 1995. *The Experiences of Tiresias: The Feminine and the Greek Man.* Translated by Paula Wissing. Princeton, NJ: Princeton University Press.

———. 1998. *Mothers in Mourning*. Translated by Corinne Pache. Ithaca, NY: Cornell University Press.

Lorde, Audre. 1984. "The Transformation of Silence into Language and Action." In *Sister Outsider: Essays and Speeches*, 40–44. Trumansburg, NY: Crossing.

Love, Jeff, and Michael Meng. 2015. "The Political Myths of Martin Heidegger." In *New German Critique* 42 (1): 45–66.

Lübbe, Herrmann. 1983. "Der Nationalsozialismus im politischen Bewusstsein der Gegenwart." In *Deutschlands Weg in die Diktatur: Internationale Konferenz zur nationalsozialistischen Machtübernahme*, ed. Martin Broszat, 329–49. Berlin: Siedler.

Luckyj, Christina. 2002. *"A Moving Rhetoricke": Gender and Silence in Early Modern England*. Manchester: Manchester University Press.

Lyon, James K. 2006. *Paul Celan and Martin Heidegger: An Unresolved Conversation, 1951–1970*. Baltimore: Johns Hopkins University Press.

Lyotard, Jean-François. 1988. *The Differend: Phrases in Dispute*. Translated by Georges van den Abbeele. Minneapolis: University of Minnesota Press.

Malabou, Catherine. 2011. *The Heidegger Change: On the Fantastic in Philosophy*. Translated by Peter Skafish. Albany: State University of New York Press.

Marafioti, Rosa Maria. 2016. "Heideggers vielsagendes Schweigen." In *Heidegger und der Antisemitismus: Positionen im Widerstreit, mit Briefen von Martin und Fritz Heidegger*, ed. Walter Homolka and Arnulf Heidegger, 277–88. Freiburg: Herder.

Marchand, Suzanne. 2003. *Down from Olympus: Archaeology and Philhellenism in Germany, 1750–1970*. Princeton, NJ: Princeton University Press.

Maurizio, Lisa. 2001. "The Voice at the Center of the World: The Pythias' Ambiguity and Authority." In *Making Silence Speak: Women's Voices in Greek Literature and Society*, ed. André Lardinois and Laura McClure, 38–54. Princeton, NJ: Princeton University Press.

McClure, Laura. "Introduction." In *Making Silence Speak: Women's Voices in Greek Literature and Society*, ed. André Lardinois and Laura McClure, 3–16. Princeton, NJ: Princeton University Press.

McNeill, William. 1999. *The Glance of the Eye: Heidegger, Aristotle, and the Ends of Theory*. Albany: State University of New York Press.

———. 2013. "In Force of Language: Language and Desire in Heidegger's Readings of Aristotle's *Metaphysics Theta*." In *Heidegger and Language*, ed. Jeffrey Powell, 46–62. Bloomington: Indiana University Press.

Meckel, Marlis. 2006. *Den Opfern ihre Namen zurückgeben: Stolpersteine in Freiburg*. Freiburg: Rombach.

Mehring, Reinhard. 1992. *Heideggers Überlieferungsgeschick: Eine dionysische Selbstinszenierung*. Würzburg: Königshausen and Neumann.

———. 2016. "Postmortaler Suizid: Zur Selbstdemontage des Autors der *Gesamtausgabe*." In *Heidegger und der Antisemitismus: Positionen im Widerstreit, mit Briefen von Martin und Fritz Heidegger*, ed. Walter Homolka and Arnulf Heidegger, 289–99. Freiburg: Herder.

Meinwald, Constance C. 1992. "Good-Bye to the Third Man." In *The Cambridge Companion to Plato*, ed. Richard Kraut, 365–96. Cambridge: Cambridge University Press.

Miller, Mitchell H. 1991. *Plato's "Parmenides": The Conversion of the Soul*. University Park, PA: Pennsylvania State University Press.

———. 2004. *The Philosopher in Plato's "Statesman."* Las Vegas: Parmenides.

Mitchell, Andrew J. 2010. *Heidegger among the Sculptors: Body, Space, and the Art of Dwelling*. Stanford, CA: Stanford University Press.

———. 2011. "Heidegger's Poetics of Relationality." In *Interpreting Heidegger: Critical Essays*, ed. Daniel Dahlstrom, 217–31. Cambridge: Cambridge University Press.

———. 2015. *The Fourfold: Reading the Late Heidegger*. Evanston, IL: Northwestern University Press.

Mitchell, Andrew J., and Peter Trawny, eds. 2015. *Heidegger, die Juden, noch einmal*. Frankfurt: Klostermann.

———. 2017. *Heidegger's "Black Notebooks": Responses to Anti-Semitism*. New York: Columbia University Press.

Montiglio, Silvia. 2000. *Silence in the Land of Logos*. Princeton, NJ: Princeton University Press.

———. 2005. *Wandering in Ancient Greek Culture*. Chicago: University of Chicago Press.

Morat, Daniel. 2007. *Von der Tat zur Gelassenheit: Konservatives Denken bei Martin Heidegger, Ernst Jünger und Friedrich Georg Jünger; 1920–1960*. Göttingen: Wallstein.

———. 2012. "No Inner Remigration: Martin Heidegger, Ernst Jünger, and the Early Federal Republic of Germany." *Modern Intellectual History* 9 (3): 661–79.

Mosse, George L. 1981. *The Crisis of German Ideology: Intellectual Origins of the Third Reich*. New York: Schocken.

Müller, Herta. 2010. *Lebensangst und Worthunger: Leipziger Poetikvorlesung 2009*. Berlin: Suhrkamp.

Nancy, Jean-Luc. 2017. *The Banality of Heidegger*. Translated by Jeff Fort. New York: Fordham University Press.

Niethammer, Lutz. 1982. *Die Mitläuferfabrik: Die Entnazifizierung am Beispiel Bayerns*. Berlin: Dietz.

Nietzsche, Wilhelm Friedrich. 1983. *Thus Spoke Zarathustra: A Book for All and None*. Translated by Walter Kaufmann. New York: Penguin.

Norton, Robert E. 2002. *Secret Germany: Stefan George and His Circle*. Ithaca, NY: Cornell University Press.

Ott, Hugo. 1993. *Martin Heidegger: A Political Life*. London: Basic.

Phillips, James. 2005. *Heidegger's "Volk": Between National Socialism and Poetry*. Stanford, CA: Stanford University Press.

Pinter, Harold. 2009. "Writing for the Theatre." In *Various Voices: Sixty Years of Prose, Poetry, Politics, 1948–2008*, 19–25. London: Faber and Faber.

Piper, Franciszek. 1994. "Gas Chambers and Crematoria." In *Anatomy of the Auschwitz Death Camp*, ed. Yisrael Gutman and Michael Berenbaum, 157–82. Bloomington: Indiana University Press.

Plato. 1991. *The Republic of Plato*. Translated by Allan David Bloom. New York: Basic Books.

———. 1996a. *Parmenides*. Translated by Albert Keith Whitaker. Newburyport, MA: Focus/Pullins.

———. 1996b. *Sophist, or, the Professor of Wisdom*. Translated by Eva Brann, Peter Kalkavage, and Eric Salem. Newburyport, MA: Focus/Pullins.

———. 1997a. *Laws*. In Plato, *Complete Works*, ed. John M. Cooper, 1318–1617. Indianapolis: Hackett.

———. 1997b. *Lysis*. Translated by Stanley Lombardo. In Plato, *Complete Works*, ed. John M. Cooper, 687–707. Indianapolis: Hackett.

———. 1997c. *Menexenus*. In Plato, *Complete Works*, ed. John M. Cooper, 950–64. Translated by Paul Ryan. Indianapolis: Hackett.

———. 1998. *Phaedo*. Translated by Eva Brann, Peter Kalkavage, and Eric Salem. Newburyport, MA: Focus/Pullins.

———. 2001. *Timaeus*. Translated by Peter Kalkavage. Newburyport, MA: Focus/Pullins.

———. 2003. *Phaedrus*. Translated by Stephen Scully. Newburyport, MA: Focus/Pullins.

———. 2004. *Theaetetus*. Translated by Joe Sachs. Newburyport, MA: Focus/Pullins.

———. 2008. *Gorgias*. In *Plato's "Gorgias" and Aristotle's "Rhetoric."* Translated by Joe Sachs. Focus/Pullins.

———. 2012. *Statesman.* Translated by Eva Brann, Peter Kalkavage, and Eric Salem. Newburyport, MA: Focus/Pullins.

Pöggeler, Otto. 1994. *Der Denkweg Martin Heideggers.* Pfullingen: Neske.

———. 2013. "The Secret Homeland of Speech: Heidegger on Language, 1933–34." In *Heidegger and Language,* ed. Jeffrey Powell, 63–85. Bloomington: Indiana University Press.

Polt, Richard. 2006. *The Emergency of Being: On Heidegger's "Contributions to Philosophy."* Ithaca, NY: Cornell University Press.

———. 2013. "The Secret Homeland of Speech: Heidegger on Language, 1933–1934." In *Heidegger and Language,* ed. Jeffrey Powell, 63–85. Bloomington: Indiana University Press.

Powell, Jeffrey, ed. 2013. *Heidegger and Language.* Bloomington: Indiana University Press.

Puschner, Uwe. 2001. *Die völkische Bewegung im wilhelminischen Kaiserreich: Sprache–Rasse–Religion.* Darmstadt: Wissenschaftliche Buchgesellschaft.

Ramet, Sabrina P. 2012. "The Relationship between Martin Heidegger's Nazism and His Interest in the Pre-Socratics." *Religion Compass* 6 (9): 426–40.

Raulff, Ulrich. 2009. *Kreis ohne Meister: Stefan Georges Nachleben.* Munich: Beck.

Redfield, James. 1995. "Homo Domesticus." In *The Greeks,* ed. Jean-Pierre Vernant, 153–84. Chicago: University of Chicago Press.

Richardson, William J. 2003. *Heidegger: Through Phenomenology to Thought.* New York: Fordham University Press.

Rockmore, Tom. 1997. *On Heidegger's Nazism and Philosophy: With a New Preface.* Berkeley: University of California Press.

Ronell, Avital. 1989. *The Telephone Book: Technology, Schizophrenia, Electric Speech.* Lincoln: University of Nebraska Press.

Rorty, Richard. 1990. "Diary." *London Review of Books* 12 (3): 21.

Safranski, Rüdiger. 1998. *Martin Heidegger: Between Good and Evil.* Translated by Edwald Ossers. Cambridge, MA: Harvard University Press.

Sallis, John. 1970. "Language and Reversal." *Southern Journal of Philosophy* 8 (4): 381–97.

———. 1984. "Towards the Showing of Language." In *Thinking about Being: Aspects of Heidegger's Thought,* ed. Robert W. Shahan and Jitendra N. Mohanty, 75–84. Norman: University of Oklahoma Press.

———. 1993. *Reading Heidegger: Commemorations.* Bloomington: Indiana University Press.

———. 1995. *Delimitations: Phenomenology and the End of Metaphysics.* Bloomington: Indiana University Press.

———. 1999. *Chorology: On Beginning in Plato's "Timaeus."* Bloomington: Indiana University Press.

———. 2002. *On Translation.* Bloomington: Indiana University Press.

Schalow, Frank. 1995. "The Topography of Heidegger's Concept of Conscience." *American Catholic Philosophical Quarterly* 69 (2): 256–73.

Schaps, David. 1977. "The Woman Least Mentioned: Etiquette and Women's Names." *Classical Quarterly* 27 (2): 323–30.

Schmidt, Raymund. 1939. "Das Judentum in der deutschen Philosophie." In *Handbuch der Judenfrage: Die wichtigsten Tatsachen zur Beurteilung des jüdischen Volkes*, ed. Theodor Fritsch, 391–401. Leipzig: Hammer.

Schmitz-Berning, Cornelia. 1998. *Vokabular des Nationalsozialismus.* Berlin: Walter de Gruyter.

Schneeberger, Guido, ed. 1962. *Nachlese zu Heidegger: Dokumente zu seinem Leben und Denken.* Bern: Buchdruckerei.

Schorcht, Claudia. 1994. "Gescheitert: Der Versuch zur Etablierung Nationalsozialistischer Philosophen an der Universität München." In *"Die Besten Geister der Nation": Philosophie und Nationalsozialismus*, ed. Ilse Korotin, 291–327. Vienna: Picus.

Schürmann, Reiner. 1973. "Heidegger and Meister Eckhart on Releasement." *Research in Phenomenology* 3 (1): 95–119.

———. 2003. *Broken Hegemonies.* Translated by Reginald Lilly. Bloomington: Indiana University Press.

Schwarz, Herrmann. 1936. *Zur philosophischen Grundlegung des Nationalsozialismus.* Berlin: Junker und Dünnhaupt.

———. 1937. *Grundzüge einer Geschichte der artdeutschen Philosophie.* Berlin: Junker and Dünnhaupt.

Seemann, Silke. 2002. *Die politischen Säuberungen des Lehrkörpers der Freiburger Universität nach dem Ende des Zweiten Weltkrieges (1945–1957).* Freiburg: Rombach.

Seier, Helmut. 1964. "Der Rektor als Führer: Zur Hochschulpolitik des Reichserziehungsministeriums 1934–1945." *Vierteljahrshefte für Zeitgeschichte* 12 (2): 105–46.

Seshadri, Kalpana. 2012. *HumAnimal Race: Law, Language.* Minneapolis: University of Minnesota Press.

Sieg, Ulrich. 2004. "'Deutsche Wissenschaft' und Neukantianismus: Die Geschichte einer Diffamierung." In *Nationalsozialismus in den Kulturwissenschaften*, vol. 2, ed. Otto Gerhard Oexle and Hartmut Lehmann, 199–222. Göttingen: Vandenhoeck und Ruprecht.

————. 2013. *Geist und Gewalt: Deutsche Philosophen zwischen Kaiserreich und Nationalsozialismus*. Munich: Hanser.

Simmel, Georg. 1969. "The Metropolis and Mental Life." In *Classic Essays on the Culture of Cities*, ed. Richard Sennett, 47–60. New York: Appleton-Century-Crofts.

Sluga, Hans D. 1993. *Heidegger's Crisis: Philosophy and Politics in Nazi Germany*. Cambridge, MA: Harvard University Press.

Smith, David Nowell. 2013. *Sounding/Silence: Martin Heidegger at the Limits of Poetics*. New York: Fordham University Press.

Sontheimer, Kurt. 1957. "Antidemokratisches Denken in der Weimarer Republik." *Vierteljahrshefte für Zeitgeschichte* 5 (1): 42–62.

Sophocles. 1960. *Antigone*. In *Sophocles I: Three Tragedies*. Translated by David Grene and Richmond Lattimore. Chicago: University of Chicago Press.

Speck, Dieter. 2015. "Vorlesungen im Phantomsemester: Die Freiburger Philosophische Fakultät in Beuron zwischen Flucht und Fiktion." In *Mittelalterliches Mönchtum in der Moderne? Die Neugründung der Benediktinerabtei Beuron 1863 und deren kulturelle Ausstrahlung im 19. und 20. Jahrhundert*, ed. Karl-Heinz Braun, Hugo Ott and Wilfried Schöntag, 169–90. Stuttgart: Kohlhammer.

Spivak, Gayatri Chakravorty. 1988. "Can the Subaltern Speak?" In *Marxism and the Interpretation of Culture*, ed. Cary Nelson and Lawrence Grossberg, 271–313. Urbana: University of Illinois Press.

Stern, Fritz. 1974. *The Politics of Cultural Despair: A Study in the Rise of the Germanic Ideology*. Berkeley: University of California Press.

Stommer, Rainer. 1985. *Die inszenierte Volksgemeinschaft: Die "Thing-Bewegung" im Dritten Reich*. Marburg: Jonas.

Svenbro, Jesper. 1993. Phrasikleia: *An Anthropology of Reading in Ancient Greece*. Translated by Janet E. Lloyd. Ithaca, NY: Cornell University Press.

Taplin, Oliver. 1972. "Aeschylean Silences and Silences in Aeschylus," *Harvard Studies in Classical Philology* 76: 57–97.

Thomä, Dieter. 2016. "Heidegger als Mitläufer des Seins," In *Heidegger und der Antisemitismus: Positionen im Widerstreit, mit Briefen von Martin und Fritz Heidegger*, ed. Walter Homolka and Arnulf Heidegger, 364–72. Freiburg: Herder.

Thurnher, Rainer. 2016. "Sondierungen zu Heideggers 'Privatnationalsozialismus.'" In *Heidegger und der Antisemitismus: Positionen im Widerstreit, mit Briefen von Martin und Fritz Heidegger*, ed. Walter Homolka and Arnulf Heidegger, 373–83. Freiburg: Herder.

Tourlamain, Guy. 2014. *Völkisch Writers and National Socialism: A Study of Right-Wing Political Culture in Germany, 1890–1960*. Bern: Lang.

Trawny, Peter. 2003. *Martin Heidegger*. Frankfurt: Campus.
———. [2010] 2014. *Adyton: Heideggers esoterische Philosophie*. Berlin: Matthes and Seitz.
———. 2015a. *Freedom to Fail: Heidegger's Anarchy*. Translated by Ian Alexander Moore and Christopher Turner. Cambridge: Polity.
———. 2015b. *Heidegger and the Myth of the Jewish World Conspiracy*. Translated by Andrew J. Mitchell. Chicago: University of Chicago Press.
Vallega-Neu, Daniela. 2001. "Poietic Saying." In *Companion to Heidegger's "Contributions to Philosophy,"* ed. Charles E. Scott, 66–80. Bloomington: Indiana University Press.
———. 2003. *Heidegger's "Contributions to Philosophy": An Introduction*. Bloomington: Indiana University Press.
———. 2013. "Heidegger's Poietic Writings: From *Contributions to Philosophy* to *Das Ereignis*." In *Heidegger and Language*, ed. Jeffrey Powell, 119–45. Bloomington: Indiana University Press.
———. 2015. "Heidegger's Reticence: From *Contributions* to *Das Ereignis* and Toward Gelassenheit." *Research in Phenomenology* 45 (1): 1–32.
———. 2016. "The *Black Notebooks* and Heidegger's Writings on the Event (1936–1942)." In *Reading Heidegger's "Black Notebooks 1931–1941,"* ed. Ingo Farin and Jeff Malpas, 127–44. Cambridge, MA: MIT Press.
Van Buren, John. 1994. *The Young Heidegger: Rumor of the Hidden King*. Bloomington: Indiana University Press.
Vernant, Jean-Pierre. 1982. *The Origins of Greek Thought*. Ithaca, NY: Cornell University Press.
Vohburger, Max. 1940. *Germanisches Volkserbe im Alamannendorf Wintersweiler: Reichsbestearbeit der Sparte "Deutsche Volksgeschichte" im 3. Reichsberufwettkampf der deutschen Studenten 1937/38*. Berlin-Dahlem: Ahnenerbe-Stiftung.
Volkov, Shulamit. 1978. "Antisemitism as a Cultural Code: Reflections on the History and Historiography of Antisemitism in Imperial Germany." *Leo Baeck Institute Year Book* 23 (1): 25–46.
Volpi, Franco. 1978. "Heideggers Verhältnis zu Brentanos Aristoteles-Interpretation: Die Frage nach dem Sein des Seienden." *Zeitschrift für philosophische Forschung* 32 (2): 254–65.
Weingart, Peter. 1995. *Doppel-Leben: Ludwig Ferdinand Clauss zwischen Rassenforschung und Widerstand*. Frankfurt: Campus.
Weinreich, Max. 1946. *Hitler's Professors: The Part of Scholarship in Germany's Crimes against the Jewish People*. New York: Yiddish Scientific Institute–YIVO.
Wieland, Wolfgang. 1962. *Die aristotelische Physik: Untersuchungen über die Grun-*

dlegung der Naturwissenschaft und die sprachlichen Bedingungen der Prinzipien-forschung bei Aristoteles. Göttingen: Vandenhoeck and Ruprecht.

Wittgenstein, Ludwig. [1921] 1989. *Tractatus Logico-Philosophicus*. Frankfurt: Suhrkamp.

Wolin, Richard. 2016. *The Politics of Being: The Political Thought of Martin Heidegger*. New York: Columbia University Press.

Zaborowski, Holger. 2016. "Licht und Schatten: Zur Diskussion von Heideggers *Schwarzen Heften*." In *Heidegger und der Antisemitismus: Positionen im Widerstreit, mit Briefen von Martin und Fritz Heidegger*, ed. Walter Homolka and Arnulf Heidegger, 428–40. Freiburg: Herder.

Zarader, Marlène. 2006. *The Unthought Debt: Heidegger and the Hebraic Heritage*. Stanford, CA: Stanford University Press.

Zeitlin, Froma. 1996. *Playing the Other: Gender and Society in Classical Greek Literature*. Chicago: University of Chicago Press.

Ziarek, Krzysztof. 1994. *Inflected Language: Toward a Hermeneutics of Nearness: Heidegger, Levinas, Stevens, Celan*. Albany: State University of New York Press.

———. 2013. *Language after Heidegger*. Bloomington: Indiana University Press.

Zimmerman, Michael E. 2010. *Heidegger's Confrontation with Modernity: Technology, Politics, and Art*. Bloomington: Indiana University Press.

Index

Mussolini, Benito, 21, 181

Nancy, Jean-Luc, 178
National Socialism: academics involved
with, 8, 10–11, 13, 37; antisemitism
of, 13, 18, 39; German essence linked
to, 33, 153; Heideggerian themes
associated with, 98–101, 177–78;
Heidegger's relationship to, 4, 5,
8, 10–17, 22–24, 29, 33, 99–100,
151–52, 159, 173–85, 190n32, 190n43,
190n46; Heidegger's remarks on,
1, 4–5, 9, 11; and language, 193n17;
moral underpinning of, 15–16, 39, 51;
philosophy and, 8–9; resistance to,
176; silence and, 9–12, 15, 17–18, 57,
151, 153–54; spiritual vs. vulgar, 101,
152–54, 179
National Socialist Student Federation,
176
neo-Kantianism, 44–45
neoliberalism, 185
Neoplatonism, 195n10
Niemeyer (publisher), 21
Niethammer, Lutz, 182
noise, 11
nonbeing, 80–81, 89–90
Nordic people, 36–38, 160, 171. See also
Aryans; German essence
Notgemeinschaft der deutschen
Wissenschaft (Emergency
Association of German Science), 46
nothingness, 74, 80

occidental essence/spirit, 10, 27, 28–29,
33, 153, 167

Panther, Der (journal), 44
Parmenides, 80, 88–89
peasants, 46–48, 160–67. See also Volk
and völkisch movement
pedagogy: Aristotle and, 117; defined,
121; in Greek culture and philosophy,
102–4; Heidegger and, 124–25; Plato's
Parmenides and, 107–14; Pythagoras

and, 105–7; selection process in, 106,
107, 117, 125; in universities, 122–23
Pericles, 130, 197n9
phallologocentrism, 149
philhellenism, 41
philosophy: Aryan vs. Jewish
influences on, 42–45; attunement
in, 82–83; and ethno-nationalism,
8; exclusions of, 148; Heidegger's
place in, 183–85; historiographical
vs. historical conceptions of,
53–54; and National Socialism,
8–9; peasant mindset and, 47–48,
163; as phallologocentrism, 149;
philosophers' lives in relation to, 9,
19, 28–30, 101, 155, 176–78, 182–83;
politics in relation to, 8–9, 153; and
silence, 148; and totalitarianism, 8,
183–84; violence underlying, 149
Pinter, Harold, 136
place. See landscape
Plato: Aristotle and, 88; conception of
being in works of, 89; Gorgias, 140;
Heidegger influenced by, 19; Laws,
127–28; Lysis, 139; Menexenus, 135;
"Myth of Er," 145; Parmenides, 104,
107–15, 120, 124, 195n10; Phaedo, 109,
133, 145; Phaedrus, 111, 131, 195n13;
Republic, 109–11; and silence, 19, 103,
104, 107–14, 135, 140; Sophist, 89;
Statesman, 113–14; and stillness, 131;
on thinking, 96; Timaeus, 128–29;
and women, 130
Pöggeler, Otto, 31
polis: Heidegger on, 147; self-mastery as
virtue of, 103, 121, 126; women's role
in, 128, 130, 133, 147
politics: of gathering, 99–100;
Heidegger's, 9, 41, 56, 153;
ontological, 168–69; philosophy
in relation to, 8–9, 153; sigetic, 99;
silence and, 7, 10
Polt, Richard, 32
polyvocality: of force, 91; of the good,
115; of logos/language/discourse, 62,

withdrawal, 74–75, 90–95, 120
Wittgenstein, Ludwig, 80
Wolin, Richard, 183, 189n23
women and femininity: absence/
   placelessness of, 128, 130–31, 138–39,
   141, 143, 147; Aristotle's notions
   of, 133, 138–39, 197n24; and being,
   128–30, 145; contradictory qualities
   ascribed to, 127–30, 140, 144;
   forgetting associated with, 130, 139,
   144–46; in Greek culture/thought,

103, 126–48, 197n15; Heidegger's
   philosophy and, 146–48; and *logos*,
   128–29, 139–40, 147; masculinity
   compared to, 103, 132–33, 140; role
   of, in polis, 128, 130, 133, 147; and
   silence, 126–32, 137–48
Woolf, Virginia, 136
work. *See* production

Zaborowski, Holger, 29
Zeitlin, Froma, 143

The authorized representative in the EU for product safety and compliance is:
Mare Nostrum Group
B.V Doelen 72
4831 GR Breda
The Netherlands

www.ingramcontent.com/pod-product-compliance
Lightning Source LLC
Chambersburg PA
CBHW030732280326
41926CB00086B/1197